# The Merchant in German Literature of the Enlightenment

**UNC** | COLLEGE OF ARTS AND SCIENCES
Germanic and Slavic Languages and Literatures

From 1949 to 2004, UNC Press and the UNC Department of Germanic & Slavic Languages and Literatures published the UNC Studies in the Germanic Languages and Literatures series. Monographs, anthologies, and critical editions in the series covered an array of topics including medieval and modern literature, theater, linguistics, philology, onomastics, and the history of ideas. Through the generous support of the National Endowment for the Humanities and the Andrew W. Mellon Foundation, books in the series have been reissued in new paperback and open access digital editions. For a complete list of books visit www.uncpress.org.

# The Merchant in German Literature of the Enlightenment

JOHN W. VAN CLEVE

UNC Studies in the Germanic Languages and Literatures
Number 105

Copyright © 1986

This work is licensed under a Creative Commons CC BY-NC-ND license. To view a copy of the license, visit http://creativecommons.org/licenses.

Suggested citation: Van Cleve, John W. *The Merchant in German Literature of the Enlightenment*. Chapel Hill: University of North Carolina Press, 1986. DOI: https://doi.org/10.5149/9781469656878_Cleve

Library of Congress Cataloging-in-Publication Data
Names: Van Cleve, John W.
Title: The merchant in German literature of the Enlightenment / by John W. Van Cleve.
Other titles: University of North Carolina Studies in the Germanic Languages and Literatures ; no. 105.
Description: Chapel Hill : University of North Carolina Press, [1986] Series: University of North Carolina Studies in the Germanic Languages and Literatures. | Includes bibliographical references and index.
Identifiers: LCCN 85014142 | ISBN 978-1-4696-5686-1 (pbk: alk. paper) | ISBN 978-1-4696-5687-8 (ebook)
Subjects: German literature — 18th century — History and criticism. | Businessmen in literature. | Enlightenment — Germany. | Germany — Intellectual life — 18th century.
Classification: LCC PT289 .V36 1986 | DCC 830/.9/355

*For Max Lorenz Baeumer
of Madison and Trier*

# Contents

| | |
|---|---|
| Preface | xiii |

## Part One: The Merchant in Society

| | |
|---|---|
| I. The Merchant in Society | 3 |

## Part Two: The Merchant in Literature

| | |
|---|---|
| II. Menace and Menaced: Haller, Schnabel | 45 |
| III. From Fool to Friend: Borkenstein, L. A. V. Gottsched, J. E. Schlegel | 70 |
| IV. Virtue in the "Jewish Profession": Gellert | 91 |
| V. The Merchant as Hero: Lessing | 109 |
| Conclusion | 137 |
| Notes | 141 |
| Bibliography | 157 |
| Index | 167 |

*The Merchant in German Literature of the Enlightenment* contains material from three previously published articles by the author; substantial revisions have been undertaken for this monograph. The articles are:

"Social Commentary in Haller's *Die Alpen*," *Monatshefte* 72 (1980): 379–88.

"A Countess in Name Only: Gellert's *Schwedische Gräfin*," *Germanic Review* 55 (1980):552–55.

"Tolerance at a Price: The Jew in Gellert's *Schwedische Gräfin*," *Seminar* 18 (1982):1–13.

# Preface

This study draws from both social history and literary criticism to detail a major change within an artistic tradition. Under scrutiny is the entry of a previously excluded segment of the population into the cultural life of German-speaking Europe. During the seventeenth century, the trauma of total war and its aftermath served to retard the development of capitalism east of the Rhine to such an extent that synchronic comparisons with France and England are of questionable worth until the later 1700s. If the political instability of the age offered the ruling nobility an opportunity to consolidate power, it simultaneously made the prince the one reliable source of funding for the various creative media. However, as the shock waves from the Thirty Years' War faded, so, too, did the old patronage system. For both artist and audience, times were changing.

Ironically enough, the governing elite provided the impetus for that change. Absolutist policies had created an ever-growing need for university-trained administrators and managers, who found natural peers among professionals: physicians, lawyers, and clergymen. Not only university experiences but also cultural expectations and income levels were similar. And from their ranks emerged those writers immediately associated with eighteenth-century Germany, from Haller and Lessing to Lenz and Goethe. But all was not sweetness and light during the rise of the middle class as the chief force to be reckoned with in German culture. Extended periods of peace in town and countryside had renewed the viability of commerce. By the early decades of the new century, merchants and businessmen usually constituted the wealthiest subcategory within the urban bourgeoisie. His often robust personal economy could easily make such a figure an object of envy in the mind of a struggling civil servant. At the same time, the beneficiary of higher education would have been tempted to look down upon a semiliterate neighbor who was far more comfortable with a simple abacus than with a challenging tome. The paradoxical combination of jealousy and superciliousness on the part of the nonmercantile middle class only increased a gap opened centuries before by the traditional suspicion of the one who lives for profit.

The investigation that follows commences with an analysis of both the historical merchant during this time of change and the highly ambivalent attitudes toward him held by the balance of his class. Then the focus shifts to literature during the early Enlightenment. It was during the quarter century surveyed that the image of the merchant underwent a metamorphosis that should be understood before broad statements are made concerning the relationship of artist and public at this point in history. Such an understanding is the goal of this study.

Albrecht von Haller's long poem "Die Alpen" is the earliest literary product of the Age of Reason to have won a place in the canon of German literature "from the beginnings to the present." The Swiss author's lyrical tour of the terrain between Berne and Zurich offers a deeply hostile evaluation of the capitalist anno 1729. A strikingly different perspective emerges from comedies published in the mid-1750s by Gotthold Ephraim Lessing; their appearance coincided with the conclusion of the first major phase of that writer's development. As Lessing moved away from *the* dramatic form of the 1740s and toward innovations in theme as well as genre, he raised the literary Enlightenment to a more sophisticated, mature plane. Nevertheless, with publication of his *Schrifften* in 1755, the young man from Kamenz had already completed yet another achievement for which the early Enlightenment deserves credit. That period has long been recognized as the breeding ground of the moral weekly and the literary periodical. It started writers on a century-long quest for professional, middle-class status. It turned the literary tradition to the service of a new patron, the bourgeois. And during the latter process, as will be demonstrated, it moved to expand the ranks of the new culture-bearing stratum of society by ushering in a long-time outsider.

The working hypothesis here is that the literary world first chose merely to depict money-making activity in the worst possible light. Then, as the economic realities of middle-class life became more apparent, such activity was presented in progressively less negative fashion. Soon, the next logical step was taken: literature proceeded from positive depiction to active championing of the businessman. The merchant came to be portrayed as a figure who is in a position to change his society for the better, as a figure who, in a crisis, can step forth as a guide, and even as a hero.

Before considering those men of commerce, flesh-and-blood as well as pen-and-ink, I would like to express my gratitude for the assistance given by a number of institutions and individuals. Research was made possible by the graduate libraries of the University of Illinois, the University of Minnesota, Mississippi State University,

Northwestern University, and the University of Wisconsin. The holdings and the staff of the Newberry Library were particularly helpful.

Mississippi State University granted a sabbatical leave that greatly expedited work on the project. Dean Edward L. McGlone of the College of Arts and Sciences has been a true champion of research in foreign languages and literatures. To my esteemed colleague in the Department of Foreign Languages, James R. Chatham, sincere thanks for moral support that has always been at the ready.

Information concerning physical characteristics of sundry European peoples was cheerfully provided by Michael Allen McNutt, M.D.

The Feicht family of Chicago has been closely involved in the preparation of the monograph. Bernice Hammann Feicht contributed generously to the financial welfare of an academician's family. My late and sorely missed father-in-law, Arthur J. Feicht, Jr., answered questions concerning the history of commerce, business practices, and business terminology with his customary good humor and genuine interest. His daughter, Judith Arden Van Cleve, offered her love and encouragement.

Nancy C. Michael of the Department of English at Mississippi State was so kind as to read the manuscript and offer suggestions for improvement.

Thanks are also due the editors and readers of the University of North Carolina Studies in the Germanic Languages and Literatures for their thoughtful guidance.

This study is dedicated to my dear friend Max Lorenz Baeumer of the German Department at the University of Wisconsin–Madison; I have benefited immeasurably from his good counsel. His generosity with his own time has been boundless; his critique has added greatly to whatever merit these pages can claim. Were I asked to cite those qualities that contribute to the making of a consummate academician of the humanities, I might be tempted to describe the indescribable—sensitivity, imagination, grace. However, I would do far better to suggest an hour beside Max Baeumer's hearth.

# Part One
# The Merchant in Society

# I. The Merchant in Society

In 1936 Leo Balet published a study of German culture in the eighteenth century that has attracted a new readership during the past decade.[1] The monograph analyzes how and why the middle class assumed responsibility for traditions in art, literature, and music previously supported by the ruling nobility. Recent scholarship has shown sustained interest in this period of change in the relationship between artist and society, interest manifest in a blossoming of secondary literature, much of which has focused on that middle class, its composition, and its expectations.[2] A common evaluation of the dynamics within the rising social stratum has accordingly emerged and found its way into primers on the period and its poets.[3]

During the late Middle Ages, a small middle class composed primarily of craftsmen and merchants consolidated its position in the towns and cities of the overwhelmingly rural German-speaking states. Trade routes to and from the Mediterranean crisscrossed a region whose mineral deposits guaranteed representation at the major markets of Europe. Balet writes: "Im 15. Jahrhundert war Deutschland ein reiches Land, besonders durch seine Bergwerke."[4] Specifically, the merchant was the man whose search for new contacts involved his city in the period of growth.[5] The situation changed drastically during the Age of Discovery, as nations with easy access to the rapidly developing sea-lanes scrambled for wealth in distant South American and East Asian colonies. Portugal, Spain, France, England, and Holland asserted their primacy during the sixteenth and early seventeenth centuries even as landlocked German states entered the economic doldrums. The once mighty Hanseatic League became a mere extension of worldwide lines of trade initially drawn by the seafaring British and Dutch. Holland parlayed its strong geopolitical influence on traffic on the Rhine and Baltic, its lucrative involvement in the Indian spice trade, and its status as primary customer for German goods into a position of dominance vis-à-vis the becalmed hinterlands. Southern cities that had played pivotal roles in the commercial alignments and cultural life of the early decades of the sixteenth century—Augsburg, Nuremberg, Vienna, Prague—were already wallowing in economic stagnation when the Thirty Years' War began. It has been estimated that those long years of devastation and chaos then left society in much of the

German-speaking region of Europe a full century behind England and France.[6]

The second half of the seventeenth century presents the historian with a new set of political, economic, and demographic realities that informed the literary life of the "Aufklärung." Any study that presents such social determinants as a guide to that period of literary history must review broad areas of human affairs and, in so doing, must risk the charge of cursoriness. If valid, such censure would be all the more damning in view of repeated calls for greater specificity in research-topic definition and less frequent recourse to the sweeping statement.[7] The goal here is a more precise understanding of the relationship between one small but significant component of society on the one hand and its literary representation on the other. It should be apparent that, if only because of his financial clout, the merchant played a vital part in Balet's process of "Verbürgerlichung." Hence, it is necessary to answer the following question in some detail: What realities, what restrictions and what opportunities, did a merchant face at the beginning of the eighteenth century?

The Peace of Westphalia provides a convenient terminus a quo for the full-blown emergence of what had been a provisional form of wartime government, a sort of martial law, as *the* political system in Central Europe.[8] Continual upheaval had severely weakened the authority of the Holy Roman Empire of the German Nation to the benefit of its constituent states and their rulers. As political and religious alliances with and against the "Reich" were made, unmade, and made again by German princes during the war, a concept of sovereignty developed that was applied with scant regard to the dimensions, population, or location of a given state. The absolutism of the century and a half following 1648 extended to several hundred governmental entities: its ascendancy over the imperium of the High Middle Ages founded on confessional differences, the growing rivalry between the houses of Habsburg and Hohenzollern, as well as the interests of hundreds of noble families in and out of power. That power took a form common throughout Europe of the ancien régime: just as God was believed to preside over all of creation, the temporal ruler directed all activities within his realm, finally answerable to no mortal. Abuses of this position of preeminence took sundry forms: corruption, extravagant life-styles, and sexual excess were well known.[9] Although the ruled were under no illusions as to the fallibility of the rulers, acceptance of the divine right of petty princes eliminated civil uprising as a recourse. Alan Menhennet notes: "The often excessive luxury in which many nobles indulged . . . was, of course, an offense to any reasonable and humane observer and it was frequently criticized. . . . But this was usually seen as a moral, rather than political question, whose solution lay in the gradual improvement of the human race."[10]

Of course, many nobles did not have the opportunity to cultivate such tastes. Typically, those not among the ruling elite served either the state, or especially in Catholic regions, the church. Positions of authority within the bureaucracies, including those of the usually disproportionately large military establishments, were entrusted to the lesser nobility, although opportunities for ambitious burghers became increasingly available as the new century began. Participation by the nobility in the profession of particular interest here was by contrast infrequent. Wolfgang Zorn has written: "Gegen Betätigung in Handel und Gewerbe wurden nach dem Kriege die Vorurteile im Adel insgesamt . . . wieder stärker."[11] The necessity of earning one's daily bread because of a lack of inherited wealth sufficient to maintain a standard of living consonant with noble rank brought a fall in status. A corresponding rise occurred when services rendered secured a patent of nobility for the well-connected bourgeois. Norbert Elias has pointed to these two phenomena as reciprocal components of the social mobility present in a society that featured rigid boundaries between classes.[12] Still, all classes were locked into economic restraints mandated by the princes, restraints that subordinated the fate of the subject to the wealth of the state.

Not only the disruption of trade routes and the destruction of industrial centers but also heavy population losses contributed to the economic prostration widespread by 1648. The body of policy legitimated at the time as conducive to recovery and now seen as uniquely supportive of particularistic absolutism was the mercantilist system. German princes considered the possession of extensive liquid assets a sure sign of political ascendancy and therefore acted to keep money and precious metals within their borders. Economic growth was managed accordingly. By means of elaborately layered taxes and tolls, a nation's commerce was directed toward the importation of raw materials along with the exportation of finished goods and away from the exchange of cheap domestic resources for expensive foreign workmanship. While trade agreements did exist among various states, stringent observation of the terms agreed upon was rare.[13] Actively supported by the ruler of each state were agricultural production, manufacturing, and internal commerce. Such support could take the form of road and canal construction, the regulation of river traffic, or the drive for full employment. In order to secure the largest possible work force, states encouraged the immigration of both individuals and groups, made emigration difficult, tolerated the use of child labor, and moved against such ancient means of avoiding employment as begging.[14] The extent to which these and other allied steps found implementation varied greatly according to the size and geopolitical status of a given governmental entity. However, as an early attempt to rationalize commerce, mercantilism has been called the first phase of the German Industrial Revolution, a development well under way in the unified nations of Europe by the end of the eighteenth century.[15] The trend toward the regulation of commerce was so strong that it found acceptance even by the state with a historical aversion to foreign trade and/or with a strictly agrarian economic base, as evidenced by the adoption of a French form of mercantilism, called Colbertism, by the canton of Berne.[16]

Of course, throughout the German-speaking area, the city dweller belonged to a minority. Whereas London could count over 800,000 inhabitants by 1800, and Paris 670,000, Vienna lagged far behind at 207,000.[17] But it surpassed Berlin's 150,000 and Hamburg's 100,000. Dresden, Königsberg, Prague, and Breslau numbered between 50,000 and 100,000. Approximately 80 percent of the population lived and worked in rural areas.[18] And, while conditions within the peasantry varied from region to region and from landowner to landowner, illiteracy was the norm.[19] Hence, the largest segment of the population must be virtually excluded from examinations of literary life until well into the nineteenth century. Those few peasants who could read usually reached only as far as the family Bible. Still quite rare was the gifted boy who was educated either by the church or by the army. In many regions, the most that society offered its working class was food and shelter, and, all too often, it did not offer that.[20]

Ironically enough, its level of education also kept much of the nobility from involvement in literary life. An adolescent son was frequently proficient at little more than dancing, fencing, and riding. As he matured, social graces were added along with a taste for travel and a tolerance for liquor. According to Rolf Engelsing, the rural nobility often remained ignorant of the means of access to intellectual pursuits: "Wie die klein- und unterbürgerlichen Schichten war der Landadel, der literarische Interessen hatte, vielfach darauf angewiesen, sich vorlesen zu lassen."[21] Throughout the eighteenth century, the "public sphere" for literature was overwhelmingly middle-class, and the composition of that social level had changed since the Age of Luther.

Absolutism of the type that developed in Germany during the course of the Thirty Years' War invested the tiny ruling elite with legislative, executive, and judicial powers that affected all aspects of human affairs. The areas of responsibility were simply too many and too varied to be tended adequately by a single human being, the prince. Accordingly, an administrative bureaucracy began to grow up around the ruler, a bureaucracy that required legal and fiscal expertise not normally possessed by the lower nobility. The demand for university-trained professionals rose, with the result that the merchants and craftsmen of the old urban middle class were joined by ever more lawyers, administrators, physicians, theologians, and of course by the teachers and professors who trained the others. Given the disparities in education and experience within the new, expanded middle class, it was inevitable that fissures would open. For example, the frequently cited "Kleiderordnung" promulgated in Frankfurt in 1731 can distinguish five separate levels within that town's population.[22] Striking is the position of the craftsman in this hierarchically arranged code: he appears at only one remove from the day laborer. Meanwhile, highly educated professionals and wealthy entrepreneurs are securely ensconced in the upper categories. The split was further widened by feelings of condescension on the one side and suspicion mixed with envy on the other.

Any survey of the economic and social status of the German-speaking merchant at this point in history that did not take local factors into account would be of dubious worth. To cite only two centers, Hamburg and Berne supported two highly divergent business atmospheres. Nevertheless, several general conditions combined to promote the rise of the man of commerce. Of mercantilist policies, the support of population growth may have contributed most significantly to the creation of a salubrious climate for business. For centuries before 1648, a number of historical factors had combined to maintain population density at levels sufficiently low that most consumer needs could be met by local farm markets and town craftsmen.[23] Eastern colonization during the High Middle Ages had served to disperse a people whose ranks were increasing. Then, as expansion reached geographic limits in the fourteenth century, the Black Death arrived on the scene. Plague swept the length and breadth of the region well into the following century, regularly decimating the hapless citizenry. Upon first consideration, it would seem logical that the trend toward urbanization during the Reformation would have occasioned a marked rise in the number of city dwellers. But, according to Friedrich Lütge, "... schon die Blütezeit der städtischen Wirtschaft im 15–16. Jh. sieht ein anderes Mittel des Korrigierens: nämlich das späte Heiraten der Gesellen, der Zwang für viele, unverehelicht zu bleiben, u. a. m. treten neben die grundsätzliche Ehelosigkeit des Klerus."[24] The dawn of the eighteenth century did not illuminate a world suddenly devoid of poor sanitary conditions, high infant mortality, and war; however, population density was rising at a rapid rate and with it the demand for goods and services at a distance from consumers. The intensification of trading that resulted not only strengthened existing routes to markets foreign and domestic but also created new ties. The major expansion of overland connections with eastern Europe and Asia Minor has been cited as one of the more significant developments in the economic history of eighteenth-century Germany.[25]

Men of commerce were adapting to changes caused by the growth of the consumer population just as the influence of the "popular philosophy" of the Enlightenment was becoming apparent. The same faith in reason that shone forth from the printed page gave less theoretically inclined contemporaries of Leibniz and Wolff the courage to act on their rational, if at times unconventional and even adventuresome, analyses by sallying forth to distant, often exotic markets. Back at home, the new optimistic attitude enjoined greater attention to the concerns of this world. The *memento mori* mentality of the Baroque faded before empiricism in the natural sciences and sensualism in the philosophies of Locke and Hume. Materialism was on the rise, and, as Friedrich Lütge has pointed out, the mercantilist German princes supported the development: "Dieses Streben [for more adequate supplies of goods] wird auch von den Landesherren für berechtigt angesehen und die Wirtschaftspolitik darauf eingestellt."[26] A burgher's concern with the "quality of life" did not lead him to indulge himself, however. The animosity directed against those engaged in meaningless activities or in no activities at all is apparent in two satirical comedies from mid-century, J. E. Schlegel's *Der Geschäfftige Müßiggänger* (1743) and Lessing's *Der junge Gelehrte* (written in 1747).[27] Each play presents a main character whose lack of initiative and drive would have appeared laughable to audiences of the day. If a member of such an audience happened to be engaged in commerce, his brow was damp during business hours not only because of such eternal variables as the weather, civil turmoil, changes of rulers, and changes of taste but also because of the nature of the governmental status quo. If his interests extended beyond the walls of his home base, he had to contend with the array of tolls and regulations that separated state from state. The absence of a central police authority meant that simply traveling among the various tolltakers involved considerable hazard. Strict limits on the money supply constituted an additional challenge to the resourcefulness of the German merchant. There was no institution similar to the Bank of England (founded in 1694) that could change the credit reserves of a powerful nation by printing money.

Despite such built-in brakes, commerce did expand during the eighteenth century under the leadership of entrepreneurs amply endowed with tenacity and flexibility. Some few did come from the nobility. Worthy of special note are the diverse activities of the rural nobility in Prussia and the other eastern states. Their large estates had long yielded grain for export westward, including to an ever more food-dependent England, and grazing supported a woolen industry. The gentry also showed a growing predilection for the establishment or expansion of industries based on available natural resources. Mills for grain and lumber, breweries, potteries, and mines produced goods that were then marketed, in many cases, by the noblemen themselves. Such industries as beekeeping and pisciculture were largely under the control of the gentry.

The most visible nobleman-entrepreneur was often the regent himself. During and immediately after the Thirty Years' War, a prince interested in developing his commercial profile usually found the local bourgeoisie in a state of disarray characterized by an aversion to time-consuming, risk-taking ventures at what was a time of depressed profitability. For his part, the ruler was typically determined to display his wealth and power in a style epitomized by the court of Louis XIV; hence the appeal of a domestic tapestry or porcelain industry. Whereas the utility of the end product may well be called into question, the taste for luxury did provide badly needed new job-opportunities for thousands.

Many of the bourgeois entrepreneurs who dominated eighteenth-century commerce emerged from the same medieval class that had produced Hans Sachs. The practitioner of a craft usually had the right to market the fruits of his labor as he saw fit. The more enterprising expanded beyond the servicing of a local clientele and began to sell their wares at ever greater distances from the workshop. Finally, a master craftsman would often leave the production end of the business to young masters and journeymen while he devoted himself to merchandising. Shopkeepers and regional retailers expanded in the opposite direction by investing in production. Then it was simply a matter of creating a demand in new markets and supplying that demand. One major requisite for developing foreign trade connections was political stability at home. As a general rule, those cities that led the way in trade were able to offer such a healthy climate for business either because of the policies of energetic, effective rulers or because of the good fortune to have missed much of the dislocation and trauma of the seventeenth century. Such cities were inhabited by real-world models for the merchants in the canon of the early Enlightenment; they also supplied increasing financial support to the literary community, support in the form of theater tickets, book sales, and subscriptions to periodicals. A number of these centers of commerce and culture deserve special attention; first, however, the several participants in the economic life of all German cities must be identified.

During the eighteenth century, a clear distinction was made between the merchant engaged in large-scale foreign trade, the entrepreneur, and the local shopkeeper.[28] The former (variously styled a "Fernhändler," "Importhändler," or "Großhändler") organized, managed, and assumed the risks of an enterprise that directed the passage of a large number of goods from the point of production or post-production storage to the point of consumption or pre-consumption distribution. Although primarily a wholesaler, he did often take part in retail trade. However, local commerce was largely the domain of shopkeepers ("Krämer"), street peddlers operating from mobile stands or booths ("Höker"), and door-to-door hucksters ("Hausierer"). Since the Middle Ages, German hucksters had offered yard goods, thread, yarn, and sewing accessories. Although they would continue to be a significant component of commerce through the nineteenth century, their function was taken over gradually by resident peddlers, the success of whose stands occasionally brought about an elevation in social status. Usually the peddlers sold groceries, housewares, and small farm implements and sustained profit levels that qualified them for membership in the petite bourgeoisie. Their goods were produced locally, whereas the shopkeeper dealt in all manner of products (hence the designation "Alleskaufmann") supplied by the wholesaler. The import-export trader exercised considerable control over the local store-owner. As participants in the governance of their cities through powerful guilds and through seats on city councils, successful wholesalers were involved in the setting of maximum retail prices and in the monitoring of business practices.

Still, despite limits imposed from above, even shopkeepers could arrive at a state of some affluence. Of them, Lutz von Krosigk writes: "Sie gehörten in den großen Handelsstädten zu den wohlhabenden Gruppen der Bevölkerung und hoben sich in ihrer Lebenshaltung deutlich vom Handwerk ab. Doch stufte sich innerhalb der Krämerei das Vermögen nach Tiefe und Breite vom Ärmsten bis zum Reichen ab."[29] Even in smaller towns, where income levels of store-owner and craftsman were virtually the same, the former saw himself as occupying a higher position in the social pecking order. However, it was the large population center that came to support both commerce and the arts during the eighteenth century, and the first among such centers was Hamburg.

The old Hanseatic town enjoyed many advantages in addition to its long history as a nexus for trade. Its highly favorable position on the Elbe featured a protected harbor near the sea and improved with the completion of the Müllroser Canal (1668) between the Oder and the Spree, which opened eastern Europe to Germany's great port. That same geographic advantage was partially responsible for Hamburg's success at avoiding most of the warfare of the seventeenth and early eighteenth centuries. The death and destruction visited upon cities and towns in the interior was virtually unknown. And Hamburg directed its gaze not toward the ongoing scenes of despair but toward its great models and rivals, London and Amsterdam. There entrepreneurs had come to have considerable input into governmental decision-making: so, too, in Hamburg, the independent city-state. Erwin Wiskemann asserts that, already in the seventeenth century, its inhabitants saw their home as a republic whose institutions contrasted happily with the status quo elsewhere in Germany: "Der Machiavellismus wird bei jeder passenden Gelegenheit abgelehnt, das freie Bürgertum zur Maxime erhoben, die Freiheit der Stadt wird als etwas Gottgewolltes betrachtet."[30] Pride in modern quay facilities that bustled with ships sailing under a wide variety of flags was matched by pride in a council system of municipal government that assured the participation of several groups within the population. The set of basic laws adopted in 1710 and 1712 provided the framework for nearly a century and a half of history in the port city. Governance was shared by two bodies: the parliament (the "Bürgerschaft") and the city council (the "Rat"). Although both participated in the drafting of new laws, the city council was invested with final executive and judicial authority. It was composed of fourteen men trained in the law and another fourteen well versed in the intricacies of commerce and sea trade. The latter were in fact principals of the larger merchant houses. The parliament did include landowners, certain members of the city's administrative bureaucracy, and representatives of the various churches; however, it was subject to both call and dismissal by a council whose members were all cognizant of the fact that the city's heart was its harbor. That facility served approximately two thousand ships per annum during the eighteenth century; between 1750 and 1800, insurance companies wrote policies covering cargoes and their conveyances that reached 120,000,000 talers.[31]

Hamburg's special position within European commerce is described with verve in an autobiographical sketch that spans the last seven decades of the eighteenth century as experienced by a merchant, his father, and their families: "Denn Hamburg ward für eine Staatstadt gehalten, und dieses Wort war von den Zeiten der Hansa her noch ehrwürdig. . . . Das eingebrannte Hamburger Wappen und der Cirkel, der in Hamburg auf die Tonnen gesetzt wurde, leistete die Gewährleistung für ihre innere Beschaffenheit, und der Kredit des so versandten Herings erhielt sich unerschüttert."[32] The father's rise coincided with the city's emergence as the herring market for all of Europe. Just as significant for Jacob Hinrich Hudtwalcker's employer and his competitors was the trade in whale oil, dried fish, and other sea products. Others handled the importation of more exotic consumables such as tobacco, tea, sugar, and coffee. After the first quarter of the century, the grain trade and an allied brewing industry began to fade; however, such natural resources as lumber and metal ore continued to support big business in Hamburg. The most significant export item was linen cloth from Westphalia and Silesia. Destined primarily for England and Portugal, it accounted for 75 percent of the city's approximately 1,640,000 marks in export trade with the English in 1713.[33]

The strength of Hamburg's economic life was manifest in the existence of a substantial social level composed of wealthy merchants who actively supported literature and the arts. When the elder Hudtwalcker left the house of von Winthem in 1743, that company could show holdings of 300,000 marks.[34] The principal was accordingly in a position to demonstrate his gratitude for sixteen years of faithful and effective service by presenting the would-be entrepreneur with a sum of 4,000 marks, which accounted for two-thirds of Hudtwalcker's initial capitalization. Such available liquidity found its way into a theater life that grew by leaps and bounds during the first half of the eighteenth century. Traveling companies such as the

Schönemann troupe enjoyed steady support, which by 1750 had begun to take the form of drama criticism in major publications.[35] Among the latter were a number of moral weeklies designed after the English model, including *Der Patriot* (begun in 1724). Edited by a son of one of the city's leading commercial families, Barthold Hinrich Brockes, *Der Patriot* was popular enough to warrant press runs of up to five thousand copies.[36] This degree of popularity can be attributed at least in part to the relative sophistication of the city that fathered the "Teutschübende Gesellschaft" and which Christian Wernicke, J. U. König, and Friedrich von Hagedorn called home. Coffeehouses similar to those in the British capital served as cultural watering holes where merchants, civil servants, and intellectuals met to read periodicals and to discuss the news of the day.[37] Mingling among the sounds of the port was the music of resident composers Telemann, Buxtehude, and Händel; opera flourished even as it introduced libretti that celebrated the accomplishments of Germanic heroes such as Arminius and Charlemagne or praised the virtues of everyday life and work in the Hanseatic town.[38] The breadth of the city's cultural activity was possible only because of the participation of a civic-minded merchant class.

In the case of Leipzig, the tie between trade and intellectual pursuits had long been institutionalized by the three annual book fairs, which went far toward making the host city the literary capital of Germany during the early Enlightenment. Particularly significant were the Easter meetings of the book-dealers, who often also doubled as publishers.[39] They paid visits to the best-known publishing houses, and trades would be arranged; generally speaking, copies of books, not money, changed hands. Of course, sales to a city hungry for the printed word were also a significant incentive to make what was for many an exhausting trip. Hence, advertisements, handbills, and title pages were displayed throughout the center of a town whose university constituted a second great support for the arts and sciences. Georg Witkowski has pointed to an example of this merging of interests: "Die großen Buchhändler boten für ideale Zwecke ihren Reichtum dar. Als der Universitätsbibliothekar in den achtziger Jahren des 17. Jahrhunderts Programmata metrica ad literatos herumschickte, um sie zur Vermehrung und Auszierung der Bibliothek 'anzufrischen,' hatte seine Bitte den besten Erfolg. Unter den 91 Porträts, den Landkarten und mathematischen Instrumenten, die bis 1687 der Bibliothek geschenkt wurden, stammten viele von Leipziger Bürgern her."[40] The university returned the favor by providing Leipzig with the likes of Pufendorf, Thomasius, Leibniz, and Wolff. Germanists immediately associate the name Johann Christoph Gottsched with the home of the "Deutsche Gesellschaft." The prominent literary theoretician, theater reformer, and rhetorician edited moral weeklies and journals of general scholarship targeted at a relatively well-educated, economically secure bourgeoisie that belonged to several local learned societies.

The heart of that bourgeoisie so active in promoting learned studies and cultural institutions beat in time to the demands of a diverse consumer population, for the affluent citizens of Leipzig were its merchants.[41] For decades Saxony had served as a crossroads for trade routes bearing a wide variety of goods north and south and, more specially, east and west. To this highly favorable geographic location were joined the traditional annual trade fairs and substantial mineral deposits. Roads were often dangerous during the few decades before and after 1700; however, merchants adapted by forming caravans and by hiring armed escorts.[42] Many trading patterns established before and even during the Thirty Years' War contributed to the prosperity enjoyed by Leipzig's commercial elite. Silk goods traveled from Italy via Leipzig to Poland, Silesia, and Russia. In similar fashion, Saxon woolens, Swabian fustian, Rhine wines, cloth from England, and housewares from the workshops of Nuremberg found their way to consumers in the east through the offices of Leipzig merchants. From Silesia came linen in great quantities, linen that represented the most significant single item in the German states' export trade with other nations.[43] The trade in tin, copper, brass, iron, and sheet metal, which had suffered greatly when the tumult of the first half of the seventeenth century closed many a mine, began to rebound as industrializing England and France developed ever greater appetites for raw materials.

Leipzig's commercial life benefited from the eastward movement of French Huguenots in the wake of Louis XIV's campaign of oppression.[44] The refugees soon established extensive networks for dealing in such "French wares" as wine, indigo, oil, and luxury items. The trade in silk, wool, and especially tobacco from the Americas was soon advanced by a minority which, however, did not receive full civil rights until the Napoleonic incursion. The same was true of the Italian community, whose merchants typically bought and sold wine, fruit, and specialty foods. Native Germans frequently developed such strong business ties to the court in Dresden, as well as to other princes in central Europe, that they became virtually indispensable. Such alliances were frequently formalized through ennoblement. For example, the wool trader Johann Ernst Kregel (1652–1731) became Johann Ernst Kregel von Sternbach in 1697. Peter Hohmann (1663–1732) rose through the ranks in the merchant house of Fleischer and Kober to become one of the wealthier financiers in the city. Because of his lucrative activity in supplying various armies, he was created Hohmann Edler von Hohenthal by Emperor Charles VI in 1717.[45] Such men built elegant Baroque townhouses, which they adorned with the immortalizing work of portraitists and engravers as well as with extensive art collections drawn together from throughout Europe. Of course, the grandest life-style was reserved for the elector himself, and, by the beginning of the eighteenth century, August the Strong was spending enormous sums in an effort to compete with the French court. According to Balet, in the year 1719 he lavished four million talers on his own need for luxury.[46] Festivals were arranged, palaces built, and mistresses kept on call. On the one hand, such a life-style meant high taxes for the entire citizenry of Saxony; on the other hand, Leipzig's merchants fared better than most since the court did bring them steady business. As Ernst Kroker notes: "Was Dresden brauchte, mußte es zu einem großen Teil durch die Vermittlung Leipzigs kaufen."[47]

No such division between centers of government and commerce existed in Prussia, where Berlin served as a single nexus for political, economic, and cultural affairs. The capital experienced a tremendous growth in population during the eighteenth century: the small garrison town of 24,000 in 1700 had swelled fivefold to 113,000 at midcentury and to 172,000 by the year 1800.[48] One major factor in the startling leap from small town to significant city was the immigration policy first enunciated by the Great Elector. The Edict of Potsdam of 29 October 1685 established an "open-door" policy for French refugees with the avowed intention of stimulating trade.[49] At the time, some form of stimulation was needed. Berlin was an isolated community inhabited largely by farmers and craftsmen whose lives conformed to patterns dating back to the Middle Ages. But for the needs of the regent, his court, and senior military officers, foreign trade would have been almost unknown. Accordingly, Berlin could not boast a class of merchants with international business connections. Stefi Jersch-Wenzel finds this to be the case "teils wegen des Fehlens eines aufnahmefähigen Marktes, teils wegen der noch wenig ausgebauten Verkehrswege und schließlich infolge der gesamten wirtschaftlichen Rückständigkeit."[50] The rulers of Prussia first tackled these hindrances by "importing" foreign-born, foreign-trained practitioners of commercial techniques and customs not yet commonplace in eastern Europe. The French immigrants brought funds with them in addition to expertise in capital-formation and credit-management. Friedrich Wilhelm reciprocated by providing armed moving teams, by lifting duties on possessions moved, by offering dwellings along with any building materials needed for repair, and by extending full civil rights.

The degree to which the second great monarch of Prussia supported economic development in his realm and, specifically, in Berlin has been the subject of some debate.[51] However, Friedrich Wilhelm I was without question an active champion of his nation's wool industry. The exportation of raw wool was forbidden under penalty of, first, imprisonment and then, in the event of recidivism, execution. Not the raw material but the finished product was to be Prussia's export. Toward this end the ruler took two steps. First, weavers and dyers were induced to take up residence in Berlin, and, secondly, an institution was created through which the state provided impoverished textile workers with raw wool. Their labors were paid for in cash when finished cloth was returned from home workshops to what was referred to as the "Lagerhaus," founded in 1723.[52] One year later, at the prodding of the king, a consortium of Berlin fabric merchants founded the "Russische Handelskompanie," which reached its export maximum of 21,511 measures of cloth in 1733.[53] As the name indicates, trade was carried on with Russia and Poland primarily; imported through this same major channel were hides, leather, and furs.

Among other companies that came into existence under the reign of Friedrich Wilhelm I, the firm of David Splitgerber and Gottfried Adolf Daum, founded in 1712, deserves special mention.[54] The partnership began as a military supplier of August the Strong and then Friedrich Wilhelm I. Cannon balls, bombs, gunbarrels, swords, daggers, and bayonets were first brought to Berlin after purchase abroad from foreign distributors; then, as the firm grew, it set up its own factories and took over the management of previously state-controlled and still state-owned armament facilities. Soon, however, Splitgerber and Daum were active in the "colonial" trade (tea, spices, cocoa, coffee) as well as in the importation of cloth and clothing from England. By the late 1720s, they owned a controlling interest in the "Russische Handelskompanie," which at their behest developed a healthy trade in the Austrian territories.

Friedrich II possessed a broader vision of economic trends, as evidenced by his stance concerning trade in wool and cotton. His predecessor had forbidden the use of cotton cloth in Prussia for fear of wounding the well-established wool industry; however, Frederick the Great not only lifted the ban but supported the efforts of those active in promoting what he saw as a commodity with export potential. It has been suggested that one of the new monarch's major interests in the War of the Austrian Succession was the textile industry of annexed Silesia,[55] not to mention the region's mineral deposits. Prussia's continual search for new markets prompted the establishment in 1751 of the "Compagnie prussienne," whose mission was the development of transoceanic ties, especially with India and the Far East. Its ships were also to take part in the rapidly growing whale-oil and tallow trade. Friedrich II took special interest in this manifestation of the rise in his land's international stature, an interest concretized in the granting of major tax and tariff reductions. In addition, the "Compagnie" was permitted to offer for domestic sale any items purchased abroad, whether or not such sale was normally proscribed in Prussia.

Clearly, the king had his pet commercial ventures, even as he had his favorite merchants, among whom Johann Ernst Gotzkowsky must be counted.[56] Gotzkowsky manufactured silk cloth from the raw material supplied by Italian merchants and then sold the finished product to customers from Russia and Poland whom he met at the Leipzig fairs. During the early stages of these endeavors, the king repeatedly helped this redoubtable man of commerce with sizable loans that ensured expansion even during such economically depressed periods as the last years of the war against Austria and then the aftermath of the Lisbon earthquake of 1755. Gotzkowsky more than repaid his ruler and his city with a blend of heroism and diplomacy during the occupation of Berlin by the Russians and Austrians in 1760.

The capital of Prussia cannot be considered a major cultural center during the first half of the eighteenth century; nevertheless, intellectual life was hardly moribund. Leading the charge were two "Staats- und gelehrte Zeitungen," the "Vossische" (begun in 1721) and the "Spenersche" (begun in 1740).[57] Both presented not only "hard news" from the courts of Europe but also reviews of new publications in the natural sciences and in the humanities. Lessing himself wrote reviews for the "Vossische" and in 1754 began to edit one of the first literary journals, the *Theatralische Bibliothek*. The citizenry that supported active presses also bought theater tickets, and in 1750 the city welcomed no less a personage than Voltaire, who paid an extended visit to the royal court. Nevertheless, as of mid-century

Berlin could not claim the well-developed cultural life of either Leipzig or Hamburg.

Literary activity in the first half of the eighteenth century was concentrated in a relatively small number of locales, notably Hamburg, Leipzig, Berlin, and German-speaking Switzerland. It is, however, impossible to pass over Frankfurt am Main, which played such a significant role in the economic life of central Europe. At this time the Frankfurt trade fair trailed that of Leipzig in significance, and the Saxon city's rate of population growth outstripped that of its old rival.[58] Still, Frankfurt had clearly established itself as the banking and financial center of Germany. Such leading financiers as de Neufville, Metzler, and the Bethmanns extended major loans to both cities and monarchs. At the end of the century, fabulous sums were provided by Frankfurt to both Russia and the Empire.[59] Of course, it was primarily through the underwriting of political entities and private entrepreneurs along the Main and the Rhine that the banking component of the city's well-to-do bourgeoisie maintained its preeminence. The commercial component was concerned with supplying the south and west of Germany with wares from Holland and France.

Income levels within the middle class in a city the size of Frankfurt go far to explain why public support for artistic endeavor came from the privileged few. Paul Münch divides that class into three categories, which correspond to the petite bourgeoisie, the professional community, and the moneyed upper middle class.[60] For these categories he cites average real-income estimates for the year 1700 at 200, 400 and 800 talers respectively. The gaps between levels have widened by 1750, when the figures have risen to 400, 900, and 2,000 talers. Clearly, by 1750 the commercial bourgeoisie had effectively separated itself from its noncommercial peers, many of whom had equivalent if not substantially higher educational attainments. In the meantime, the petite bourgeoisie was struggling to keep ahead of the rising cost of goods (especially, food) and services. According to Münch: "Im Durchschnitt mußten fast 75% des Einkommens für die Ernährung aufgewandt werden, so daß de facto schon für den geringsten Luxus (z.B. Bücher) kein Geld vorhanden war."[61] It is only logical to assume that German literature's passage from an institution for the nobility to an institution for the middle class must have passed through a number of stages on its way down the social ladder. This assumption is borne out by the financial conditions that obtained within that lower level. As will be shown, writers became increasingly sensitive to the needs of their merchant-patrons.

Three smaller localities that played significant roles in both commercial and literary life were Bremen, Berne, and the county palatine Stolberg. By the eighteenth century, Bremen had been far surpassed by Hamburg in nearly all forms of human activity. It serviced only one-quarter as many trade vessels as the larger city,[62] although its merchant community did figure prominently in the movement of specific goods. Lumber, North German foodstuffs, and linen from Westphalia enjoyed strong consumer-demand abroad and hence exercised a major influence on the city's export standing. Tobacco came to be a colonial import immediately associated with the old Hanseatic town, which therefore benefited from the development of Britain's North American colonies. A sizable fleet maintained routes to Britain and Scandinavia, whose shores were frequented by representatives of such consortia as the "Englische Kompanie" and the "Bergenfahrer-Gesellschaft."[63] Still, the intellectual atmosphere of Bremen was considerably less vibrant than that of larger cities. As an example, Pamela Currie cites the failure of the *Bremer wöchentliche Nachrichten* to find a large enough readership for a literary supplement.[64] Two attempts were made, complete with pieces by such popular writers as Hagedorn and Gellert; however, any great interest in poetry and moral essays was lacking. That the city comes to mind among the specialists in literature of the "Aufklärung" is largely due to the *Neue Beiträge zum Vergnügen des Verstandes und Witzes*, the literary journal that served as an organ for apostate followers of the literary pope Gottsched. However, the only strong tie that Gellert, Rabener, the Schlegels, and later Klopstock had to Bremen was the location in that city of Nathanael Saurmann, publisher of the *Bremer Beiträge*.

A small city with one direct tie to the eighteenth-century canon was Berne, the home of Albrecht von Haller.[65] Both town and canton had long enjoyed an underlying economic stability based on agriculture. However, by the end of the seventeenth century, foreign imports had come to play a dominant role in the local economy. As judged by mercantilist standards, Berne was declining in political as well as commercial significance. The oligarchical governing institutions that reacted to this development were the "Great Council" and the smaller executive cabinet, both of which were controlled by approximately seventy wealthy families. The first major step taken was the creation of a "Kommerzienrat" (1687) charged with fostering the establishment of new industries and trade connections. Hans Rudolf Rytz has demonstrated that the rigorously mercantilist policies of the French finance minister Jean-Baptiste Colbert provided the Swiss with a highly visible model.[66] Silk, wool, leather, and linen industries were developed with the express intention of creating a strong foreign trade in finished goods. In 1719 the importation of such products was forbidden by a canton ordinance which also set in place mechanisms for governmental surveillance of local markets. Rytz summarizes official policy as follows: "Dem Beispiel Frankreichs und der reformierten Nachbarn folgend, sah die Regierung des Agrarstaates Bern nun plötzlich die Einführung von Manufakturen als den Weg zu Reichtum, Macht und Glück."[67] The relatively abrupt change in the canton's course advocated by its ruling circles met with organized resistance from traditionalists during the Davel uprising in 1723 and then again during the brief revolutionary career of Samuel Henzi, who was arrested and executed in 1749. Henzi's plot had as its central aim a broadening of the franchise and a reorganization of the Great Council. Although the established order prevailed and indeed became even more entrenched in the aftermath of the revolts, the latter constitute an accurate barometer of the tension produced when Bernese experimented with the "path to wealth, power, and happiness" followed not only by France but also by the German states.

Quite the opposite situation obtained in Stolberg, where the ruling count was also the tiny state's leading entrepreneur.[68] He presided over lucrative export industries developed since the sixteenth century, industries that exploited abundant natural resources located along the southern apron of the Harz Mountains. Iron mining supplied a local smelting operation, while copper deposits guaranteed commercial distinction to an area that was rather isolated. In addition, the regents directed timber and milling operations from the midst of their heavily forested realm. From 1724 until mid-century, Count Christoph Ludwig had in his employ as barber-surgeon, travel companion, and court functionary Johann Gottfried Schnabel, the author of the first highly successful German "Robinson novel." *Insel Felsenburg* was written in Stolberg.

Schnabel's employer must have been the envy of merchants who came to know him professionally, for the man was both proprietor and prince, his sphere of activity both company and country. In general, bourgeois contacts could not have helped but muse on the apparently ideal conditions enjoyed by aristocratic colleagues, whose youthful training was more often than not as relaxed as their mature dealings were extensive. The making of a man of commerce within the middle class proceeded in definite stages, none of which assumed either inherited land or substantial liquidity. By the third decade of the eighteenth century, a consensus was emerging as to the form that the education of a would-be merchant without title should take. In his highly perceptive article on bourgeois class-consciousness during the early Enlightenment, Wolfgang Martens cites a fictitious character-portrait published in 1726 as an article in Hamburg's *Der Patriot*.[69] The exemplary young entrepreneur who emerges has been the recipient of a thorough, well-rounded, "liberal" education provided by the public schools of the city on the Elbe. Through his nineteenth year, Pasiteles has attended grammar and secondary schools and spent two years at the "Gymnasium." Topics of concentration at the latter institution include history, geography, mathematics, law, modern foreign languages, Latin, ethics, and philosophy. An extensive European tour follows which is designed to make the young man conversant with the manners and mores of other peoples on the continent. Two institutions are conspicuous by their absence from the curriculum vitae of the worthy. Although his family is sufficiently wealthy to fund a "Studienreise," the youth has not studied under private tutors, the "Hofmeister" to whose often dubious ministrations children of the nobility were normally commended. Likewise, the *Patriot* does not have its flawless creation attend the university; if anything, the careful enumeration of formidable courses of study suggests some small insecurity, the grounds for which are made clear below. At any rate, his formal education complete, Pasiteles immediately throws himself into business and civic activities. Indeed, his dedication to the city is described in particularly strong terms: "Er entbrach sich nicht nur seinen eigenen Geschäfften, sondern, auch seiner nöthigen Ruhe, so offt er der Stadt zu dienen wuste."[70] In the course of such service, the young man's altruism guides an informed, moderate, thoughtful voice that is sought out by others. In fact, *Der Patriot* creates a figure so involved in the common weal that the reader is left wondering how the merchant can possibly find time for his calling. Strikingly absent are descriptions of business involvements: his apprenticeship, position within a firm, relationships with superiors and colleagues, or attitudes concerning business as a profession. The image that emerges is that of an erudite, civic-minded cosmopolite, who also happens to be a merchant. Such was the published ideal.

The living reality was frequently just the opposite. For instance, the social historian Rolf Engelsing sketches the life of the Bremen merchant Konrad Wilhelmi (1730–1803), whose obituary describes the man's early education as deficient.[71] Beyond training in mercantile subject areas, only the bare rudiments of Latin were offered in his schools. Wilhelmi did acquire some French during a prolonged stay abroad; however, he possessed only a very weak reading knowledge of his own native tongue, a knowledge that failed him more often than not. Engelsing comments: "In den Jahren, in denen er hätte lesen lernen können, schien die Zeit dafür zu kostbar und war zu knapp. Dabei war Wilhelmis Lesefertigkeit am Durchschnitt gemessen noch nicht einmal allzu gering ausgebildet. Denn es gab zahlreiche Kaufleute, die jedenfalls die Bibel und die Erbauungsliteratur nicht selbst lasen, sondern von Jüngeren vorgelesen bekamen, wohl weil sie selbst zuviel Mühe mit der Lektüre gehabt hätten."[72] The gulf between Pasiteles and these semiliterates is huge. Particularly noteworthy is the fact that Wilhelmi did have the opportunity to learn how to read adequately but instead put profit-margin before intellectual improvement—over a period of years. Engelsing asserts that the typical man of commerce could read, write, and cipher to the extent required to certify him as a member of the middle class.[73] Of course, the paperwork produced by professional activity (e.g., correspondence) rendered true illiteracy too great a liability for any entrepreneur with even modest trade connections. However, the period of apprenticeship in an office was not calculated to imbue a young man with a burning desire to widen his horizons. He was expected to pick up the rudiments of his future vocation from a master who was often both ill equipped and disinclined to articulate the dos and don'ts of commerce, let alone to undertake any sort of broader pedagogical role. That the situation could become frustrating for a gifted youth is clear from the comments of Johann Daniel Noltenius (born in 1726), who wrote in 1744 concerning the less than rewarding situation at his master's office in Bremen: "Dieses Alles wollte ich mich noch nicht verdrießen lassen, wenn ich nur gute Unterweisung hätte. Was ich kann, muß ich von mir selber lernen. Mein Herr selbst kann nicht viel."[74]

A closer look at the formal education obtained by members of two rising merchant families during the first half of the eighteenth century is provided by Johann Michael Hudtwalcker (1747–1818) in his autobiographical writings. These reminiscences date from 1795 and 1811; however, they detail the life of their author's father, Jacob Hinrich (1710–1781), and describe the childhood of Johann Michael up to 1763.[75] The elder man was himself the son of a marginally successful owner of a cheese shop in Altona and received instruction only in the basic skills, reading, writing, and arithmetic, in addition to study of the catechism. Johann Michael comments:

Das war die Erziehung der damaligen Zeit bis ins 15., 16. Jahr bei den meisten Menschen, besonders in Kleinstädten, wie derzeit Altona war. Aber die Erfahrung und Beispiel waren auch damals, was sie noch sind und ewig bleiben werden, die eigentliche Erziehung. Die Schule fängt erst recht an, wenn man die sogenannten Schulen verläßt. Auch in der vorigen Generation gab es gute und große Männer, wie in der jetzigen. Sie bildeten sich selbst, wie in der jetzigen.[76]

Certainly the state of affairs recounted here as generally applicable is fully consonant with Engelsing's portrayal of a merchant whose education was humble at best. The editorializing in the sentences cited suggests an eagerness on the part of the boy destined for trade to leave formal schooling behind, the willingness of elders to accede to such wishes, and finally a mild contempt for institutionalized learning. Hudtwalcker implies that schools are actually obstacles in life's path. His faith in experience as the most able teacher would hardly have been shared by the young Noltenius.

In the year 1727, the sixteen-year-old Jacob Hinrich Hudtwalcker began his apprenticeship in the establishment of Meinert von Winthem, a wholesaler in herring, train oil, and fish. The youth's father had just died; hence, to two guardians devolved the task of extending a signed guarantee to the merchant with regard to their charge's execution of responsibilities. Johann Michael reports with apparent pride: "Sie klopften ihm auf die Schulter, sagten: 'Junge, mach' uns nicht Schanden'—und unterschrieben."[77] Their faith was more than justified. For four years the young man strained his somewhat delicate constitution with heavy manual labor during daylight hours and devoted long evenings to writing in the office. Although Jacob Hinrich provided his employer with such extensive, demanding service, his compensation was minimal, and his treatment befitted the most humble of menials. He took meals with the house servants, and in fact had to shine his master's shoes as well as those of the senior employees. His tasks also included helping the cook clean out the kitchen and holding a lantern for von Winthem whenever the latter went visiting in the city after dark. No formal education was offered by the merchant during an apprenticeship that the biographer describes as the early eighteenth-century norm. "Die Lage des Kaufmannsburschen war derzeit nicht von der Lage eines Handwerksburschen verschieden und vielleicht in mancher Rücksicht noch schlimmer."[78] The elder Hudtwalcker is described as meeting such treatment with large amounts of fortitude, some disgust, and not a few tears.

At age twenty Jacob Hinrich was rewarded for his diligence with a promotion to the rank of junior assistant. Although strength and sweat were still demanded, his rise brought him under the daily scrutiny of von Winthem himself, to whose table Hudwalcker was now admitted. As the firm came to value the young man more highly, it began to initiate him into the mysteries of commercial practices. Detailed instruction was provided in bookkeeping and correspondence even as he was made acquainted with market conditions and environmental factors that affected the harvest of the ocean's bounty. That is to say, during the course of his apprenticeship, Jacob Hinrich's further education was strictly limited to subject areas vital to the pursuit of success in his vocation. That he viewed this state of affairs as unsatisfactory is apparent in his son's mention of an ongoing commitment to self-improvement: "Mein Vater fing früh an, seine Prediger zu wählen, sich an keine Kirche zu binden und zu Hause sich den Inhalt aufzuschreiben. Er bildete dadurch seinen Stil und seine Sprache; er tat, was er konnte, sich zu bilden."[79] However, long hours of work within a profession that did not foster intellectual growth inevitably took its toll. Even a young merchant so clearly desirous of a well-rounded education faced considerable difficulty; his peers could not appreciate such endeavors. "Mein Vater konnte [meine Muttersprache] nicht allein weder richtig sprechen noch schreiben, sondern auch von meiner anderen Umgebung fast niemand, den einen Lehrer ausgenommen."[80]

Johann Michael writes these last lines with reference to the situation he faced as a boy in the mid-1750s. His father's business had expanded to such an extent that the family now numbered seven and occupied a large three-story house in the center of Hamburg. At the time the elder Hudtwalcker enjoyed financial success and material well-being; however, his dissatisfaction with very real deficiencies in his education persisted and found new, positive expression in support for his son's academic career. By age three the child was babbling forth the alphabet for his parents and was attending a "Leseschule" with his older sisters for three hours during the morning and two during the afternoon. The boy's teacher had studied theology in Marburg; after moving to the Hanseatic town, he had undertaken the instruction of over twenty pupils when Johann Michael began to take lessons in 1754. Herr Junck emphasized reading from the Bible, Latin, grammar, and geography and won over his young charges with an unorthodox, informal approach. Nevertheless, at least one pupil found the teacher wanting: "Bei dem allen war dieser Unterricht sehr leer und mangelhaft; an Sachkenntnis, an Begriffe von Recht und Unrecht, an Historie, an Bildung der Urteilskraft oder des Geschmacks und an unsere Sprache wurde gar nicht gedacht."[81] A far deeper impression was made on the boy by excursions shared with his father, whom Johann Michael credits with being his best teacher. Filial devotion is immediately apparent, as is the first step in the making of a merchant. However, when Junck showed himself to be more interested in the social whirl of the big city than in his professional duties, Jacob Hinrich did not take the opportunity to discontinue all lessons but rather engaged two new instructors, one for French and one for Classics. The latter also introduced his teenage student to the better German writers of the day. When young Hudtwalcker began to work in his father's firm in 1762, his studies continued; indeed, English was added at the cost of another instructor. As the firm took more and more of his time, Johann Michael allowed his studies to suffer; however, when compared with that of his father and most of his contemporaries, the formal education sketched here was little short of extraordinary.

The standard level of training attained by a young apprentice emerges from a royal Prussian decree of 16 July 1755, which constituted yet another attempt by Friedrich II to regulate commercial life for the good of his nation.[82] Here the goal was to impose some uniformity on the requirements for admission into the fraternity of commerce. The generally accepted age of fifteen was accordingly fixed as the minimum. The wording of the decree makes clear the fact that unprincipled merchants had taken younger children into their firms —doubtless in order to have additional years of service at the mindless jobs familiar to Jacob Hinrich Hudtwalcker. Also, a local pastor was to examine such fifteen-year-olds in three subjects: writing, arithmetic, and Christian dogma. Finally, provision was made for the evaluation of a young man's progress after a four-to-seven year period of apprenticeship. Testing by a committee of local merchants was clearly designed to bring peer-pressure to bear on the merchant-master as a means of ensuring that some actual training was provided. The decree paid special attention to the vulnerable position of youths from towns outside of Prussia and sons of the peasantry. In sum, it is clear that the junior Hudtwalcker's situation was completely unknown to many a boy entering the world of trade, a boy whose master was not related by blood. The familial tie *was* most often the case in villages, where shopkeepers occupied positions of prestige within the middle class.[83] Their sons began service in the early rather than middle teens as errand-runners, stock clerks, and janitors. After five or six years of strict supervision and periodic instruction, they entered public-contact positions behind the counter. Although such small-town men of commerce enjoyed relatively comfortable life-styles and great respect among their rural clientele, status did not accrue as the result of any formal education of consequence, which was in fact rare.

Wherever he found himself, the German youth headed for a business office had an easier time securing an education, however humble, than did his female contemporary. When the ideal merchant Pasiteles presides over a growing family, he plays an active role in the education of his sons.[84] He alternately encourages and threatens with the express intent of making them independent, responsible citizens of a republic. The daughters of the house have received instruction in French; however, it is not this bow to modish francophilia that wins general approval, but rather their demure personalities and domestic capabilities. From young girlhood on, women were not presented with an alternative to subaltern status. Even in the *Patriot*'s ideal case, it is readily apparent that marital relationships between men and women so reared rested on a set of exploitative, even abusive assumptions. Curt Gebauer writes: "Eine weitere Ursache der ehelichen Mißstände war in dem zurückgezogenen Leben der meisten Mädchen aus bürgerlichem Stande zu finden, das einer kurzsichtigen und tyrannischen Sitte entsprach."[85] In the country, the woman who could read and write her native language was a novelty. Fathers justified their support for a kind of ongoing Dark Ages for half of humanity with such intriguing reasons as the possibility that amorous correspondence would occur.[86] Given the extremely narrow range of intellectual activity permitted young women and the ennui that must have resulted, this particular fear seems well founded. The catechism was normally the greatest conceptual demand placed upon what was clearly perceived as the "second sex." The situation within a merchant family in a trading town of any size was little better. "Mit der weiblichen Erziehung war es um diese Zeit in Hamburg schlecht bestellt, und meine Mutter war als Mädchen nicht mehr, als was fast alle ihre Zeitgenossinnen damals waren."[87] Johann Michael Hudtwalcker's mother mastered just enough reading and writing to enable her to discharge the duties of a housewife. While Pasiteles's daughters learned French as their bit of culture, this woman took piano lessons and learned some dance steps. All of which, her somewhat supercilious offspring reports, the lady soon forgot. Her son does dutifully report that Frau Hudtwalcker had learned the catechism and had become adept at cooking and sewing: that is, precisely the same accomplishments as her many sisters in isolated rural areas. So complete was the woman's ignorance that she did what she had been brought up to do without reflection, "ohne sich um etwas, was außer Hamburg in der Welt vorging oder vorgegangen war zu bekümmern."[88]

The great discrepancy in education, experience, and worldview between merchant and wife had major implications for the institution of marriage and, more generally, for family patterns. Modern views concerning the equality of spouses had no currency in Germany during the first half of the eighteenth century. Again concerning his mother, Hudtwalcker writes: "Sie wußte nicht, was Liebe als Leidenschaft war; aber Jugend, Treu und Anhänglichkeit machten sie zu einer vortrefflichen Frau, und die Ehe meiner Eltern war sehr glücklich."[89] The picture that emerges is that of a childlike person completely under the domination of an authoritarian patriarch. She is the "gute Hausfrau" to whom a later age would assign the provinces "Kinder, Küche, Kirche."[90] As is apparent from Hudtwalcker's observations, the bond of deep affection was not necessarily present within successful marriages. In fact, the very concept "family" had quite a different aspect before the beginning of the nineteenth century.[91] The "nuclear family" so integral to contemporary society was preceded in prosperous eighteenth-century homes by a broader, less close-knit group bound together by joint habitation and economic necessity. Live-in servants as well as blood relations occupied positions in a pyramidal unit better designated by the word "household." The private, warm, caring atmosphere, the intimacy now associated with things domestic, was hardly the norm, and not only because of the educational and experiential gap that separated man and wife. Emotional satisfaction with one's choice of profession was of considerably less consequence than was appropriateness vis-à-vis social standing, preference or need of one's father, and professional possibilities open within one's native city or region. Reason and cool logic prevailed here; hence, it was only natural that they should dictate the course of a marriage from its very inception, from the determination of spouses. During the first half of the eighteenth century, the traditional means of regulating courtship were affirmed—both the strictures regarding mésalliance and the corollary custom of investing parents or guardians with the right to select spouses for their young charges. The literature of two centuries bears eloquent witness to the tension and sorrow that resulted when love and logic were at cross-purposes. Not only Lessing and Schiller but also Fontane and Thomas Mann create plots that pivot on this traditional point of conflict between generations. Of course, circumstances often conspired to obviate discord. The prospective bridegroom was often somewhat older; his parents deceased. Or, he might have been the first of his line to attain a higher social status. Each of these circumstances obtained when Jacob Hinrich Hudtwalcker proposed matrimony at age thirty-five. His son reports that the man had always intended to marry; however, the advance of time weighed heavily in the final decision: "Er . . . hatte also keine Zeit zu versäumen. Er wußte, daß der Vater der Mädchen [there were three sisters] zwar im Ansehen, aber nicht reich war und wählte dieses Mädchen Sara Elisabeth zu seiner Gattin."[92] The eighteen-year-old brought her husband a dowry of some three thousand marks. Hudtwalcker's concerns in the matter were as dispassionate, as rational as those any father might have harbored. Above all, the choice was "appropriate"; considerations of status and financial gain were clearly taken into account. The age discrepancy made for an impressionable, even malleable, and altogether unsophisticated wife.

A typical day at the house in Hamburg began when the paterfamilias rose in the early morning to say his morning prayers and to read his daily devotional. He then proceeded to an adjacent room where he dressed and, pipe in hand, surveyed the waking city. Soon his wife appeared with hot tea, and the children trooped in to greet their father before dispersing to school or nursery. Johann Michael reports that his father then headed for the office in all good humor. Upon his return from the exchange at 1:30, dinner was served to the entire family. At the conclusion of the meal Jacob Hinrich was accustomed to receiving the attention of those assembled for a brief moralizing lecture. By the mid-1750s, two clerks from the growing office also dined at the Hudtwalcker table. The shorter period of business and schooling then lasted until five-o'clock tea, which the parents shared with their older children. The younger offspring were under the watchful eye of a "Französin" throughout the day. "So nannte man damals jede weibliche Person, die in Handarbeit Unterricht gab, die Sitten der Kinder, ihr An- und Auskleiden u. dgl. unter ihre Aufsicht nahm."[93] Despite the title given to this nanny, nationality was not a primary consideration; the five children under this particular roof were tended by an unmarried Hamburg native in her late twenties and thirties whose still-respected family had seen better days. The children played for an hour or so before joining her for a lighter evening meal; by 7:30 they had retired. Striking to the latter-day historian is the formality of parent-child contact, in addition to its relative brevity. To be sure, Jacob Hinrich did later take his sons along on walks through the city. However, it is clear that within this household three spheres of activity coexisted. The merchant had his office and the exchange. The housewife had her kitchen, the sewing-room, and the market. The children had their teachers and their "Französin." Such was the structure of a "happy marriage" at mid-century.

Considerable caution must be exercised in the course of a consideration of the cultural expectations and attainments of an eighteenth-century German merchant and his family. The broad span of educational experiences cited above suggests that the desire for intellectual stimulation outside of the business office and the sewing-room did vary greatly among individuals. Among the less educated, there were some who made an effort to improve themselves. For example, the elder Hudtwalcker found that his ability to read served him well in business dealings, while it also enabled him to satisfy an interest in the world of ideas. His piety was sustained through regular study of the Bible and extensive memorization of favorite passages.[94] Through newspapers and magazines he kept abreast of political and social events in Hamburg and followed controversies that flared up within the Lutheran church. Although his library was quite small, it did contain the works of Brockes, among whose writings the merchant particularly treasured panegyrics on the beauties of nature. It is instructive to note than an urbanite immersed in the affairs of men would turn to literature for an aspect of existence beyond his daily ken. His son may be guilty of some exaggeration in describing Jacob Hinrich's devotion to natural splendor as "sein ganzes Leben durch die Quelle seiner reinsten Freuden"; however, an admixture of idyllic escapism clearly informed the older man's perception of literature.

Whatever the motivation, reading as a form of participation in the cultural life of German-speaking societies faced other hurdles besides deficient or altogether absent formal education. Literacy did not translate into financial support for the publishing trade if potential consumers could not afford the merchandise. Books and periodicals were relatively expensive; their cost alone served to limit audience size. Pamela Currie comments as follows on the average price of a Hamburg magazine during the 1720s: "To the poor, 6 Pf. represented perhaps two days' food and would hardly be spent on a weekly periodical."[95] In fact, to the vast majority of the population—peasants, unskilled workers, servants, and the petite bourgeoisie—even the occasional purchase of reading material would have been an extravagance. Subscription sales were made almost entirely to the moneyed bourgeoisie and the nobility.[96] Prohibitive prices provided a strong incentive for the formation of reading circles, private lending libraries, and reading societies. Later in the century, reading societies became large, democratically organized institutions; they frequently occupied their own buildings, which contained rooms for books and periodicals as well as halls set aside for the discussion of readings. Earlier in the century, however, the Enlightenment had just begun to suggest the importance of ongoing education and to work at forging a consensus support of its optimistic program. Reading societies did not begin to emerge as a significant phenomenon until after 1750.[97] Although a few scattered forerunners did exist, the public discussion of new publications during the earlier decades was usually reserved for the coffeehouses and for the book-review sections of periodicals.

Doubtless one of the better-known, highly organized forms of leisure activity during the eighteenth century was freemasonry.[98] Merchants usually belonged to the lodges, in which class distinctions were suspended by a conscientiously enforced egalitarianism. Noble and burgher met on common ground that was carefully apolitical and nondenominational. The movement was imported from England to Hamburg, where the first lodge was founded in 1737. German masons pursued the cosmopolitan ideals of fraternity, tolerance, and ethical improvement, ideals based upon the assumed perfectibility of man. Each member passed through three major stages as his adherence to masonic teachings strengthened. But from apprenticeship through fellowship to mastership he was sworn to secrecy concerning the ritual observances and philosophical aims of the local lodge. For him the secret society was a tiny safe haven which promoted the self-fulfillment that a turbulent outside world with its capricious monarchs, inflexible superiors, and unreliable business connections often denied.

Another cultural institution that enjoyed considerable prominence within the urban bourgeoisie was the newly "purified" stage. Numerous theater troupes circulated among the larger northern towns and performed plays from a growing repertoire of translations from the English and French as well as native dramas, all of which benefited from the support of the great arbiter of public taste, Gottsched. Since comedy had been set aside by long tradition as the appropriate dramatic forum for treating the problems of non-ruling-class individuals, it is not surprising that the genre experienced a wave of popularity as the growing middle class began to cast about for a literature that addressed its condition. The list of comedies produced during the 1740s and early 1750s is impressive if only for its length.[99] That theater attendance was perceived as an appropriate, respectable activity even by a less-educated member of the bourgeoisie is apparent in Johann Michael Hudtwalcker's recollection of accompanying his father to watch the Koch troupe stage *Miß Sara Sampson* in 1756. Jacob Hinrich and his nine-year-old were blithely unaware that they were witnessing a drama to which Germanists would later accord epochal significance: "Von einem Trauerspiel hatte ich keinen Begriff, und mein Vater hatte es wahrscheinlich nicht bemerkt, daß es ein Trauerspiel gäbe."[100] The son comments laconically that the original stimulus for an afternoon at the theater may have been the word "Sara," even then the shorthand form of the title and Frau Hudtwalcker's first name. Apparently such conjugal veneration had its limits—the lady herself was not invited. Implicit in the biographer's gentle condescension is a fair degree of sophistication with regard to belles lettres, a sophistication that came later in life. Although no account is offered of the older man's reaction to the play, his estimation of the theater as an institution was obviously high enough for this traditional father to take along a child then at a highly impressionable point in life. However insensitive Jacob Hinrich may have been to the niceties of genre, he had clearly joined the audience that developed around the reformed German stage; he expected worthwhile entertainment. He and his son represented one of the four elements Karl Guthke has pointed to as forming the basis of "literary life" as it came into being during the second third of the eighteenth century; that element was the literary public: "In dem Maße, wie [das Bürgertum] seit den ersten Jahrzehnten des Jahrhunderts in seiner wirtschaftlichen und gesellschaftlichen Stellung und in seinem moralischen Selbstbewußtsein erstarkt, entwickelt es zunehmend Interesse an seiner philosophisch-literarischen Bildung, bis es, spätestens seit der Jahrhundertmitte, zum führenden Träger des literarischen Geschmacks wird."[101] One member of that "culture-bearing" bourgeoisie was a half-educated but intellectually alive Hamburger who never spoke fluent High German and who could attend a cultural event for reasons both noble and naive. A literary life supported by Hudtwalcker and his colleagues inevitably responded to them, to their strengths, and to their weaknesses.

Any assessment of the merchant's condition during the German Enlightenment must recognize the fact that he was often Jewish. By mid-century, tolerance had been propagated as an ideal by educators and writers for decades, and yet Christian burghers still experienced mixed emotions when confronted with the existence of the minority. George Mosse has written: "There can be no doubt of the ambivalence of the Enlightenment toward Jews and Jewish emancipation. Judaism was immoral, superstitious, and produced an undesirable Jewish stereotype. The individual Jew could be made fit for participation in society only through reeducation."[102] During the process of becoming enlightened, the Jew was expected to drop many of his religious and social practices as archaic customs. Of course, such expectations were hopelessly naive. German Jews and their culture had lived apart from the rest of society for centuries, separated by ghetto walls, discriminatory laws, language, and dress as well as religious belief.[103] Although the new intellectual atmosphere was hardly congenial to its growth, anti-Semitism survived thanks to its deep medieval roots. The stereotype that flourished during the Age of Reason has been described in these terms: "Even the few Jews whose lives were easier by virtue of wealth or fame were greatly limited in their personal freedom. In general, the Jew was an object of scorn. In the common view they were a race of beggars, peddlers, usurers; they were unlikable, deeply superstitious, uneducated, and grotesque in appearance and behavior."[104] The great majority of Jews lived in a state of penury and social ostracism; the latter condition was enforced not only by Christians but also by better-situated Jews.[105] City-dwelling Christians doubtless had difficulty reconciling the dictates of mature reason with childhood impressions that often coalesced with the stereotype. For instance, Mosse cites a prominent Frankfurter's still vivid recollection of a youthful visit to that city's "Judengasse" during the 1750s: "Die Enge, der Schmutz, das Gewimmel, der Akzent einer unerfreulichen Sprache, alles zusammen machte den unangenehmsten Eindruck, wenn man auch nur am Tore vorbeigehend hineinsah."[106]

The "throng" of humanity that Goethe remembered was also characterized by poverty. Only a few rose to wealth, influence, and even fame, usually as merchants, industrialists, financiers, and economic advisers. However, it should be emphasized that during the eighteenth century the great majority of German Jews knew only want from cradle to grave.[107] Above them on the social scale of this society-within-a-society were two very thin levels. Rabbis, teachers, and physicians belonged to an urban middle class. Truly wealthy members of the minority often adopted a supercilious attitude toward poor Jews, a feeling of distinction that was to become apparent in the use of German as opposed to Yiddish.[108]

Jews who were lucky enough to be involved in commerce had a long tradition behind them. Since the early Middle Ages, many Near Eastern peoples had actively participated in Europe's overseas trade.[109] Successful entrepreneurs located in the larger German cities frequently added money-lending and money-changing to their portfolios of activity. Here, Christianity's prohibition against the charging of interest effectively set aside increasingly important aspects of finance for control by that small minority within the Jewish population. During the first half of the eighteenth century, the presence of Jewish traders was particularly noticeable in Hamburg and Leipzig. Because they frequently handled such luxury goods as silk, gems, and precious metals, these men enjoyed ready entrée into the homes of the nobility. There they frequently met other Jews who were engaged by many German princes as business managers, bankers, and armament dealers. These "Hofjuden" or "Hoffaktoren" exercised considerable power; however, their positions were rarely proof against the whim of a monarch or the hatred of a mob.[110] Members of the minority also serviced the small towns and villages of the countryside as wholesale buyers, sales representatives, and as money-lenders. However, the greatest impact of Jewish people in general and the Jewish merchant in particular was felt in the cities, several of which witnessed flowerings of literary culture during the early Enlightenment.

Hamburg's Jewish community underwent a major transition in the early decades of the new century. Since the late 1500s, Sephardim from Portugal had settled in the city on the Elbe as merchants.[111] Gradually the city council had granted them limited rights pertaining to residency and religious observance. Doubtless a portion of this grudging tolerance was due to the excellence of several physicians, including Henrico Rodriguez and Rodrigo de Castro, of whom the last named served all of the city's citizens with extraordinary valor during plague years in the early 1600s. Of course, the "Portuguese," as they were always styled, also played a decisive role in Hamburg's emergence as a trade center not just for North Germany but for all of Europe. They established ties to both the Iberian peninsula and to that region's colonies in the New World. Hence the appearance of sugar, tobacco, spices, cotton, and other "exotic" goods at the Hamburg market. Sephardim founded the Amsterdam bank in 1609 and the Hamburg bank in 1619 while developing a money exchange at the same time. The more successful entrepreneurs soon built refineries, which were frequently supplied by shipping fleets owned by Sephardim. The community also provided goldsmiths and stonecutters who contributed to a boom in the city's luxury trade. Throughout the seventeenth century, such families as the Texeiras and the Abensurs guaranteed the old Hanseatic town an ever higher commercial profile. However, decline set in during the last three decades of the century as a result of internal strife over the appearance of the false Messiah Sabbatai Zevi and external pressure from Christians for restrictions of rights that had evolved over the years. As many leading Sephardim left the city, the growing significance of the Ashkenazim became apparent. The latter were not allowed the right of settlement in Hamburg proper until 1710, when an imperial commission moved to lessen discord among the city council, the senate, and the two Jewish populations with a "Reglement der Judenschaft in Hamburg Sowohl Portugiesischer als Hochdeutscher Nation." However, central European Jews had lived in Danish-administered Altona and then in Wandsbek since the 1620s. In 1657 a number of such families fled to Hamburg before advancing Swedish armies, and their presence was met with unofficial tolerance and high taxation for the remainder of the century. These people were primarily retailers, dealers in gems, and money-lenders; however, they also established small industries in tobacco and luxury items such as lace. The circumstances of the mercantile Ashkenazim at the beginning of the eighteenth century are detailed vividly by Glückel of Hameln in memoirs originally intended for her children and descendants. She began the project shortly after the death of her first husband in 1689, by which point she had borne fourteen children, several of whom were still in infancy. Undaunted, the widow continued a business in seed-pearl trading, money-lending, and retailing, about which she had always been consulted: "My business prospered, I procured me wares from Holland, I bought nicely in Hamburg as well, and disposed of the goods in a store of my own. I never spared myself, summer and winter I was out on my travels, and I ran about the city the livelong day."[112] Glückel ascribes a similarly busy, even hectic life-style to other "German" Jews involved in Hamburg's commerce. Their travels took them in seach of profit to trade fairs at Braunschweig, Frankfurt, and above all Leipzig.

Electoral Saxony did not allow Jews to settle, even unofficially, within its borders. However, they were admitted for fairs, around which the economic life of not only the country but also the entire central European region revolved. Estimates place 82,000 Jews at the fairs between 1675 and 1764; by the end of the eighteenth century, they constituted between one-quarter and one-half of total participants.[113] The variety of goods traded equaled that which passed through Hamburg. The same colonial wares were present, in addition to items ranging from horses to feathers—all brought to the city by Jewish merchants. Leipzig's position as the commercial "Door to the East" was apparent in the activity of Jews from Poland, who arrived laden with textiles and, above all, furs.[114] Such traders were subjected to rigorous surveillance and burdensome taxes. At the gate to the city, they had to register by name and place of origin and receive an entry pass and a bit of yellow cloth. Within the city, they had to produce upon demand the pass and the bit of cloth as well as a document from the authorities of their home cities certifying their status as merchants. At the marketplace, they were required to proceed to the "Ratswaage," where the city collected various fees totaling ten talers four groschen.[115] At the conclusion of the fair, each Jew was required to pay duty on at least six hundred talers' worth of merchandise bought and/or sold, whether or not he had enjoyed that volume of business. In short, Leipzig viewed Jewish merchants as a necessary evil. That they were deemed pariahs is strikingly apparent in the practices followed when a Jew was so unfortunate as to die while attending the fair. Glückel of Hameln reports this to have been a source of particular dread among her merchant colleagues, since the city's response was to confiscate all property and to deny burial in a Jewish cemetery. She cites one such incident during the course of which friends and relations had to beg influential men and spend in excess of one thousand talers in order to have the body released and transported for burial at Dessau some thirty miles away.[116]

Of course, Leipzig's animosity toward these merchants did not comprehend one institution, the Court Jew. August the Strong used the advice and connections of a procession of such figures in order to develop Poland as a market for Saxony's growing textile and china industries and to ensure participation by all of European Jewry at the fairs. Bernd Lehmann, Jonas Meyer, and Assur Marx were accordingly granted special residency status as well as permission to deal as a firm in goods and money—all of this by royal decree and over the objections of municipal authorities.[117] Finally, however, August's Christian ministers voiced such vehement opposition to the rising influence of the firm, which handled much of Saxony's foreign trade as of 1728, that the ruler found himself forced to renew the total prohibition of Jewish trade, except at the fairs.

Berlin experienced a marked increase in Jewish population and trade as a result of the economic policies established by the Great

Elector and Friedrich III.[118] Residency in the Prussian capital was permitted, however limited through quotas and special tariffs. Specifically, an edict promulgated in 1671 granted the privilege of domicile to fifty families newly banished from Vienna. The personal predilections of the kings played a far smaller role in such decisions than did their common desire to greatly expand trade with the outside world, to accelerate the circulation of money, and to develop credit and monetary customs already well established in other German-speaking countries. At the pinnacle of the minority community stood the king's Court Jews, whose business interests ranged from luxury items to lumber, from grain to goods from the New World. Services rendered to the state by such families as Gompertz, Liebmann, and Itzig did not, however, precipitate a loosening of strictures applied to Jewish participation in human affairs. In Berlin as elsewhere, Jews were forbidden to practice most trades and professions. Their direct contributions to Prussia were a matter of public record: in 1705, the Jewish community paid over three times as much in excise taxes as the Christian merchants of Berlin.[119] Despite this, despite the general effectiveness of the community in guiding Prussia's entry into the mainstream of European trade, and despite the rise of the Enlightenment with its emphasis on tolerance, Jews in Berlin were just as susceptible to governmental caprice as were their coreligionists elsewhere. This is starkly evident in the action taken in 1737 by the generally less well-disposed Friedrich Wilhelm I in reducing the quota of Jewish families in residence from 180 to 120, with the result that some 584 people suddenly had to leave the city.[120] Such periodic bursts of hostility also characterized the soldier-king's illustrious successor, despite Friedrich II's renown as the "enlightened despot." The historian Selma Stern has written of this monarch: "[He] kept the Jews fettered with medieval restrictions, divided them into 'ordinary' and 'extraordinary' Jews, restricted their freedom of movement, limited their numbers, laid heavy taxes upon them, introduced the principle of collective responsibility, which made each member of the Jewish community responsible for any legal violation committed by another, and promulgated laws that regulated their lives from birth to death."[121] The cornerstone of this policy was the harsh "Generalreglement" of 1750, which did not, however, prevent the king from giving all manner of support to those individual Jews whose trade activity was deemed potentially beneficial to the state. Through such offices, highly favorable ties with Poland were established, ties which ensured a continuous flow of less expensive raw material into Prussia and more valuable finished goods out of Friedrich's domain. Jews were actually invited to settle along the Polish border. The capital had its Jewish bankers, industrialists, merchants, and Court Jews, all of whom the regent "tolerated" in the usual sense of that word for pragmatic reasons. Peter Baumgart points out that the king's men were often more truly devoted to the ideals of the Enlightenment in their dealings with the minority; hence the following from the privy finance minister Manitius in an internal memorandum from 1745: "Handel und Wandel kennet keinen Unterschied der Religion, sondern erfordert nur Treu und Glauben und wäre zu wünschen, daß dieser, nach proportion der Anzahl der handelnden Christen, mehr bey diesen als bey den Juden zu finden sein möchte."[122] However, the discrepancy in perspective between such usually university-trained career civil servants and the great majority of Christian merchants and tradesmen was vast. Stern documents a history of continual, formal complaints about the advances made by minority members and supported by the rulers of Prussia into areas of commerce previously under the control of the majority.[123] In effect, a sort of accelerated economic Darwinism had arisen. When a prince perceived that one individual or one type of individual fostered the rapid development of an aspect of his nation's economy, he had at his command all the means of supporting such individuals while at the same time thwarting weaker competitors who threatened to retard growth. And support them he did, often to the extent of creating monopolies. The concomitant rise of the Court Jews with their international connections inevitably attracted the attention of Christian counterparts. The Jewish response to complaints and accusations was frequently a simple enumeration of the virtues requisite for success in business—industriousness, tenacity, flexibility, watchfulness—and the suggestion that Christian colleagues try harder.[124] In his highly controversial monograph, Werner Sombart advances the thesis that Judaism as a system of beliefs enhanced the ability of its adherents to advance in a capitalistic system.[125] Sombart's dangerous tendency to simplify and generalize has been apparent to recent scholarship, which has emphasized the Jews' place in historical social stratification. Stefi Jersch-Wenzel argues convincingly that the determined search for economic independence and security resulted from the uncertainties built into minority status.[126] During the eighteenth century, this did give rise to tension within the merchant community, a tension that partook of a still more general difficulty faced by all who practiced the profession—the cloudy reputation of commerce itself.

The pursuit of profit, the dedication of a human life to the amassing of wealth, has met with consistent opposition since the advent of the Christian era. The Stoic Seneca, whose teachings had a profound effect on the early Church, writes: "Riches produce shamelessness. The things which are goods give us greatness of soul, but riches give us arrogance. And arrogance is nothing else than a false show of greatness."[127] In the eyes of this moral philosopher, wealth is a sure catalyst of inappropriate, unethical behavior. The same concerns underlie the attitude of the Apostle Paul, who emphasizes the transitory, uncertain nature of material possessions (1 Timothy 6:17–19). As the systematic, lifelong pursuit of such material gain devoid of any inherent restraints in the form of public or private charity, the occupation of merchant was viewed with grave displeasure by such medieval authorities as Thomas Aquinas, who castigates the "acquisitive urge" which is always one step away from money-making activities.[128] In medieval theory, a trader was to receive only that remuneration consonant with services rendered in storing, transporting, and supplying goods. However, when payments outstripped the merchant's efforts and needs, his profits were viewed as unethical, as "filthy lucre," *turpe lucrum*.[129] This fundamental aversion to trade continued into the late Middle Ages. As the wealth of the New World began to enter the Old, opportunities abounded for those few with both money and energy to invest. The resultant widening of the gap between rich and poor, the phenomenal wealth piled up by successful entrepreneurs provoked bitter commentary against the commercial sphere from, among others, Martin Luther:

> Erstlich haben die kauffleut vnter sich ein gemeyne regel / das ist yhr heubtspruch vnd grund aller fynantzen / da sie sagen / Ich mag meyne wahr so thewr geben alls ich kan / Das hallten sie fur eyn recht / da ist dem geytz der raum gemacht / vnd der hellen thur vnd fenster alle auffgethan / . . . / Es kan damit der kauffhandel nichts anders seyn / denn rawben und stelen den andern yhr gutt.[130]

Even when allowance is made for the turbulent historical background of such a statement and for the reformer's lifelong penchant for strong rhetorical weapons, the sweeping condemnation still arrests the attention of a modern reader. Aquinas is delicate in comparison with a text that effectively accuses all merchants of unscrupulous practices, asserts their solidarity with thieves, and consigns them to hell.

It does not necessarily follow that an age of absolutism so firmly bound to economic advance as pursued through mercantilism sought to launder the reputation of the figure at the economic vanguard. In fact, much of the traditional suspicion, the hesitant tolerance of a necessary evil, persisted. The prince eager to increase trade for the sake of his nation cast a jaundiced eye at the subject whose first concern was profitability.[131] The merchant's natural inclination was to travel as little as possible and to sell at the highest markup possible; hence the local marketing of imported luxury items possessed great appeal. Of course, such a practice stood in direct opposition to mercantilist policy. If tension characterized the relationship between the man of commerce and the ruling elite, outright contempt colored the reputation of the merchant among the lesser nobility and the university-educated middle class. Infected with francophilia during much of the century, the lesser nobility echoed the French aristocracy's estimation that any sort of participation in trade was far beneath its dignity.[132] Academicians and civil servants considered the merchant's education deficient, his interests too mundane. They responded to his presence in society with no great warmth, when not with outright, even printed ridicule.[133] Localities newly committed to the revival of stagnant economies could not effect overnight change in private attitudes so as to ensure concord with public policy. To traditional hostilities directed against those who pursued wealth were added ancient rural-urban tensions exacerbated by the gradual demographic movement into cities. Rustic idylls of the contented life of the farmer or herdsman lived on tenaciously—all the more so in the minds of arriviste burghers whose immediate ancestors had led a pastoral existence. Hence the reluctance of the citizenry of a smaller city such as Berne to embrace Colbertism. The social reflexes, the interests, the very life-style of the merchant flew in the face of local tradition, with predictable results. Hans Rudolf Rytz expresses it in stark terms: "Die Berner Bürger verachteten Handwerker und Kauflleute."[134] The venerable agrarian foundations of many a state would simply not be razed in order to suit economic exigency.

It should be apparent that the merchant's status in German-speaking Europe was fraught with contradictions even as the Enlightenment began to gain momentum. Ambivalence within the general population was reflected in no less a figure than Friedrich II. While many of his decrees facilitated export trade, his personal opinion of the agents of such activity is apparent in references to one of the founders of the house of Splitgerber and Daum as "Spitzbubegerber."[135] The substantial services rendered by that leading merchant had obviously failed to dissociate him from the entrenched stereotype.

The historical stereotype, the flesh-and-blood merchant, and the tension between them could not be ignored by the literary world—not by a middle-class literary world then in its infancy. The still-weak, highly sensitive institution of "bourgeois literature" had to come to grips with a decidedly uncomfortable presence. The result was a series of images of the merchant. Given the wealth of conflicting attitudes, that series displays remarkable diversity.[136] Nevertheless, literary historians have shown no great interest in the appearance of the man of commerce in the Enlightenment canon. The few available studies are either poorly executed or primarily directed at later periods.[137] One noteworthy exception examines the highly influential English tragedy that presents the fall of an apprentice from a position of trust to the very gallows. In George Lillo's *The London Merchant* (1731), Peter Szondi finds a veritable apotheosis of world trade, which serves to redistribute the earth's natural resources in a reasonable, humane fashion.[138] However, the highly flattering portraits of merchant virtue in such characters as Thorowgood and Trueman had been anticipated: "Was in dem Stück über die soziale Rolle des Kaufmannsstandes gesagt wird, ist bereits zwanzig Jahre früher gesagt worden und . . . sogar in prononcierter Form."[139] The reference is to articles by Joseph Addison in the *Spectator*, articles that trumpeted the value of commerce and its practitioners to English society. The programmatic enunciation of the Enlightenment's logical position vis-à-vis trade thus found its way into the literary canon only after a substantial delay.

So it was in Germany. Wolfgang Martens has amply documented the support extended to the merchant community by the moral weeklies, particularly by early Hamburg journals such as the *Patriot*.[140] However, major literary genres were slower to admit the wealthiest segment of the bourgeoisie. And, when the merchant does appear, literary convention must be taken into account. In the chapters that follow, examples of drama, poetry, and prose are studied—each example bearing the stamp of expectations regarding genre held by artist and audience alike. The idyllic verse of Haller and the utopian epic of Schnabel drew from long traditions rooted in archetypes that have strongly antimaterialistic and anticommercial traits. At first, this might suggest that attitudes voiced by the writers in question are less deeply felt or that they are less timely. However, it was of course the writer who selected the genre. Haller reached for the idyll in part because he wished to assail his own nonidyllic society. Cast by Vergil and honed by Tacitus, that literary sword had been wielded for centuries—still, it was but one weapon of the many available to the young Swiss in 1729. In similar fashion, the satiric comedy with its fool at center stage offered a convenient hook on which to hang the traditional hostility to trade and trader. As the literary image of the merchant changed during the 1740s, the locus of objectionable behavior shifted to other stereotypes.

Finally, particularism itself acted as an impediment to any common effort among artists, let alone support for a hitherto suspect segment of the population. The German-speaking area had no single cultural center; a writer's attitudes toward society and its constituent elements developed in and, to varying degrees, reacted to local conditions far removed from those in a London or Paris. The written record is accordingly more varied; several stages of development can be detected from Haller to Lessing. Again, it is during this quarter century that the process Leo Balet called "Verbürgerlichung" achieved clear definition. Only when the literary tradition had finally made its peace with the merchant could it hope to speak to the entire middle class. And only then did that class have its own literature.

# Part Two
# The Merchant in Literature

## Part Two
The Merchant in Literature

# II. Menace and Menaced: Haller, Schnabel

In the summer of 1728, a young Bernese of redoubtable intellect trekked through the Alpine center of his native land to Zurich. The experience gave Albrecht von Haller a close familiarity with mountain flora and provided German literature with "Die Alpen," one of the early monuments of its Enlightenment period. At age nineteen the poet could already claim a finished professional education as well as a firsthand acquaintance with the customs of much of Europe.[1] The year before, he had taken a doctorate that completed studies at Tübingen and Leiden; two "Bildungsreisen" had introduced him first to North Germany and then to England and France. Hence, it is hardly an ingenuous Swiss provincial but rather a young cosmopolite who comments on the manners and mores of two peoples, the mountain peasants he came to know and the city dwellers among whom he had spent his formative years.

Berne was ruled by a closed oligarchy of the wealthy and long established bourgeoisie. Not only did powerful families control the actions of the two major governing bodies, but they also placed members in most of the rural governorships, which effectively guaranteed their control over the entire canton. Their family fortunes made by the 1720s, these patricians concentrated on governmental duties and considered mercantile or professional involvement beneath them. Versailles provided the inspiration for many a splendid residence as well as for the elegant dress and carefully schooled French to grace it. While in Zurich and Basle guilds and local companies supplied most of the decision-makers, Berne's merchants, professionals, and lesser officials found themselves in much the same position as their counterparts in the German states. The same gulf yawned between the true bourgeois and the physician, the teacher, the civil servant; however, the trappings of power were disseminated among a number of families rather than concentrated in the hands of a single prince. As a result, wealthy households usually could not approach the palace life-style of Germany, although costly amenities were displayed on the streets of Berne. The more comfortable merchant might contemplate the purchase of such luxuries both to raise himself closer to the leisure class and to gain status vis-à-vis his less affluent neighbor. Affected foreign manners could easily follow. Colbertism inevitably boosted the number and the prestige of merchants in the city, with the result that status-seeking was more visible and the status sought more prominent. If the patricians of Berne were discomfited when this new state of affairs occasioned critical commentary, they had only themselves to blame. By changing economic policy, they had breathed life into the mercantile bourgeoisie. Considerable demographic displacement was assured.

Niklaus Emanuel Haller was a lawyer by profession who entered governmental service in 1713. His son Albrecht displayed the powers of a formidable mind at a tender age and proceeded through formal schooling with dispatch. From 1721 through 1722, the youth was attending the "Gymnasium" in Berne just as an insurrection was brewing in a remote, largely rural district of the canton. The French-speaking Vaud had been ruled by Berne since the Reformation, and its inhabitants had gradually come to resent a distant, German-speaking government that taxed without granting a meaningful amount of self-determination and whose members lived in what was perceived as a state of outrageous, degenerate opulence. In the early 1720s, the pious former army officer Abraham Davel gathered a following that demanded freedom for the Vaud and a return to simple, agrarian-oriented, Christian governance. Davel led a march to Lausanne in early 1723 to plead for the formation of such a new, purified state, only to suffer a death penalty eventually imposed by the Berne-controlled city council.

Davel's rejection of the political and ethical status quo focused on conditions repugnant to the social level from which Haller emerged. On the other hand, true common ground was limited: Davel's French reflexes, his naive religiosity, and his lack of trepidation at the thought of civil disturbance were not attributes that could gain favor among many residents of the city. However, his actions did serve to give concrete form to or, at least, a point of departure for the open analysis of social ills perceived by the new, moderate, virtuous, educated—that is, "enlightened"—middle class. That dissatisfaction with life in the canton continued to find strong expression is apparent in the reformist and, in the end, revolutionary career of Samuel Henzi. Berne did have its critics; with "Die Alpen," Haller became one of them.

In the very first stanza, the poet establishes the identity of his intended audience as well as the critical posture that he will maintain throughout:

Geht, eitle Sterbliche, erfüllt die Luft mit Schlössern,
Teilt nach Korinthens Lehr' gehaune Berge aus;

Belebt der Gärten Pracht mit steigenden Gewässern;
Bedeckt mit Samt den Leib und mit Porphyr das Haus;
. . . . . . . . . . . . . . . . . . . . . . .
Wird schon, was ihr gewünscht, das Schicksal unterschreiben,
Ihr werdet arm im Glück, im Reichtum elend bleiben.[2]

The audience addressed has regular contact with splendid houses, gardens, fountains, with all the benefits that accrue to city dwellers from international trade connections and technological expertise. It purchases luxury goods, velvet and porphyry, traditionally associated with the aristocracy. Porphyry, the purple rock from the Mediterranean coast, was long reserved for the adornment of royal chambers—and coffins. Not only were such items rare and expensive but their presence in a home whose owners were not aristocratic would have borne mute testimony to a drive for status, for a semblance of nobility via possessions. With the second word, judgment is pronounced upon those who live for such rewards. Here, and throughout the poem, Haller draws on both the pathos and the rhetoric of baroque poetry.[3] The lines actually ascribe an externalized, transitory way of life to not one but two types of "mortals": by implication, those who have already built their palaces and, in so many words, those who wish to be in a position to do so one day. That the emphasis is to be on the latter is apparent in the last two lines quoted above. Because he describes a sorry state of affairs that has not yet come to pass in final form, the poet casts himself in the role of prophet to a wayward people, or, more precisely, a people whose errant ways have begun to find physical expression. Berne's experiment with Colbertism had begun at the turn of the century. By the time the young citizen set off on his Alpine tour, the new, official emphasis on foreign trade, industrialization, and the accumulation of private wealth had had ample opportunity to bear fruit, or, in the words of the poet, entire gardens. Haller's dire warning at the conclusion of the stanza proceeds from a position diametrically opposed to his city's course during the first half of the century. The elaboration of that position begins when the poet turns to his ostensible subject.

In the first ten stanzas, the simple, virtuous mountain folk are presented as a clear antithesis in a strongly worded moral lecture. Their perduring, spiritual values contrast sharply with the superficial, ostentatious goals pursued by their urban counterparts:

Wohl dir, vergnügtes Volk, dem ein geneigt Geschicke
Der Lastern reiche Quell', den Überfluß, versagt!

> Dem, den sein Stand vergnügt, dient Armut selbst zum Glücke,
> Da Pracht und Üppigkeit der Ländern Stützen nagt. (A, 311)

It is a passage with which upright, pious individuals like Abraham Davel could immediately sympathize. Satisfaction and peace of mind are presented as the happy lot of the burgher who is as comfortable with his station in life as are the mountain people. The inclusion of "ein geneigt Geschicke" permits an anagogical interpretation of the passage: here, destiny is not a fickle, inscrutable force in human existence but rather the active agent of a grand design. It guides those in harmony with a materially impoverished but metaphysically charged environment. Quite a different image is applied to the quest for wealth; the use of "nagen" suggests a great parasite that endangers not just individuals but entire nations. In the second line cited, Haller uses an appositive to recall the old, medieval response to those in search of profit levels above and beyond personal need. Who belongs to the afflicted group? In the first instance, those dissatisfied with their condition—those who desire "Pracht und Üppigkeit" but do not yet have them. The poet is reaching beyond the long-established Bernese bourgeoisie to include those who fully understand an arriviste standard of living through daily observation and who covet it. Haller's upbringing, with its optimistic faith in the strength of virtue, shines forth in the unstated assumption that the foundations of any society are laid in the same mores so carefully tended in the Alps. A return to such foundations is his fervent, conservative hope for the society he knows best, an urban society drained of its vitality by "excess."

Haller scholarship has frequently cited "Die Alpen" as a harbinger of Rousseau's epochal call for a rejection of decadent modern civilization in favor of a state of harmony with nature.[4] Such "history of ideas" investigations have emphasized the importance of city/country and society/nature polarities—with ample reason. The poet addresses the following to the Alpine populace:

> Laß sein, daß die Natur der Erde Ranft versteinet,
> Genung, dein Pflug geht durch, und deine Saat errinnt;
> Sie hat dich von der Welt mit Bergen abgezäunet,
> Weil sich die Menschen selbst das größte Elend sind. (A, 312)

The two symbols of fertility constitute a strikingly direct means of equating rustic life with the eternal order of nature. In fact, nature is cast as an active protector: it has used the mountains to build a protective barrier around its chosen people. The barrier is more effective than any castle wall because it is not viewed from the outside as defensive in intent. The same combination of forbidding exterior and idyllic interior is employed by Schnabel when he rings Felsenburg with craggy peaks. At first consideration, the final line here is confusing because it implies that all human communities, regardless of size, promote harmful interpersonal relationships. However, "die Menschen" is in fact being employed as a *variatio*: large numbers of people living in close proximity constitute a potential danger to themselves in the sphere identified as "die Welt." Of course, the use of both nouns to refer to those who live below the mountains serves to emphasize the sparseness of the Alpine population, the "otherworldly" pattern of their existence, and the isolation from their countrymen below. In the city, the great attraction of congregating has been the potential for material gain; hence the poet's praise of isolated, honest poverty:

> Der Bergen tiefer Schacht gibt dir nur schwirrend Eisen,
> Wie sehr wünscht Peru nicht, so arm zu sein als du!
> Dann, wo die Freiheit herrscht, wird alle Mühe minder,
> Die Felsen selbst beblümt und Boreas gelinder. (A, 312)

Even the mineral deposits beneath the surface of this haven are such as will not invite the exploitive encroachments of "civilization." The potential for disaster in the event of such contact is adumbrated through reference to Peru, whose treasures had attracted the outside world to a terrain just as formidable and to a people just as simple as those described in "Die Alpen." The exotic component of the comparison magnifies the danger: thousands of watery miles and fear of the unknown could not prevent the fall of the Indian cultures. If Switzerland had ever had highly valued resources, it, too, would have been ransacked—mountains or no mountains.

In these lines, Haller invests the term "Freiheit" with a double significance, and one of the meanings can easily overshadow the other. He has in mind political freedom, of course; Swiss history demands such an understanding. However, in context, the poet is also speaking of freedom from greed, ethical freedom from peer pressure to strive after more and more possessions. Both freedom from political oppression and freedom from greed are, by implication, absent from civilization. The significance of the two forms of freedom is underscored rhetorically by the two oxymora in the final line, which reanimate the "dead metaphor," that is, "Freiheit herrscht," in the preceding line. That freedom would indeed reign was of particular concern to the level of society to which Haller belonged, and the importance attached to the less apparent freedom is evident in the lines immediately following:

> Glückseliger Verlust von schadevollen Gütern!
> Der Himmel hat kein Gut, das eurer Armut gleicht. (A, 312)

The virtual apotheosis of poverty bespeaks both youthful naiveté and lack of firsthand experience with the human condition under discussion. The poet's traditional suspicions concerning those whose lives are spent accumulating wealth also informs his attitudes toward interpersonal relations: any agglomeration of property guarantees discord when harmony should be the rule. Mention of "Eintracht" strikes a note in resonance with the Enlightenment's tendency to foster the development of clubs and societies in urban areas; hence the popularity of the masonic movement later in the century. In holding up the concept of an ethos grounded in material sufficiency and mutual supportiveness, the poet offers not only the observations of a traveler in *terra incognita* but also the encouragement of a committed participant in the intellectual life of urban Europe. He shares the hope that, under the auspices of carefully nonpolitical institutions, the Enlightenment can eventually proceed from the hearth to the meeting hall to the seat of power.

Earlier in the stanza just quoted, the human faculty dearest to the "Aufklärung" appears in rural glory. Of the Alps Haller writes:

> Hier herrschet die Vernunft, von der Natur geleitet,
> Die, was ihr nötig, sucht und mehrers hält vor Last.
> Was Epiktet getan und Seneka geschrieben,
> Sieht man hie ungelehrt und ungezwungen üben. (A, 312)

While the direct statement in these lines concerns the human condition among isolated mountains where nature rules, the writer also indicates which aspect of nature must provide the model for behavior in all areas of human commerce. Not the wild, "excessive" nature of the Alpine avalanche but rather a pacific, balanced nature whose various components accomplish what is necessary for the smooth functioning of the whole—and nothing more. To follow this grand example and to obey the dictates of reason is to avoid desire for personal property not needed for the functioning of the individual in either urban or rural society. Just as Abraham Davel had extrapolated a purified, ideal world from rural beliefs and traditions, so Haller holds up the "natural" pattern to his fellow citizens, and not in general, all-embracing terms. Here he is attacking not civilization as a whole but rather one destructive side of urban life as it affects his own social level. The materialism indirectly but powerfully supported by Colbertism had as its prime exponents the very merchants and manufacturers whom the new economic policy put at the forefront. Young Haller's reaction against rising, ostentatious members of the middle class typifies the standard response of his well-educated peers. However, this is no mean aversion. The poet has effectively charged a considerable segment of the population of his hometown with behavior at odds with the order of the cosmos. Mention of Epictetus and Seneca ranges the pre-Christian philosophy of Stoicism against what Haller suggests is a new era of decadence sadly reminiscent of the first two centuries of the Christian era. In fact, the attitude assumed in these lines and throughout the poem recalls a third denizen of Rome during the early phases of decline—Tacitus, who also used observations of a remote, hardy race to preach to his wayward friends and neighbors back home. Of course, Haller cites the two ancient authorities in the hope that his peers will recognize the parallels and therefore the magnitude of the menace that confronts them.

Haller's rejection of what he presents as an artificial pattern of social stratification is one of the more arresting features of the first stanzas of the poem:

Hier herrscht kein Unterscheid, den Hochmut hat erfunden,
Der Tugend untertan und Laster edel macht. (A, 312)

The drawing of class distinctions itself is not necessarily rejected, only the set of criteria applied in one environment. Of course, pride was a quality reserved by rhetorical decorum for a ruling class perpetuated in power by right of birth; hence, it is hardly surprising that pride is characterized here by opposition to reason and nature. The parallelism of the second line cited suggests that a new ordering for human society should be guided by the same impulse to virtue so carefully fostered among the powerless in town. The clearly audible note of complaint would have been incongruous if uttered by a member of Berne's growing merchant community. Haller speaks for those who have grimly watched the rapid advancement of a calling apparently dedicated to ideals at odds with those of the Enlightenment. The frustration expressed here as the poet looks down from the Alps is palpable; however, if he provided only the exposition of a lamentable state of affairs, he would indeed be guilty of painting an idyllic landscape solely to promote escape from the real world.[5] Poetry would be functioning as a substitute for life. But such an interpreta-

## 52   The Merchant in Literature

tion ignores Haller's unmistakably didactic bent. In "Die Alpen" he is at pains to reinforce the educated, middle-class notion of how man should act in society—in a diseased society. His implicit wish would have the impulse to virtue within individuals eventually diffused into an increasingly "natural" nation. Lines such as those quoted above are less confrontational (and, therefore, given the "Realpolitik" of 1730, less idyllic) than they appear at first glance because they speak directly to the subject class.

In fact, the young Bernese applies the Alpine test for virtue to three phenomena affecting those who share his station in Swiss society, and in each instance his urban contemporaries are urged to return to simpler ways. First, these words concerning the quality of day-to-day life:

> Hier macht das Glücke nie die Zeiten unterschieden,
> Die Tränen folgen nie auf kaum gefühlte Freud'.
> Im ganzen Leben herrscht ein nie gestörter Frieden;
> Heut ist wie gestern war, und morgen wird wie heut. (A, 313)

Sudden change was hardly an everyday reality for those on the upper and the lower rungs of the social ladder in the early eighteenth century. It did, however, characterize life within a professional community dependent upon poorly policed trade routes, upon some degree of international peace, and upon uninterrupted financial support from the ruling oligarchy. Nothing could be more utopian than the suggestion that a class of people who live by their wits and under such conditions could possibly adopt a pattern of life that guarantees continuity and tranquility. It is, quite simply, the pipe dream of a young man who has been protected from the harder realities of his times. If Haller appreciates the occupational diversity that characterizes his middle class, he does not accept all of those occupations as worthy. Naturally enough, his intellectual posture here is that of the insulated civil servant; before him lay an academic career that offered the same high degree of stability and security that his father's position had provided. In uncritical fashion, Haller finds salaried service to the state comparable to contented self-sufficiency in the mountains. Still, he *is* attempting to use the Alpine model to improve middle-class life. And it could be argued that the household that experienced extreme fluctuations was headed by a paterfamilias who pursued excessive goals—whatever his calling. Nevertheless, the poet's hostility is directed at least in part against a clearly definable group held dangerous to an entire culture. To say "Heut ist wie gestern war, und morgen wird wie heut" smacks of a traditionalism inherently opposed to the canton's new economic program.

The nineteen-year-old stands on more familiar ground when treating a second discrepancy between the Alps and Berne, namely that involving courtship and marriage customs. Here he touches upon a point of friction between Enlightenment ideology and upward mobility:

> Die Ehrsucht teilet nie, was Liebe hat verbunden,
> Die Staatssucht macht sich nicht zur Unglückskupplerin.
> Die Liebe brennt hier frei und förcht kein Donnerwetter;
> Man liebet vor sich selbst und nicht vor seine Väter. (A, 314)

On the one hand, family life was just beginning to take on new meaning for the middle class. A man's home was becoming his castle. Whereas in his occupational activities and in his capacity as citizen he was accorded only limited authority, beside the hearth he was a prince who ruled with an eye to those widely discussed categories, reason and virtue. To establish a family was to stake out a private but sovereign realm, hence the rise of romantic love during the first half of the century as a major determinant in human affairs, a development that culminated in "sentimentality."

On the other hand, long tradition stood behind the extended "household" with its detached spheres of activity. The man whose existence revolved around his ledger did not hesitate to subordinate familial considerations to financial gain. It is the marriage of convenience that arouses the poet's ire when he declares, "Die Liebe brennt hier frei." The economic reality was brutally clear: marriage could furnish a means of achieving a jump in wealth and status. The cost of making a strategic match for one's offspring was negligible, particularly in view of the low standing of women. The return on such an investment could take the form of an alliance between two commercial houses, or a direct tie to the often impecunious lesser nobility.

Having previously urged a return to a more peaceful, steady pattern of life consonant with Berne's relaxed bucolic past, Haller now mounts an assault on, of all things, an old patriarchal custom. A portion of his opposition to arranged betrothals is the inevitable product of his age and sex. However, equally apparent is the canny combination of the primitive with the progressive in an effort to dislodge the traditional. The threefold mention of love in the lines above is ranged against prescriptions for behavior made by generations of "Väter," this within a poetic environment steeped in intellectual independence and unbiased inquiry. The older generation is being confronted with an element in human affairs long considered random and destabilizing. For the poet, love's claim to special status is verified by its respected position in a society stripped of the complications of modern civilization. Here, that claim is staked anew with the aid of an emerging worldview founded on critical, if not iconoclastic, analysis. It goes without saying that what was evident to the young university product was without doubt news of a distinctly unwelcome nature to the middle-aged Bernese merchant.

Haller also conjures forth the vision of a rustic golden age as a counterpoint to the unhealthy ambience of modern life:

Entfernt vom eitlen Tand der mühsamen Geschäften,
Wohnt hier die Seelenruh und flieht der Städten Rauch.
Ihr tätig Leben stärkt der Leiber reife Kräften,
Der träge Müßiggang schwellt niemals ihren Bauch. (A, 315)

More clearly than any other, the passage in which daily commerce is described as "eitler Tand" shows that Haller is a beginning artist who does not yet know his audience, its importance, and what will offend it. The point he wishes to make is clear—the hectic pace generated by business concerns tends to destroy peace of mind. However, instead of arriving inductively at a position that would be understandable, if not acceptable, to all, the poet attacks with strong rhetorical weapons. Both the mountains and the valley work, but one sphere's "invigorating activity" is the other's "drudgery." Relaxation leads to inner peace ("Seelenruh") for the Alpine folk, to indolence for the town dwellers. The use of "Tand" testifies to a hostility to modern man's desire to better his material condition; the reference to air pollution reinforces that stance by casting the Bernese as ravagers of nature. The last two lines cited suggest that Haller correctly associated "der Städten Rauch" with long-term physical maladies. Those who follow the negative life-style constitute a threefold menace: to the world around them, to their fellow man, and to themselves. The wording of the final line reaches out for those who are not yet fat but who are already swelling, that is, for those who have recently "arrived" only to abandon themselves to leisure and opulence. The statement to those immediately beneath such swollen figures on the economic scale is that such a state is definitely not to be envied. It would be far better to be content with a humbler, healthier lot.

These opening monitory observations are followed by the main body of the poem with its descriptions of flora and fauna, mountains and mores. Here, the traveler establishes his authority as a reporter and as an empiricist. In the course of these stanzas, the reading audience is meant to exchange its initial impression of Haller as social critic for one of Haller as guide. The poetic strategy is brilliantly conceived; a concluding reprise of the opening theme should seem less repetitive and more convincing since the narrator has assumed a more trustworthy role. However, execution falls short of conception, if "Die Alpen" is to be considered as didactic poetry. Again in the final lines, the poet-guide evinces no great sensitivity vis-à-vis significant component groups within what was an already small literary public. Opposition to commerce finds even more direct expression:

Noch vor der Sonne reißt die Ehrsucht ihre Knechten
Nach der verschloßnen Tür geehrter Bürgern hin,
Und die verlangte Ruh' der lang erseufzten Nächten
Raubt auch der stete Durst nach nichtigem Gewinn.
Der Freundschaft himmlisch Feu'r kann nie bei euch entbrennen,
Wo Neid und Eigennutz auch Brüderherzen trennen. (A, 323–24)

The new, enlightened age would have nothing to do with witches, goblins, and demons, but Haller sees the danger posed by excess so vividly that he allows himself the use of imagery that strongly suggests demonic legions able to threaten the honored citizen even when he thinks himself most secure. The poet finds that, all too often, the pursuit of material well-being has been rewarded by public accolades oblivious to private tortures. Earlier in the poem, he concentrates on deflating the seductive trappings of power and, in particular, wealth; here attention is focused first on the resultant lack of emotional peace and then on the paradoxical isolation of the individual within a major population center. The latter development is manifest in the imperiling of friendship as an institution, the very institution that provided a basis for the century's "secret" and learned societies. Rhetorical parallelism with a blood bond ("Brüderherzen") indicates the depth of commitment Haller expects of that relationship. Finally, of course, the appearance of "himmlisch" adds divine disfavor to inner emptiness and self-imposed loneliness; what would otherwise be a flat hyperbole is deftly anticipated by the nocturnal servants of an almost hellish Ambition.

The bedeviled family presented in the first four lines as characteristic of modern civilization is easily identifiable as that of a merchant. As previously indicated (p. 38), the search for profit had long been portrayed as a destructive physical need—whether an "urge," a "hunger," or a "thirst"—by those who disapproved of it. While it is possible that Haller might also be thinking of civil servants and professionals who put personal income before all else, the use of "stet" implies single-minded activity during waking hours. In addition the highly judgmental "nichtig" would hardly have occurred to the poet as a fitting adjective for the work of the lawyer, the teacher, the government official. However venal his motivation, such a figure performed a service the value of which would have been apparent to the son of Niklaus Haller. The depth of his concern is indicated by the final couplet: the poet moves directly from lines about the merchant to a broad statement that carries implications for all who come into contact with the man of commerce. His professional activity injects envy and selfishness into all of his relationships; clearly the implication is that the disease may be contagious. And, even if such destructive qualities remain strictly self-destructive, they deprive "healthy" citizens of life-enriching friendships. Either actively or passively, trade threatens human happiness.

The very next stanza concludes with a close variation on the same theme:

Der Geiz bebrütet Gold zu sein und andrer Plage,
Das niemand weniger, als wer es hat, besitzt.
Dem Wunsche folgt ein Wunsch, der Kummer zeuget Kummer,
Und euer Leben ist nichts als ein banger Schlummer. (A, 324)

Here again, the prospect of wealth occasions harm in the form of another of the deadly sins, and Haller specifies that others will suffer the consequences of greed. As to any benefits that might be expected to accrue from the possession of gold, they are revealed to be illusory. Vision and reality ("Wunsch" and "Kummer") are poles apart. With its reference to troubled sleep, the final line cited joins this passage to the lines featuring Ambition and its cohorts. The underlying question in the later lines as to the true nature of the verb "besitzen" applies most directly to the one who lives by "ownership." To possess more is to enjoy fewer of the benefits of life so well known to the people in the mountains. By extension, the poet would agree that the wider a merchant's profit margin, the greater his assets—and the greater the menace he constitutes to himself and to his friends, neighbors, and associates.

Haller devotes considerably less space to the censure of a second social level:

Dort spielt ein wilder Fürst mit seiner Dienern Rümpfen,
Sein Purpur färbet sich mit lauem Bürgerblut.

Haß und Verleumdung zahlt die Tugenden mit Schimpfen,
Der giftgeschwollne Neid nagt an des Nachbars Gut. (A, 324)

The wild prince was certainly not a Swiss phenomenon and would tend to support an interpretation that equates the Alpine folk with Switzerland itself.[6] However, the poem's essential polarity is not "free Switzerland" versus "absolutist Europe" but the healthy mountains versus the diseased cities. The first sentence here stands alone; the third line is not class-specific, and the fourth has returned to relations between neighbors, i.e., to a decidedly middle-class sphere. Monarchs are under attack for the same reason the luxuriating Bernese bourgeoisie is under attack: as ruling classes, both provide harmful examples for their university-educated subjects. The resultant status-seeking nourishes "der giftgeschwollne Neid" and allows it to grow outside of society's elite.

The aggressive, highly critical posture assumed by the poet bespeaks deep dissatisfaction; however, Haller's vitriol should not be taken as evidence of "Kulturfeindlichkeit."[7] Quite the contrary is true! He storms because in the final analysis he is optimistic about human society. He believes that, when shown the way, it can better itself and eventually provide happiness for its members. Andreas Müller accurately describes him as "im Tiefsten ein politischer Mensch," a "leidenschaftlicher Kämpfer und Hasser."[8] He hates the city of Berne as it is, dominated by corrupt wealth and power, by greed and status-seeking, a dirty and infected nexus of unhappiness. His prescription is adherence first to the ways of nature—that is, to the natural balance of needs and capacities—and secondly to reason as the control which will keep man in touch with that balance.

Of course, any change in society of this magnitude would have shifted decision-making responsibility toward those trained to approach human affairs with abstractions such as "nature" and "reason." In charging the ruling class with ethical bankruptcy, Haller indirectly suggests its replacement by peers of the Hallers, father and son. This position places its author at the vanguard of an expanding, progressive social level; he feels free to assess the motivations of his "betters" as well as those of his equals. Hence the poem's warning not to be tempted to imitate the prince or the bourgeois, but to become good friends and neighbors, to be as supportive of one another in society at large as were members of private salons and clubs when sheltered behind institutional walls. The poem's great flaw lies in its author's perception of those friends and neighbors. The warning is ill-conceived at its basis because of the economic realities facing its audience, an upwardly mobile class. The last two lines provide another illustration:

Der seinen Zustand liebt und ihn nicht wünscht zu bessern,
Gewiß, der Himmel kann sein Glücke nicht vergrößern. (A, 324)

Whether by pursuing advanced education or by developing new business operations, the middle-class citizen responded to a need to better his own condition, a need instilled by society. Furthermore, dissatisfaction with the current state of affairs and dedication to improvement based on the application of reason characterized the worldview of Haller's fellow burghers. Had young Albrecht himself practiced in life what he preaches in verse, he never would have gone into the Alps on a journey of discovery. The course of his later career testifies not to a poet entrapped in pastoral conventions but rather to a highly flexible, inquisitive mind constantly pushing back the bounds of ignorance.[9]

Why then does he miscalculate here? Youthful inexperience must be mentioned. For all of his travels, studious habits and a devoted family militated against any broad and deep knowledge of the human condition. Bookish idealism has yet to come to terms with mature common sense. Still, in fairness to Haller, it should be recalled that extraordinary sensitivity and exceptional powers of observation would have been required to detect what was in 1730 an incipient change in the composition of the literary public. The Bernese merchant community and the city administration that had thrown in with it would have rejected out of hand a statement such as the couplet above. The depiction of trade as a menace to peace of mind, as an ally of dark powers and mortal sins was guaranteed to keep commerce disinclined to offer its support to or to become involved in literary culture. Although Haller has learned Enlightenment thinking well enough to give it effective expression, he shows no awareness of what might be termed the diplomacy of poetry—that is, the reconciliation within the text of message and audience. Haller sees message and audience pulling in opposite directions and chooses to castigate the latter. Whereas his decidedly negative perception of the merchant may well have been shared by poets still to be surveyed, they did not allow themselves to cast the man of trade in the same nefarious role. In fact, given the initial position established by Haller and, to a lesser extent, by Schnabel, the speed and thoroughness of change in the nature of the poet's appeal to the reader could hardly be greater. Even the author of *Insel Felsenburg*, which appeared just a year before publication of "Die Alpen," even Johann Gottfried Schnabel does not allow his obvious antipathy to trade to find expression as open hostility. The presentation of the effect of commerce on humanity is as integral to the plot as is the case in Haller's poem; however, Schnabel shifts his emphasis from the malefactor to the victim. In the process he takes a step away from Haller's vision of Ambition and its cruel agents.

Details concerning Schnabel's life are so few and far between that they can all be presented—including his interminable baroque titles—on a printed page or two.[10] He was born in 1692, the son of a pastor and his wife who were both dead by the infant's second birthday. Matriculation records from a "Lateinschule" in Halle suggest that the boy was raised by relatives or close family friends determined that he should live up to his potential. For a five-year period through 1712, Schnabel served in the army of the dashing Prince Eugen of Savoy, whose campaigns in the Netherlands during the Wars of the Spanish Succession may have employed the novelist-to-be as a medical corpsman. During the following decade, the young man may have secured additional training as a barber-surgeon; however, no activity can be documented before 1724, when the duke of Stolberg engaged a new "Hofbalbier" for service at his residence in the Harz Mountains. There Schnabel gradually became a sort of general factotum whose titles included "Hofagent" and "Kammerdiener" and whose services included the editorship of a weekly newspaper, the *Stollbergische Sammlung Neuer und Merckwürdiger Welt-Geschichte*. It is recorded that a wife was buried in 1733 and that Schnabel sent a personal petition to his regent in 1744; however, further details, including a date of death, have eluded scholarship.

The first volume of the work that was to assure its author a not insignificant place in the history of eighteenth-century German literature appeared in 1731 and bore a title that encompassed over one hundred words. The novel *Wunderliche Fata einiger See-Fahrer, absonderlich Alberti Julii, eines gebohrnen Sachsens, Welcher in seinem 18den Jahre* [. . .] grew in 1732, 1736, and 1743 by sequel volumes, each of which has in its title the phrase "auf der Insel Felsenburg." It was Ludwig Tieck's edition of 1828 that firmly established the work's canonical status and shorthand title, *Die Insel Felsenburg*. The writer's great model was of course Daniel Defoe's *Robinson Crusoe* (1719), which enjoyed unprecedented popularity as measured in numbers of translations, adaptations, imitations, and continuations.[11] *Insel Felsenburg*'s four volumes were each reprinted regularly during the middle decades of the century: the first no fewer than seven times.

Readers were enthralled by the world unfolded before young Eberhard Julius, university student and scion of the fabulous centenarian Albertus Julius. When still in his teens, the latter accompanies the nobleman Carl Franz van Leuven as personal servant on the Dutchman's elopement with Concordia Plürs, daughter of a wealthy Englishman. The lovers' hopes of sailing off to a bright new beginning on the other side of the globe, in Ceylon, are dashed against the cliffs of a remote, uncharted island. There the treachery of the ship's captain Lemelie occasions not only his own death but also that of van Leuven. Concordia and Albertus Julius find themselves solitary castaways on an island whose forbidding exterior surrounds an Eden-like interior.[12] Soon, friendship between the two becomes love, and a family is founded. As years pass, the island is cultivated, children grow to maturity, and periodic contact is made with Europeans; however, the family resolves to remain where it is. Of those outsiders, the worthy seaman Leonhard Wolffgang becomes a valued friend who is trusted to bring Europeans to the island in his ship in order that the community might be made complete.

In a recent study of utopian literature during the "Aufklärung," Dietrich Naumann uses two headings in his treatment of *Insel Felsenburg*: "Europa" and "Felsenburg."[13] Such a detailed consideration of the novel's structure inevitably takes up this fundamental polarity, whereas an analysis of the role played by a specific social group might seem restricted to "Europa." Certainly, the impact of the merchant is apparent throughout the first (and best) volume of the novel. Three episodes can serve to illustrate the writer's attitudes concerning trade. Then the question must be raised as to whether "Felsenburg" is innocent of any and all resonance with commercial life in Schnabel's Germany.

The tale of high adventure in exotic locales actually begins with words from young Eberhard Julius that describe his own rather prosaic origins. He is the son of a wealthy merchant who lives in a German city never described more specifically than as "eine gewisse berühmte Handels-Stadt" (F, 236). However, when Eberhard is sent off to a university, it is to Kiel and then, for more advanced study, to Leipzig. Given the boy's age at the commencement of his career in higher education (sixteen; he leaves home with a trusted guardian), it is reasonable to posit a native city at no great distance. Schnabel means the reader to assume that the setting is in fact one of the internationally renowned trading towns of North Germany. Bremen, Lübeck, or Hamburg would have occurred most quickly to Schnabel's contemporaries; and, of the three, Hamburg already did the most business by far. In addition, Eberhard's father makes reference in a letter to an Indiaman that he had outfitted (F, 16)—which is to say, he alludes to East Asian markets whose German trade (for instance, in tea) was primarily recorded in Hamburg offices. Finally, the departing father writes his son: "In Hamburg bey Hrn. W. habt ihr vielleicht mit der Zeit Briefe von meinem Zustande zu finden" (F, 16). Again it is tellingly easy to draw a conclusion—that the older man would correspond from the ends of the earth back to his hometown.

Eberhard's brief description of his boyhood deserves notice on two counts. First, his characterization of the manner in which he was raised: "etwas zärtlich, jedoch christlich und ordentlich" (F, 14). The conjunction "jedoch" attests to the distance between parent and child that was customary at the time: the young man feels a need to reassure his audience that a somewhat unconventional home atmosphere has not adversely affected his character. Secondly, he relates that his parents decided while he was still a small child that their son would attend the university. To that end the growing boy was furnished with effective teachers who worked with a diligent pupil. His strong commitment to formal education is reminiscent of Jacob Hinrich Hudtwalcker (see above, pp. 24–26); however, it should be recalled that the latter's relationship with his son was atypical. Equally unusual is the influence wielded by Eberhard's mother: the student decides to prepare for a career in law out of deference to her wishes. Frau Julius is described as the daughter of a prominent attorney. Marriage with her no doubt raised her merchant-husband's social status, and it has raised his expectations for the education of his offspring. They have been raised to such an extent that he has accepted the possibility that Eberhard, his firstborn son, may decide not to carry on in a successful family business. The senior Hudtwalcker clearly expected his son to follow in the paternal footsteps; however, the only fatherly involvement in career choice evident in the Julius family is the commitment to university education.

The perceptions that give rise to Schnabel's sharp deviation from the standard practice of his day emerge when the student's father suddenly takes leave. Frantz Martin Julius, who has only recently lost his wife, reports in a letter than he has gone bankrupt. Three blows have been too much for his "Reputation und Wohl-Stand": his partner has lost a fantastic sum and filed for bankruptcy, the Indiaman mentioned above has been taken by pirates, and his stocks have suffered reverses totaling 50,000 talers. Further losses are intimated before the merchant reveals his decision to leave Europe for either the East or West Indies. The actual farewell is highly instructive: "Lebet wohl, und bedauert das unglückliche Verhängnis eures treugesinnten Vaters, dessen Redlichkeit aber allzustarcker *hazard* und Leichtgläubigkeit ihm und seinen frommen Kindern dieses *malheur* zugezogen" (F, 16). Frantz Martin presents himself as a victim; destiny has treated a decent ("treugesinnt") man badly. His business has trapped him between irreconcilable character traits: "Redlichkeit" on the one hand and "*hazard* und Leichtgläubigkeit" on the other. Volker Meid and Ingeborg Springer-Strand define the foreign borrowing in this context as "Waghalsigkeit."[14] The man is dealing harshly with himself in a *mea culpa* statement. However, naiveté is a character flaw only when exploited by another, and "recklessness" is a shattered man's term for the sort of risk-taking that has always been essential for success in business. From the character's perspective, he has brought ruin upon himself and his family. From the writer's perspective, a dangerous occupation has brought about that ruin, an occupation that seeks out any potential human weakness and then uses it to lead the victim, his associates, and dependents to disaster. Rolf Allerdissen has argued that the novel offers a Hobbesian view of European civilization; accordingly, each person pursues his own advantage even when that pursuit destroys the weak.[15] The inclusion of Frantz Martin's partner's fate as one of the major blows puts commerce in a still more dubious light: even if the entrepreneur boasts a personality devoid of weakness, his future course is at least partially determined by others, over whom he has little or no control. Whereas Haller concentrates his attention on the nature of the evil introduced into human society by trade, Schnabel focuses on effects.

A second episode in the novel underscores the magnitude of those effects. It is an attempt to assert the father's traditional prerogative to control the selection of his offspring's spouse that eventually sets Albertus Julius on a ship bound for the rocky shores of Insel Felsenburg. He is extracted from a financially and emotionally embarrassing situation by Carl Franz van Leuven, the youngest son of a wealthy Dutch nobleman. Van Leuven's father has extensive business connections in England, and, with the two older sons engaged in military service, it is Carl Franz who represents his family interests abroad, and who does so with considerable success. During his time in England, the young man meets and falls in love with the beautiful Concordia. When matrimony is discussed with the two fathers, however, each answers in the negative: "Der alte Herr *van Leuven* hatte schon ein reiches Adeliches Fräulein vor seinen jüngsten Sohn ausersehen, wolte denselben auch durchaus nicht aus dem

Ritter-Stand heyrathen lassen, und der Kauffman *Plürs* entschuldigte seine abschlägige Antwort damit, weil er seine jüngste Tochter, *Concordiam*, allbereit in der Wiege an eines reichen Wechslers Sohn versprochen hätte" (F, 77). The elder van Leuven is acting to prevent mésalliance that would lower the standing of son and family. Ironically enough, the younger man's acumen as a businessman has effectively demonstrated to his father that the family does not need an infusion of bourgeois pragmatism in the form of an alliance with the highly successful Plürs. With the other two bearers of the family name engaged in a life-threatening profession, he has already taken steps to safeguard the life of the third. Hence the position as business representative in a nearby country; hence the mild noblesse oblige evident when Carl Franz hires young Albertus on the spur of the moment and without any recommendations. The fact that the Dutchman is accustomed to having his own way is apparent in his act of disobedience at a watershed event in his life, even though he had been raised to put his own feelings and desires behind those of his father.

The elopement is also a setback for the merchant Plürs, although he has already advanced to a life-style rivaling that of the English gentry. He lives at a distance of some three miles from London in lodgings spacious enough for himself, his wife, six children, and many houseguests. During his brief participation in the novel's plot, he gives two large parties at this estate, each party lasting a week and featuring a great selection of edibles and amusements. Schnabel's attentiveness to establishing the wealth of the Plürs family actually jeopardizes verisimilitude in the presentation of European conditions. By rights, Plürs should see his daughter's marriage into the nobility as the crowning glory of his own rise—all the more so in that the noble family in question has no need of subvention from the outside.

Whether or not he is consistently true to European mores regarding marriage, Schnabel does use the elopement of young van Leuven and Concordia Plürs to present commerce as inimical to happiness. Considerations of wealth set generation against generation. Neither father actually needs to profit by marrying off his child wisely; however, both are trapped in conventions that grew up even as trade ascended the social ladder of the professions. Plürs is executing a decision made twenty years before the elopement; an arranged marriage with a wealthy colleague's son would have seemed an irresistible means of obtaining future security. But twenty years later what had seemed a "vertical" move is now only "lateral." Schnabel misses an opportunity to give Plürs emotional depth by not making him aware of what should be a quandary for him. His intransigent insistence upon the old betrothal does, however, contribute to the author's portrayal of commerce as a factor in human life that cannot be controlled by reason. The situation for the senior van Leuven is quite different: if his son were to insist upon a middle-class bride, the older man's aristocratic reflexes would provide an easy solution by turning his attention to another young male relative as principal heir. Schnabel has in fact provided him with two other sons. Plürs's devotion to his own business needs—whether that devotion is misdirected or not—makes him the unyielding wall against which Carl Franz's and Concordia's dream of a traditional wedding and marriage must be dashed.

Forced elopement and, in the case of Frantz Martin Julius, personal ruin are small episodes that cast light on the novelist's attitude toward commerce. With the life history of Captain Leonhard Wolffgang, a more complete image of the merchant emerges. While a young university student at Frankfurt an der Oder, Wolffgang kills a man during a drunken brawl. News of the incident causes his father to have a fatal stroke. Suddenly, financial support is not forthcoming, and the family unit back home breaks up. When he goes to work for a successful merchant in Lübeck, young Wolffgang's self-image is as cloudy as his financial status. During two years in the service of the Lübecker, Wolffgang's rise from the depths is rapid. Soon he travels as the representative of his employer in those seaports whose business is most crucial. In Amsterdam he is offered a more remunerative position that includes the opportunity to advance his own cause as well as that of his new employer in the Eastern trade. A measure of pride in the new-found autonomy is evident: "Mein Vermögen, welches ich ohne meines vorigen *Patrons* Schaden zusammen gescharret, belieff sich auf 800. Holländ. fl. selbiges legte meistens an lauter solche Waaren, womit man sich auf der Reise nach Ost-Indien öffters 10. biß 20. fachen *profit* machen kan, fing also an ein rechter, wiewol annoch gantz kleiner, Kauffmann zu werden" (F, 30). He has in fact given himself over to the pursuit of goals eschewed by the inhabitants of Insel Felsenburg. Not only profit but even money itself are foreign to the domain of Albertus Julius. That Wolffgang is adept at his profession is made clear at the conclusion of his journey to the East: "Nechst dem so *marchandirte* zwar so fleißig, doch nicht so schelmisch als ein Jude, und erwarb damit binnen 3. Jahren, ein feines Vermögen. Denn so lange waren wir auf dieser meiner ersten Reise unterweges" (F, 41). He has now risen to a position of some wealth and feels obliged to immediately distinguish his own *modus operandi* from that employed by merchant members of the pariah caste. The prospering young entrepreneur is concerned that his quick success has left him open for a pattern of ostracism normally reserved for Jews. In other words, Schnabel's merchant is fearful that his area of expertise, his (pecuniary) means of gauging success, and his professional ethics may be identified with the tiny Jewish "upper class." Wolffgang's backhanded compliment characterizing Jews as industrious effectively leavens the anti-Semitic content of the passage. For him and for his creator, the presence of the Jew in commerce is profoundly unsettling because both subscribe to the negative stereotype. Schnabel sets the whole problem aside by limiting his island paradise to Christians and by prohibiting commerce. In the ruthlessly competitive outside world, trade leads its practitioner Wolffgang to what would have been a fatal situation but for the intervention of the Felsenbürger.

In the course of his voyages, the young man also rises in the ranks as ship's officer. His success at one calling ensures continued advance in the other. Finally, at the height of his wealth and prestige, he becomes a captain, outfits a ship, and sails forth in search of treasure as a freebooter. However, as a man totally committed to the pursuit of profit—here, pure profit: "free booty"—he neglects to exercise care in the selection of his associates. In the middle of the Atlantic, the crew mutinies and sets its unhappy captain in a boat with just three days' provisions. When he lands on what appears to be a craggy deserted island, he has given up all hope of surviving. That is to say, the course of Wolffgang's life as a merchant engaged in foreign trade has led him step by step to a miserable, unmourned death. Schnabel has traced the path of a basically decent man whose values have been endangered by his chosen profession. Just before the captain sets sail, he decides to settle the matter of the killing in Frankfurt an der Oder. Wise to the ways of the world, he attempts to bribe a pardon from the appropriate civil servant: "Weil nun mehrentheils auf der Welt das Geld alles ausmachen kan, so war auch ich in diesem Stück nicht unglücklich, sondern erhielt nach Verlauff etlicher Wochen den verlangten *Pardon*-Brief" (F, 54). The attitude that money can do anything, that it is the strongest factor in human affairs, is presented as a natural by-product of Wolffgang's commercial career. It is only when he follows this dictum through to its logical consequence—his own death is perceived by the crew as a step toward its enrichment—that he can appreciate its insidious effect. His final decision to remain at a place in which money can do nothing amounts to a thoroughgoing rejection by the author of the profession of merchant as a calamitous misuse of human energy. Wolffgang has climbed the ladder of success, has learned his calling with exemplary speed and diligence, only to be set adrift at sea.

*Insel Felsenburg* is a collection of interwoven life stories, most of which are strongly affected by trade and its practitioners. Captain Wolffgang actively seeks his own advancement through the management of commerce. Virgilia van Cattmers's passivity cannot, however, insulate her against the capriciousness introduced into human affairs by money-making activity. Orphaned at an early age, she and her inheritance are taken into the family of a merchant related to the young girl's mother. Within ten years, the man of the house has lost his ward's future financial security, a sum of 18,000 talers. The classic vice of such a household appears in pure form as the merchant's spouse: "Allein die Frau meines Pflege-Vaters war, nebst andern Lastern, dem schändlichen Geitze dermassen ergeben, daß sie meine schönsten Sachen unter ihre drey Töchter vertheilete, denen ich bey zunehmenden Jahren als eine Magd auffwarten, und nur zufrieden seyn muste, wenn mich Mutter und Töchter nicht täglich aufs erbärmlichste mit Schlägen *tractir*ten" (F, 212). This dishonest entrepreneur's career ends in the same dismal fashion as that of Eberhard Julius's honorable father: in bankruptcy. Virgilia finds herself abandoned to a fate that becomes progressively less agreeable and more threatening. Even before her upright husband meets an untimely end, she is being pursued by an amoral womanizer: "Dieser *Severin Water* war ein junger Holländischer, sehr frecher und wollüstiger Kauffmann, und hatte schon öffters in Amsterdam Gelegenheit gesucht, mich zu einem schändlichen Ehe-Bruch zu verführen" (F, 222). And, before a shipload of Felsenbürger can arrive on the scene, Water has threatened to use force in the effort to secure the beautiful woman as his consort. To the decent, virtuous Virgilia such a destiny would have been intolerable. Whereas Wolffgang experiences a precipitous decline in personal fortune, her miseries are persistent and cumulative; however, thanks to commerce, both have arrived at a life-threatening nadir when the "Altvater" enters their lives. Water's evil is mitigated only by his status as a minor character; in him Schnabel's (and Haller's) worst expectations concerning the dehumanizing effects of trade are briefly realized. Still, the novel's major creations are victims rather than villains.

Captain Wolffgang and Virgilia van Cattmers blunder into an isolated realm whose mountainous borders render entrance and egress difficult. The land is small both in population and in surface area;

however, it is blessed with mineral deposits that contribute significantly to the general welfare. It is ruled by a benevolent despot who involves himself personally or through lieutenants in all executive decision-making. No great cities or large towns mar a landscape that alternates tilled fields with forest groves. At the center, overseeing settlements and work sites, stands the residence of the regent.

It is a description that applies equally to the island and to the county palatine Stolberg, and reasons other than authorial convenience and familiarity can be found for the striking similarities. Although Schnabel filled a number of positions at court, the available evidence suggests that he was paid little more than subsistence wages.[16] In all probability, he nurtured the hope that his activities as a writer and editor would result in tangible expressions of the count's esteem. A well-known literary figure would be seen as an invaluable support of the country's international prestige. In addition, although Albertus Julius is of middle-class origins, any comparisons drawn between him and the count palatine would have been highly flattering to Stolberg. After all, the fictional character is a personification of honesty, fairness, and decency; he has earned the love and admiration of his subjects and has enjoyed a remarkably long life and reign. No republican revolution has erupted. To the contrary, the form of the regime and the rights and responsibilities of the ruler would have been acceptable to all but the most traditional of the German princes.[17] The "Altvater" does make periodic reference to "meine Regierung" (e.g., F, 25), a reign whose course he alone determines. By the time of Eberhard's birth, the sons of Albertus constitute a council of elders that performs an advisory function. The most senior of their ranks will replace the common sire upon his demise; however remote this principality may be, primogeniture still obtains. Taken collectively, the possible successors of Albertus Julius constitute a tiny privileged class on the island. Like the lower nobility back in Europe, they supervise work done by skilled tradesmen and professionals, who must be imported in ever increasing numbers to meet a growing population's ever more sophisticated needs. The development and prosperity so apparent to Eberhard Julius would have been the envy of any German monarch.

In effect then, Schnabel has created a world based on mores dear to the middle class but structured in a fashion acceptable to his prince. The duke of Stolberg is indirectly urged to look upon his subjects as Albertus Julius looks upon his—as family members, dependents whose comfort and happiness should constitute a father's primary concern. It should be recalled that eighteenth-century families were larger, looser units than the modern "nuclear" family. Hence, the parallel between Stolberg and Insel Felsenburg would have been all the more apparent to contemporary readers.

Less apparent to Schnabel himself, due to a conviction that commerce endangers its practitioners, is the fact that both the "Altvater" and the count do business with the outside world.[18] The novelist makes no attempt to reconcile his woeful image of the merchant with Albertus Julius's ongoing importation of goods and services from the continent. European trade brings books, implements, domesticated livestock, and skilled laborers to the island. In similar fashion, the count's trade connections provided the economic basis for his realm. Like Haller before him, Schnabel is either unwilling or unable to affirm the role of commerce as such a basis for country and family. From the very outset, the island society is supplied with the object of mercantilist economic policy: extensive liquid assets in the form of precious metals, coins, and priceless gems. The buried treasure of Don Cyrillo de Valaro, a Spanish noble marooned and entombed on Felsenburg well before Albertus Julius's shipwreck, enables the community to dispense with normal import-export policies. Through this facile device, the novelist ducks any confrontation with or critique of economic reality in the early eighteenth century. The reader is left to wonder how Felsenburg's demand for goods and services would have been satisfied without those unearned riches.

Nevertheless, Schnabel does present the possibility that wealth can be used to improve human life. To cite another, particularly revealing example: acting as Albertus Julius's financial agent, Wolffgang engages a Lutheran pastor to tend the flock of faithful back on the island. Even what the novel presents as the loftiest aspect of life on earth is not disjunct from monetary considerations. Whereas Schnabel echoes Haller's rejection of the merchant, the man from Stolberg does not castigate trade and the accumulation of wealth wherever he finds them. Active animosity has been replaced by a combination of formal disapproval when confronted by the profession in pure form and tacit acceptance in the face of practitioners who have taken on broader responsibilities. Unlike Haller's sleepless victims of demonic visitations, Schnabel's characters can deal with money without being doomed to perdition. While the effects of such dealings can be painful, they are seldom either fatal or damning. Van Leuven's demise is hardly a direct result of the elopement but rather an encounter with a debauched man whose attitudes constitute a negative image of Albertus Julius's purity.

If the novelist's depiction of commerce is more diversified and marginally more sympathetic than that of the young Swiss hiker, the image established by both as a precedent for literature at this early point in the German Enlightenment is uniformly dark. Regardless of its increasing visibility in the social and cultural life of population centers large and small, the merchant community was not accorded immediate acceptance by the literary world. That tiny world had yet to shed its conditioned reliance on the nobility for artistic direction and support. Similarly, the moneyed bourgeoisie with its large commercial component was viewed with a disfavor rooted in medieval Christianity.

The chapters that follow trace a complete reversal of this conservative initial position taken by the literary Enlightenment. The dark image is lightened in readily perceivable gradations until the man of commerce is finally portrayed as the sound heart of German society. Particularly intriguing is the rapid pace at which this central aspect of "Verbürgerlichung" proceeds. Within just two and one half decades, precedent has been established for the complete reconciliation of the middle class with the literary tradition. Such a reconciliation could only eventuate upon total acceptance of the previously most repugnant element of that social level. The first step away from outright antipathy entailed a de-emphasis of the supposedly dangerous or menacing quality of business life. Here, developments in theater life were to prepare the way for a substitution of the ridiculous for the nefarious. As comedy came into vogue, the merchant rendered himself morally and socially acceptable by donning the fool's cap.

# III. From Fool to Friend: Borkenstein, L. A. V. Gottsched, J. E. Schlegel

Of comedies written during the German Enlightenment, only Gotthold Ephraim Lessing's Minna von Barnhelm (1767) remains a standard fixture in the repertoires of performing companies. Terminological somersaults involving the concepts "comedy" and "Storm and Stress" might allow for the inclusion of plays by J. M. R. Lenz on what still would remain a very short list. It is, therefore, ironic that plays by Borkenstein, L. A. V. Gottsched, Uhlich, J. E. Schlegel, Gellert, and Weiße should occupy such a vital position in literary history. They made possible one of the major watersheds in the annals of the German stage. They provided a body of experimentation with dramatic structure upon which the great work of the final third of the century could be based. They offered the middle class a literature tailored to its entertainment needs and intellectual goals. And finally, they provided the ideal medium for a literary about-face. A sampling of four comedies from the 1740s can demonstrate just such a startling change in the poetic presentation of the increasingly numerous and increasingly prominent men of commerce.

Even as Schnabel was producing sequel volumes that extended the publication of the epic Insel Felsenburg into the fifth decade of the century, Johann Christoph Gottsched was promoting his reform or "purification" of the stage. He did so by publishing his epochal Versuch einer Critischen Dichtkunst vor die Deutschen (1730), by attempting to banish the harlequin from the stage of his hometown (1737), and by supervising the first widely distributed attempt at a published canon for drama, Die Deutsche Schaubühne (1741–45). The pugnacious academician's subsequent reduction to a laughingstock by Lessing has been overcome by scholarship only within the past decade.[1] Gottsched's call for new and radically different German-language dramas was met by a surge in composition for the tragic and, especially, comic stages. Comedies written during the 1740s and early 1750s assailed common human failings against the background of the Enlightenment's insistence upon behavioral patterns dictated by reason and dedicated to virtue.[2] Typically, each play features a character

From Fool to Friend 71

whose actions are rendered ludicrous either by a single fault, such as secretiveness, or by a set of related flaws, such as ignorance, pride, and religious hypocrisy. The age referred to such debilitating traits as "Laster," and its comedies attacked both major and minor varieties. The object of censure is usually a middle-class member of the *dramatis personae*; as it laughed at his negative example, an audience was supposed to gain a perspective on attitudes and actions of which the playwright found it all too often guilty. As both main and supporting characters, merchants and businessmen appear in many of these comedies; and, although the suspicion and outright hostility evident in Haller and Schnabel do persist, new and strikingly different attitudes are also present.

It was perhaps inevitable that Hinrich Borkenstein's only lasting literary effort should deal with newly acquired wealth and a family's response to it. He was himself a merchant and the son of a merchant. Born in 1705, he worked as a bookkeeper in his native Hamburg until he traveled to Spain and stayed there during the second half of the 1740s and throughout the 1750s.[3] Not until 1764 did he return home a wealthy citizen content to retire from the business world. Borkenstein's oeuvre of eight comedies appeared during the four years prior to his departure for the Iberian peninsula in 1746; of them only *Der Bookesbeutel* (1742) has attracted scholarly interest. An examination of the piece must begin with the title. "Bookesbeutel" can be translated as "book-bag" or "book-pouch"; it refers to an object used by the women of Hamburg during the seventeenth and early eighteenth centuries for carrying their hymnals to church.[4] By 1742 this fashion was somewhat dated; hence the word has the additional, figurative meaning of "outmoded, laughable routine," or what in English might be termed "old hat." With the etymology of "Bookesbeutel" borne in mind, the intent behind the title becomes clear. The playwright wishes his audience to be immediately on the watch for views and dispositions that are ridiculous, anachronistic, and/or harmful.

This tight constellation of responses is to be triggered by the family of Grobian, a Hamburger whose success at business has enabled him to rest on financial laurels kept fresh by the practice of usury. As the action begins, Grobian, his wife Agneta, and daughter Susanna are visited by their son and brother Sittenreich, a student at the university in Leipzig. The young man has been accompanied on the journey home by his best friend and fellow student Ehrenwehrt and by the latter's sister Carolina. At the conclusion of the visit and the play, two betrothals are announced: Sittenreich to Carolina and Ehrenwehrt to Charlotte, an impoverished friend of Susanna. This outcome is a severe disappointment for Grobian, who had hoped for not one but two marital links between his family and that of the fabulously wealthy Ehrenwehrt senior.

The plot is enlivened by the tension produced when two philosophies of life clash; the main bone of contention is the value of education. What the new arrivals from Leipzig look upon as an absolute necessity is seen by the Hamburg family as a highly suspicious and presumably dangerous innovation. Agneta grumbles forth their position with these words: "Es kommen so viele neue Redensarten, so viele neue Moden bey Tische und andern Gelegenheiten vor, daß man bis an sein Ende lernen müste. Wozu soll die Unglegenheit? Wenn man bleibt, wie man ist, so darf man sich den Kopf nicht zerbrechen" (B, 47). In order to ensure that his son would "remain as he was," Grobian refused to finance Sittenreich's university career at its beginning, some three years before the play's action. Into the breach stepped Agneta's brother Gutherz, whose presence in the cast of characters suggests that narrow-mindedness is not necessarily peculiar either to Hamburg or to the older generation. The interest in pursuing studies amazes Sittenreich's family because they view the learning process as a continual inconvenience. The prospect of ongoing change and development dismays Agneta, who can foresee only discomfort as a result. Her household has adopted a regimented laziness that even extends to the daily menu. Each meal fits into a weekly cycle from which no deviation is permitted. Since invited guests are rare and unexpected guests unheard of, the thought of feeding company from Leipzig without advance notice creates pandemonium. In order to save money, the larder has been stocked with only minimum portions of the day's menu items. The woman of the house reacts neither with embarrassment nor with intent consideration of possible courses of action but rather with consternation at the fact that she must deal with what is perceived as a major inconvenience.

While his wife fumes behind the scenes, Grobian has an initial conversation with his three young visitors. It is here that the businessman's provincialism and ignorance become so laughably apparent that the character is quickly reduced to the status of a clown. He first expresses wonder at the great distance traversed by the threesome:

> *Grobian*: Von Leipzig bis hier sollen doch über hundert Meil Weges seyn.

*Ehrenwehrt*: O, nein, es sind nur einige vierzig.
*Grobian*: Ich habe mich mein Tage nicht um die Wege bekümmert, den ich bin nicht Willens gewesen zu reisen. Hamburg ist ja doch der größte und beste Ort in der ganzen Welt. (B, 15)

The assertion that Hamburg is the center of civilization, the largest city in the world, would have struck both university-educated audience members and those with international professional connections as absurd. Merchants and businessmen had profited for decades by the city's responsiveness to the outside world's needs for goods and services. Grobian's statement suggests a level of general sophistication far below their own. When young Ehrenwehrt responds with a reference to larger cities such as London and Paris, Grobian continues to render himself ridiculous by recalling a cousin who visited those cities only to discover strange customs and an absence of familiar consumer items.

*Grobian*: . . . und was das merkwürdigste; unter hundert Personen ist manchmal kaum einer gewesen, der deutsch verstanden. Kann man das grosse Oerter nennen?
*Ehrenwehrt*: In Paris und London haben sie dagegen hunderterley Sachen, die uns in Deutschland fehlen und unbekannt sind. Unter hundert von unsern Landsleuten wird auch kaum einer englisch oder französisch verstehen.
*Grobian*: Ey, wozu ist das nöthig. Nach meinem Willen sollte die ganze Welt deutsch reden. Was Teufel, die deutsch Sprache kostet ja nichts. Die andern muß man vor Geld und mit grossem Kopfbrechen lernen, und alsdenn klingts, als wenn Hunde und Katzen heulen. Kein Mensch verstehts. (B, 16)

Later, Grobian is surprised to learn that the "howling" is in fact two different languages; he has assumed that the world is either German and intelligible or foreign and incomprehensible—*and* inconsequential, for he must be told that the two great capitals are not as close together as are Hamburg and Altona. Because it plays such a small role in his life, that non-German portion of the world must be equally small. Grobian cannot share in the society of his intellectually alive fellow citizens because of an aversion to the experiences and perspectives of others. Ignorance alone would not have accomplished what uncritical self-satisfaction has produced, a loss of humanity. Now, however, he wants to reenter that society and arrange it in accordance with his familial and economic interests. Long, self-imposed isolation has made such reentry impossible. As a matchmaker, he is a bull in a china shop, a caricature whose actions suit his name.

Grobian reveals himself to be a buffoon through his inability to carry on intelligent conversation, an activity that is in fact unknown in his household. Agneta reports that by midevening, when the neighbors sit and talk, her family is already in bed so as to spare lighting fuel. She has heard laughter from those neighbors' conversations and comments self-righteously: "In unserm Hause wird gar nicht gelacht" (B, 46). The results of this silence have been serious enough for Grobian, who nevertheless has his business contacts; however, they have been disastrous for the daughter of the house, who is terrified to betray her profound ignorance to the young man who has traveled to her door expressly to make her acquaintance. Inevitably, her ineptitude and stupidity cost her the handsome Ehrenwehrt. Poor Susanna has been victimized by her father's reactionary traditionalism: she can do little more than sew, cook a few dishes, and sing popular songs with her mother.[5] Otherwise, the girl is completely uneducated as she prepares to enter upon matrimony. She contrasts sharply with her friend Charlotte and with Ehrenwehrt's sister Carolina, both of whom can hold their own in polite conversation. Of course, Borkenstein's target here is the total denial of education and its potential for human enrichment on the basis of sex, a species of discrimination well known in Hamburg of the mid-eighteenth century. The plot also has men suffering, albeit indirectly: because of that discrimination, Ehrenwehrt cannot fulfill his wish for the strongest of unions between himself and his friend.

Agneta does mention that her neighbors have hired teachers for their daughter, even though the parents in question are by no means affluent: "Mein Mann hat ausgerechnet, wenn man jährlich hundert Reichsthaler an einem Kinde ersparet, daß solches in einer Zeit von zwölf Jahren, nebst der Zinse, die er mit diesem Gelde erwerben kann, wenigstens dreytausend Reichsthaler betrüge. Wenn man die zum Brautschatze legt, ist das nicht besser als alle Wissenschaften?" (B, 46). Here is the impetus that has isolated Grobian from the rest of society and destroyed family life under his roof: greed.[6] The profit motive has replaced concern for his daughter's well-being. Borkenstein's assault on the practice of placing human lives on a business ledger is at least as direct as those conducted by Schnabel and Haller; in fact, it is more fully developed. Grobian's active influence is not restricted to a portion of the play. In addition, here the excessive wealth that twists personalities appears in pure form. Grobian has not purchased a luxurious life-style; liquidity, not opulence, means everything to him. Quite simply, the man is a miser. When his family must attend a formal celebration at which fine dress is the rule, the women order jewelry on approval, wear it to the gala, and then return it to the shop as unsatisfactory. The man of the house has a horror of spending his only source of pleasure. From these words to Sittenreich, his philosophy of life emerges in particularly sharp detail: "Gelt, du bist nach gerade mit mir einerley Meinung, daß nichts mehr Vergnügen bringet, als wenn man viel Geld hat, und täglich was dazu erobert" (B, 36). This is the worldview held up to ridicule in *Bookesbeutel*, a play set in the same Hamburg that had been made great by decades of concern about daily profit. The playwright is admonishing his Hanseatic audience that a full life entails a far broader range of activities and interests.[7] His allotment of personalities within the cast of characters strongly suggests that the younger generation has found a better way through education. The one positive, older character is a model not of refinement but of open-mindedness, fairness, and generosity; hence the somewhat condescending appellation "Gutherz." He accepts the following evaluation of wealth by Ehrenwehrt's sister: "Das Geld ist freilich eine schöne Sache, weil man dessen nicht entbehren kann; der Ueberfluß aber, welchen man einsperret, und welchen man nicht geniesset, ist schädlich; und wer einen Abgott daraus macht, der handelt gar thöricht" (B, 68). Grobian's response to money has made him just such a fool; however, he does retain one significant source of power over his intellectually superior son. The element of danger that money-making injects into society is not as strong as in "Die Alpen" and *Insel Felsenburg*; the very genre militates against that. However, parental control over the selection of conjugal partners still stands as a major obstacle in the path of the happy conclusion. Grobian will not approve of Charlotte as a bride for his son because the young woman hails from a poor family. A subplot involving the uncle Gutherz separates this potential couple without anguish and awards each member to a wealthy, acceptable partner; its clumsiness in addition to the absence of psychological character development has limited the appeal of the play. Still, the reason cited for Sittenreich's drive to marry has a familiar ring. As confidant, Gutherz offers Sittenreich the following argument in favor of switching fiancées: "Ihre Hauptabsicht ist doch nur, sich des verdrießlichen Umganges ihrer Angehörigen zu entziehen" (B, 39). Grobian's greed has developed to such an extent that it is now forcing a family member to abandon the common hearth. The destructive potential of a career in money-making could not be presented more forcefully to an eighteenth-century audience.

Not only is the family destroyed from within but it also risks forfeiture of its position in society. Sittenreich is sufficiently comfortable with his own understanding of the requirements for middle-class status that he does not hesitate to tell his family members that their assumptions in that regard are out of touch with reality. The following is addressed to his sister:

> Ich habe euch wohl hundertmal sagen hören, irh wäret eine von den vornehmsten Jungfern in der Stadt? Wisset ihr aber wohl, worin alle eure Vorzüge bestehen? In euerer und anderer Leute schlechten Einbildung, und in dem Reichthum, den ihr besitzet. Sonst seyd ihr nichts weniger, als vornehm oder edel; und derjenige, welcher euch mit dem rechten Namen nennen will, heißt euch den reichen Pöbel. (B, 59)

The young man is careful to include unspecified "others" among the reasons for his family's outmoded attitudes. The audience must not consider Grobian atypical but should see him, instead, as representative of an educationally and spiritually deprived segment of the population. Because of its archaic thinking concerning the place and function of money, this segment cannot be tolerated; in fact, it must be reduced in size. Accordingly, Borkenstein creates a clown family and invites derisive laughter. At the same time, he provides a bare outline of an alternative with flattering portrayals of the young people who will inherit. Of course, the name "Ehrenwehrt" is applied to the dead father as well. Even in his absence, that man offers a contrast to Grobian. He has not been written into the play because the resultant change in the comedy's structure would divert the audience's attention from the fools at center stage. However, awareness of the possibility of a reasonable alternative effectively parenthesizes the danger posed by greed. It has definite limits. Grobian's sphere of influence is largely restricted to his family, although the case of Susanna demonstrates just how pernicious such influence can be.

The education of a businessman's offspring is also the point at issue in a comedy by Luise Adelgunde Viktoria Gottsched, and again the dramatic vehicle is a family of fools. This time, however, the aberrant behavior is opposed by powerful factions within a family that is larger and whose financial interests are more complex. And this time the behavior is stopped. The playwright's career developed in the large shadow cast by her famous husband.[8] A case can be made for the assertion that her poetic talent outweighed his; however, in view of the infamy assigned by generations of Germanists to Johann Christoph's oeuvre (e.g., *Sterbender Cato*, 1730), the significance of such a case would be dubious at best. It is at least as appropriate and unquestionably more telling to argue for her central importance in the rapid expansion of the canon for comedy, that is, the genre to which middle-class themes were traditionally assigned.[9] During the late 1730s and throughout the 1740s, she was a principal source of adaptations from the French and of "original" pieces in German.

The five-act comedy *Die Hausfranzösinn, oder die Mammsell* first appeared in the fifth volume of *Die Deutsche Schaubühne* (1744). The plot is set in the home of the widowed merchant Herr Germann, who shares the direction of a firm with his half brother Herr Wahrmund. The latter has at least two sons, one of whom, identified only as "der junge Wahrmund," takes part in the action. Herr Germann's middle child is a son, Franz; his other two children are daughters. All three have been under the care of French domestic servants as the action commences. Mademoiselle la Fleche is the "Hausfranzösinn," and as such, the person responsible for overseeing education under the family roof (see p. 28). She and her two male compatriots repeatedly voice a profound contempt for all things German, a contempt inculcated into both Franz and his younger sister Hannchen. The firstborn Luischen and the two Wahrmunds rail against such expressions even as preparations are being completed for an extended Parisian sojourn to be undertaken by Franz with the three natives as chaperones. The trip falls through when the elder Wahrmund learns that the three are in fact a family of extortionists sought by the police in their native land. At the play's conclusion, the "Französin" and her colleagues make an unsuccessful attempt to hold little Hannchen for ransom; their escape by ship is doomed when the two brothers notify the authorities at the miscreants' port of arrival.[10]

Like Borkenstein, Luise Gottsched offers a plot that is sustained by tumult within a businessman's household, tumult for which the paterfamilias is directly responsible. Each play is so constructed as to direct the laughter of theatergoers and readers against scenes of chaos presided over by a father who struggles to reassert authority. Again in *Die Hausfranzösinn*, the cast of characters can be divided into two groups, the sensible and the foolish. However, this time the apparently aberrant behavior of fully half of the comical group is shown to be rooted in an abject villainy not present in Borkenstein's play. With regard to the other half, it is revealing to establish what causes foolish behavior, what does not, and finally how such behavior manifests itself.

Germann is a partner in a business firm with extensive trade connections from Spain to Russia and from Sweden to Italy. The history of the family firm is briefly adumbrated in a sarcastic comment from the half brother Wahrmund concerning the utility of mastering such foreign languages as French: "Unsere Väter haben das kauderwällische Zeug auch nicht gewußt; und sind doch ansehnlich und reich geworden: ihre Enkel aber lernen es; damit sie arm und verachtet werden."[11] Here Wahrmund speaks from the perspective of the middle generation: his father and stepfather developed a business "from the ground up." Those now deceased entrepreneurs established the family fortune and in the process attained a measure of respect and prestige. As children, Wahrmund and Germann always had a dynamic, effective, successful figure before them as a role model. Both sons learned the business from their predecessors, but only one, Wahrmund, learned how to rule a family. Two of his sons have joined the firm and have begun to make contributions; the one who appears in the play maintains a thoughtful, courteous demeanor that would be a credit to any father. On the other hand, Germann has been inattentive to the traditional duties of a "Hausherr." His wife had long nurtured a love of French culture when she died at an early age. Through a dying request, she acted to keep her children under French tutelage. Of course, in her absence and with Germann off to the office each morning, the way was clear for a calculating "Französin." Contemporary readers doubtless would have understood how such a situation could come to pass in the wake of a tragic death. Still, eighteenth-century fathers were burdened with final responsibility for everything that occurred under their roofs. As lord of his domain, Germann is expected to step in and right any imbalance or smooth any disruption. Instead of doing so, he has both temporized and taken half measures. So much is apparent when he divulges to his half brother the startling reason behind his acquiescence to his young son's impending trip to Paris. Wahrmund is at the end of his patience after a protracted attempt to learn the truth; the pronoun refers to Franz:

> *Hr. Wahrmund* (stampft mit dem Stocke): Je! so sagt den Plunder doch einmal heraus!
> *Hr. Germann*: Er schläft – – – er schläft noch bis jetzt bey der Hausfranzösinn.

*Hr. Wahrmund*: Bey der Hausfranzösinn? Je zum Henker! wer sollte sich das einbilden?
*Hr. Germann*: Und das wird mir in die Länge bedenklich. (H, 99)

Franz is fifteen years old. His father's indecision has allowed a ludicrous situation to continue unchecked. Germann believes that during the tour the four will have to arrange for traditional bedding accommodations. The boy will share, if at all, with his male servant. Wahrmund expresses his mortification and then hotly urges his brother to fire the woman—only to run into his sister-in-law's deathbed plea.

The implied temptation of a young adolescent is only one of the many consequences of Germann's lack of assertiveness and common sense. The preparations for Franz's trip have been elaborate and extraordinarily expensive. Both the youth and his companions have procured new wardrobes. Various presents have been purchased for those going as well as for those staying at home. And finally, the coach itself has been constructed to the specifications of the French employees. Aghast at the total cost, Wahrmund warns Germann that he is risking the family's professional reputation by indulging his son: "Glaubt nur, lieber Bruder, unsere ganze Handlung wird Schaden von dieser närrischen Reise haben. Was werden sich unsere Correspondenten für einen Begriff von der Sicherheit eines Handels machen, der solche übermäßige und unnütze Verschwendung unternimmt? Wenigstens werden sie unsern Kindern einmal nach unserm Tode nicht trauen" (H, 96). Wahrmund clearly expects Franz to take a place in the firm at some future time and worries that trading partners may become hesitant to put their trust in a wastrel. That Germann's business instincts have been dulled by his family problems is evident in his gift of a blank check to the four travel companions, a check that passes into the hands of the "Französin." If the father can be compromised in this fashion, what of young Franz?

Still, the prospects for a disastrous future pale before immediate dangers. Not only is the governess leading Franz down the path to moral turpitude but she is offering virtually no true education. The two younger children can neither read nor write German with any facility. While they do liberally sprinkle their speech with isolated French expressions, Franz and Hannchen cannot speak that language. Their conduct when among their elders is usually inappropriate, ridiculous, and even intrusive. Both have learned to parrot disrespect for their own native language and culture, a habit that infuriates the upright Wahrmund all the more because he has observed it in other families. He charges that the German fatherland has been damaged by widespread French influence on child-rearing (H, 94).[12]

Among the more noticeable results of such an upbringing is an insensitivity to traditions governing interactions among social superiors and inferiors. Although the three expatriots are employees, they regularly treat the younger children like servants, and they are periodically rude to Luischen. Early in the action, Luischen discovers to her great surprise that, despite large expenditures at a haberdashery, Franz has not been provided with any shirts. The governess suggests that the young man can borrow anything else he may require from his male servant. The very thought of such a scene is too much for Luischen: "Das mag nun so französisch seyn als es will, Jungfer, so sage ich ihr: daß einer deutschen Seele nichts verhaßter ist, als solche Vertraulichkeiten zwischen Herrschaft und Gesinde" (H, 90). The entire social order has been perverted when family members regulate their actions at the behest, whether stated or implied, of servants. Rather than having the most power, Germann has the least. Only one final step toward total chaos has yet to be taken: Franz's loss of respect for his father. This the author elects not to include; however, it is a final logical ramification that could not have escaped a discerning eighteenth-century reader's imagination. Such a reader would have winced as the old German servant Erhard plays outrageous tricks on the three foreigners and laments their influence on Germann, Franz, and Hannchen: by rights it should be left to the anguished merchant to move against those who would ruin his household.

Luise Gottsched is the fourth writer considered here, and she is the fourth to cast the man of trade in a critical light. However, the manner in which Germann behaves, or, rather, the manner in which he does not behave testifies to a change in the artist's portrayal of the merchant. The character is consumed neither by greed nor by any other serious vice. Nowhere does he express interest either in hoarding liquid assets or in acquiring the luxury items that would give clear notice of personal prosperity. Germann's conversations with others give no hint of intransigent adherence to fixed attitudes. Just the opposite is the case: much of the man's distress results from the almost excessively tolerant, compliant posture he assumes in relationships with others. Nor is this merchant's outlook on life in any way parochial. Both in his business and beside his hearth, Germann shows himself to be open to contact and exchange with people from far beyond the borders of his hometown. Finally, he betrays no lack of higher instincts. This is a man who holds to a deathbed promise as a point of honor. He can still express love for his wife and express it in the presence of another (H, 100). His concern for the welfare of others is most apparent in his rising fears concerning the raising of his two younger children. While his foolishness has rendered him ineffectual, there can be no doubt as to his good intentions.

In sum then, the numerous, serious complications in the plot have a relatively minor character flaw—a situational suspension of common sense—as their cause. The man of trade is fundamentally decent; his profession threatens neither himself nor those around him. If stripped of his debilitating weakness, Germann would have no place in the environments created by Haller, Schnabel, and Borkenstein. Still more out of place would be the two Wahrmunds, particularly the older man. In him Luise Gottsched sketches the first completely completely positive merchant considered here; but the half brother is no more than a secondary character, and not a well-developed one at that. Still, the reader quickly observes that he and Germann have a close, trusting relationship founded on deep similarities of personality. Wahrmund's open, garrulous opposition to the French influence suggests a thorough appreciation of the duties of a father. His efficacy as such is manifest in the faultless, self-confident bearing of young Wahrmund, a merchant in the making. When to this pair are added Luischen and the two first-generation fathers, the larger picture of an upright merchant tradition begins to emerge. The three temporarily under tow by French charlatans constitute an aberration, and their condition is only temporary. At the play's conclusion, the children's affectations are slipping away, and Germann has resolved to commit their future care to native-born teachers and servants. He has learned the lesson that the playwright wishes to teach her audience. Like Borkenstein's Grobian, Germann is the object of the audience's scornful laughter. However, by the final scene, this prototypical German merchant (his name!) has put aside the fool's cap—and the laughter has stopped.

While Luise Gottsched's *Die Hausfranzösinn* does show evidence of inchoate change in the manner in which one member of society is presented in literature, no such deviation from the historical norm is apparent within a separate but related set of attitudes. At one point, the governess's dog is induced to enter a large bird cage only then to be hoisted above the floor, which is meant as a joke on the woman. The bewildered hound's situation prompts this comment from one of the pranksters:

*Wahrmund:* Der arme Teufel! da hängt er wie der leibhafte Jude Süß. (Sie lachen alle.) (H, 145)

The tragic fate of a famous man of business, the Court Jew Joseph Süß-Oppenheimer is viewed as inherently comic by characters presented throughout as positive, even exemplary. The stage direction indicates that the others then present, Luischen and the servant Erhard, share Wahrmund's opinion. The event they are recalling occurred in 1738, just six years before the publication of the play.[13] Oppenheimer came from a wealthy, well-educated Frankfurt family. At the court of Karl Alexander, duke of Württemberg, he had assumed the position of "Kammeragent" and the role of chief financial adviser. Soon, the duke followed his counsel in all matters economic and political. Oppenheimer advocated a concentration of state wealth in the hands of the duke as a means of rationalizing commerce, a policy guaranteed to arouse the ire of those estates which had retained at least a semblance of some power during the Age of Absolutism. Insult was added to injury when not only the duke and his adviser but also the adviser's relatives were so foolish as to display their new riches in extravagant fashion. The citizenry became restive, and the duke feared for his throne. Finally, in order to pacify his subjects, the pusillanimous ruler acquiesced when public execution was demanded.

While Wahrmund's words here may be explained as an isolated response to one unique historical individual, another comment suggests a more general attitude. When his son hears that little Hannchen is missing and that kidnaping is a possibility, the young man exclaims: "Die Franzosen werden doch nicht die Kinder stehlen, wie die Juden" (H, 173). At this point in the action, the full scope of the villainy perpetrated by the three French servants is apparent to young Wahrmund; however, he hesitates to impute to them the loathsome activity that he expects as a matter of course from Jews. All too apparent is his deep anti-Semitism with its aggressive, medieval overtones. And it is tied to a posture hostile to trade that is so deeply entrenched in Christian society that even a merchant-to-be will express it. After all, the charge is that Jews trade in human flesh. The presence of this ancient enmity in the lines of two positive characters (positive even in name—they are men who "speak truth") points to naive authorial acceptance. While Luise Gottsched does lighten the image of the Christian merchant, it was left to more gifted contemporaries to lighten the image of his Jewish counterpart.

Another comedy from *Die Deutsche Schaubühne* whose action transpires in the home of a merchant is *Der Geschäfftige Müßiggänger*, published in 1743 by Johann Elias Schlegel.[14] This best-known member of the older generation of the famous Schlegel family is remembered for his founding participation in the *Bremer Beiträge*, the first major apostasy from the teachings of Gottsched.[15] In what must now be seen as one of the more mirthless and tedious of comedies, Schlegel presents an afternoon in the life of young Fortunat. This stepson of the fur merchant Sylvester has completed his education in the law but still lives at home, where he spends his time pursuing a wide variety of hobbies in a shallow, fickle manner. During the course of the action, the fool misses two appointments which could have given purpose to his life: one with a potential employer and one with a potential spouse. Both opportunities are irretrievably lost, to the particular consternation of Sylvester. Before making his final exit, the harried man of the house spells out for his wife the source of the family's ever-present anxiety and its cause: young Fortunat expends great quantities of energy and accomplishes relatively little because, quite simply, his mother has spoiled him.[16] If Sylvester's role in the play is limited, it is because the character is too observant and too worldly-wise to take part in the inane, interminable conversations between Fortunat and his indulgent mama. Sylvester's final words also testify to his candid, forthright nature; in a play that offers no major characters worthy of emulation, the furrier maintains his integrity during infrequent but trying appearances and his sanity during long absences. He is able to lay blame for Fortunat's aimlessness at his wife's door because he was not present for the son's early upbringing. During the eighteenth century, a merchant father usually spent time on the vocational guidance and professional training of sons. However, Sylvester has noted that any such strong male hand has been absent: Fortunat has been raised exclusively by his mother, a typical, undereducated eighteenth-century "Hausfrau."

The businessman has tried to talk what he considers to be common sense into his ward—with no success. The following exchange is typical of the two; there is obviously no common ground.

*Fortunat*: Herr Vater, ich thue niemals was Unrechtes.
*Sylvester*: Ey! was unnütze ist, das ist unrecht. Ich bin ein alter Mann geworden, und habe manchen Groschen erworben. Aber ich kann Euch auf mein Leben versichern, ich kann nicht mehr als einerley. Ich handle mit Pelzen, und kenne meine Pelze, und die recht, und sonst nichts auf der ganzen Welt; insonderheit aber die

> Fuchspelze, und der soll noch gebohren werden, der mich betriegen wird.
> *Fortunat*: Nichts, als Pelze? Ich wüßte nicht! Ich stürbe doch vor langer Weile, wenn ich mit nichts, als mit Pelzen, zu thun haben sollte. (M, 52)

Sylvester emerges here as a secure, self-confident individual. He is proud of his professional competence, even as he is quite cognizant of its limited breadth. When he says that he knows only his trade, the exaggeration is comic, but the assertion's foundation in contemporary reality is sound. A merchant's training was highly focused, if he received any training at all. Still, Sylvester points with pride to what he takes to be two indications of a successful career: he has made money, and he has lived a long life. His highly directed approach to human activity makes him Fortunat's opposite number. Schlegel prevents him from appearing ridiculous as the other extreme personality type by limiting his time on stage and by investing him with clear-eyed objectivity. Thus, when the young man suggests that Sylvester spend a few days sitting for a portrait, his stepfather not only rejects the suggestion because of business commitments but also takes it as an indication that Fortunat's mind is wandering from those all-important appointments (M, 56). Sylvester accordingly reminds the fickle one of his obligations and stresses their significance. While the irresponsible Fortunat cannot comprehend another person's perspective, the furrier can anticipate Fortunat's.

A further instance in which the merchant takes responsibility for the progress of another's affairs occurs during the visit by Frau Richardinn and her daughter Luischen, the prospective fiancée. Sylvester arrives on the scene after these two have engaged the woman of the house in an endless exchange of pleasantries over coffee. After he has extended greetings, the furrier quickly gets down to business at hand:

> Jungfer Lieschen, ich will Ihnen doch was sagen. Sie werden doch auch einmal einen Mann nehmen wollen? Ich habe allezeit recht viel auf Sie gehalten. Sie sind ein feines, hübsches, ordentliches Mädchen. Ich wollte Ihnen einen Mann zuführen. Freylich, so ordentlich ist er nicht, wie Sie. Er ist auch wohl, wie ich es heiße, ein Bißchen unordentlich. . . . Aber man kriegt doch auch die Männer nicht allezeit gemalt. (M, 123)

When his stepdaughter tries to retard him with levity, Sylvester will have none of it: "Du sollst itzo nicht reden. Ja, Jungfer Lieschen, so dächte ich nun, Sie nähmen meinen Stiefsohn. Wollen Sie ihn haben? Sagen Sie mir es aufrichtig. . . . Antworten Sie doch. Sagen Sie Ja, oder Nein?" (M, 123–24). To his wife's objection to the unflattering description of her only son, he replies with a telling analogy: "Wenn ich die Hasenfelle für Fuchspelze verkaufte, so sprächen die Leute, ich wäre ein Betrüger. Und wenn ich sagte, mein Stiefsohn wäre so ordentlich, als Jungfer Lieschen, so sollten sie sprechen, ich wäre ein Lügner" (M, 124). The man's attempt to cut through traditional niceties, verbal sparring, and the jockeying for position by two mothers brokering an engagement is comic. An instinctively forthright bearing makes him laughably out of place. His mistake lies in the transferral of business mores to family situations: as he will not be guilty of deception in his enterprise, so he will not "sell" his stepson on false terms. Of course, the audience knows that a certain amount of mendacity is expected of the mothers; it is the custom to exaggerate the virtues of one's child. That audience is equally aware of the stereotype of the merchant as a "Betrüger." Schlegel has elected to use the first preconceived notion for comic effect—but not the second. Sylvester does play the fool in this scene, but it is not because of character flaws (as in *Der Bookesbeutel*) or because of weakness (as in *Die Hausfranzösinn*). In this instance, it is actually virtue that makes the merchant foolish. This man would be an honest trading partner, a reliable associate, and a good neighbor. True friendship would be difficult because he divides all of his time between family and business concerns. In addition, he lacks any sensitivity to the subtleties of interpersonal relationships; people are not pelts. Still, Schlegel's man of commerce remains a sympathetic, likable fellow. One more step remained to be taken before the merchant could step forth in a completely positive light: the audience had to stop laughing at him altogether.

Luise Gottsched's one-act comedy *Der Witzling* (1745) is set in the house of Herr Reinhart, identified as "ein reicher Kaufmann in Leipzig."[17] While the title refers directly to a young man who has come to live under Reinhart's roof during his studies at the university, the playwright is also firing an indirect salvo at the *Bremer Beiträger*. The plot features not just one "Witzling," the student Vielwitz, but three, including a wretched poet and a woefully educated scholar. The central intent is a lampoon of the opposing literary camp, its lack of erudition, poetic ability, linguistic reflexes, and common sense. Luise Gottsched goes so far as to draw a clear connection between Vielwitz and Johann Elias Schlegel.[18] The foil for these trenchant caricatures is the family composed of Reinhart, a son identified as "der junge Reinhart," and the merchant's ward Lottchen. The family's reactions to its guest are made clear in the first two scenes. The elder Reinhart considers him gifted and well educated; he reveals a desire to arrange a betrothal between Lottchen and Vielwitz, only to be surprised by the girl's expressions of horror at the idea. Both she and young Reinhart consider the student an arrogant, half-educated boor. In deference to her foster parent's wishes, Lottchen agrees to give a tea so as to become better acquainted with Vielwitz. Of course, the occasion serves only to confirm the young woman in her original opinion. Vielwitz and the other two "Witzlinge" prattle on in badly flawed German about learned topics in which they are obviously unversed. Finally, as a test of the student's poetic ability, Lottchen proposes to open an envelope of lyrics sent her by the young man. When she does so, she discovers that Vielwitz has mistakenly enclosed a letter to his father that reviles each member of his host family. As the comedy concludes, the chagrined student decides to take leave of Leipzig.

*Der Witzling* is an accurate barometer of the rising intensity of literary life during the 1740s. The savaging of the three would-be writer-scholars indicates the depth of defensiveness and hostility within the previously unchallenged Gottsched camp. In the process, the play also affords another perspective on a merchant's household. Separating that perspective from those of the three comedies considered above is the identity of the fool; here, he is an outsider. To be sure, Vielwitz is himself the son of a close business friend of the elder Reinhart. Therefore, the young man must have been brought up in a home environment structured not unlike that which produced young Reinhart. However, his absurd behavior is nowhere reflected by members of the Leipzig family. They are well-spoken, civilized, considerate people—the perfect dramatic foil. Placed in their midst, Vielwitz is an anomaly, a fundamentally hostile foreign intruder.

The father sets the tone under this roof—that much is apparent in the deference shown him by both son and ward. Even Vielwitz indirectly recognizes that authority when he decides to leave before the incriminating letter can reach Reinhart. The older man's natural courtesy and sensitivity are apparent in the play's first speech: "Nun, wie stehts, Jungfer Lottchen? Ich habe heute zu Mittage unmöglich zu Hause speisen können. Ich fand auf der Börse einen guten Freund aus Siebenbürgen, den ich mit in den blauen Engel nahm: denn ich bin meiner Frauen nicht gern mit unerwarteten Gästen beschwerlich. Ist Ihnen auch bey Tische die Zeit sehr lang geworden?" (W, 9). He is apologetic for having missed dinner, which is to say, he assumes that other family members have schedules which he respects and does not wish to inconvenience. The man is aware of the effort expended by the women of the house in preparing meals and states his desire not to burden them with unannounced guests. His last question suggests a real appreciation of the time spent together at the table and an expectation that such time will offer all members the opportunity for an enriching exchange of experiences and impressions.

The playwright has created a character to whom friendship means a great deal and for whom business affairs have created opportunities to strike up such friendships. Reinhart has given up a valued portion of his day in order to spend time with the professional colleague from Siebenbürgen. A more substantial proof of Reinhart's generosity is the very extension of room, board, and a place in the family to Vielwitz, the son of another business friend. The paterfamilias has risked disruption of his domestic routine for the sake of an enduring commitment to a friendship first founded in commerce. The strength of this trait is, however, most apparent in his decision to assume responsibility for the upbringing and financial welfare of Lottchen, the daughter of a colleague who died at an early age. Opening the door to young Vielwitz proves to be a mistake that, nevertheless, can be rectified since the youth still has a father of his own. No such avenue of escape was open when Reinhart took Lottchen; regardless of how well or ill she fit into the household, the guardian's decision was irrevocable. Of course, that gamble has paid dividends because the young woman has come to look upon Reinhart as a second father.

In three separate instances, then, Reinhart's profession has enriched his life with friendship, a commodity whose worth the man repeatedly affirms. The amassing of great wealth does not dominate the merchant's thoughts; fulfillment comes through relationships with other people. Still, liquidity does play a role in his scenario for family life. Speaking to Lottchen, he says:

> Ihr Vater war ein braver ehrlicher, reicher Mann; und wußte, daß ich wohl mein Leben für ihn gelassen hätte: darum hat er mich auch zum Vormunde über Sie gesetzt, und zwar mit einer Bedingung, die sehr selten ist: daß nämlich, wofern Sie in Ihren unmündigen Jahren wider meinen Willen heirathet, ich Ihr von Ihrem Vermögen keinen Häller auszahlen darf. Weis Sie das, Jungfer Lottchen? (W, 10–11)

At first, Reinhart's words of praise and even love for his dead friend may well strike a reader as inconsistent: in what sense is "reich" regarded as a laudatory adjective? As the balance of the speech makes clear, this man of commerce views wealth as synonymous with security for family members. Given the inherent instability of his and Lottchen's father's profession, the perception is all the more understandable. Both men have demonstrated a determination that the young woman's inheritance will insure her financial stability, rather than the attentions of gold-digging fops. The foster father is well disposed to Vielwitz not only because of the personal tie but also because of a conviction that wealth marrying wealth guarantees against the possibility of chicanery on the part of a bridegroom.

As the dialogue continues, Lottchen argues against an alliance with one to whom she refers as "ein eingebildeter Thor" (W, 11). Clearly, she has been raised in a home atmosphere supportive of free and frank exchange; Reinhart has not demanded silent acquiescence to his every wish. This open-mindedness is particularly apparent when the conversation turns to a recent quarrel between young Reinhart and Vielwitz. The older man is surprised to hear first of the episode and then of the point at issue—J. C. Gottsched's Deutsche Schaubühne.

*Jungfer Lottchen*: Ja, sie redeten von der Gottschedischen Schaubühne. Da machte nun der Vielwitz alle Stücke darinnen herunter.

*Herr Reinhart* (schüttelt den Kopf): Nun! das wußte ich doch nicht. Ich lese manchmal des Abends darinnen. Alle Stücke gefallen mir zwar auch nicht; aber einige sind doch recht hübsch, und ich denke immer: was mir nicht gefällt, das kann doch wohl einem andern gefallen.

*Jungfer Lottchen*: Das macht, Sie denken wie ein vernünftiger Mann; aber nicht wie ein junger Witzling. (W, 13)

First, it should be noted that this is a merchant who can read and that for him reading is not merely a vocational skill. In fact, he has gone to the trouble of collecting all six volumes of an anthology whose contents assume no small educational background on the part of a reader. Reinhart indicates that this activity is for pleasure and is his regular custom. The selectivity reported suggests that he does not spend time with books only to garner prestige in the eyes of others but rather that he has actually developed definite preferences, tastes for tragedy and comedy. This sophistication extends to a recognition that other readers will have other tastes which he may not share but which he will respect. The man is as interested and as tolerant in intellectual pursuits as he is in interaction with family and friends. In sum, the elder Reinhart displays a wide variety of personality traits critical to the Enlightenment. Rather than putting him forward as a crude, avaricious object of contempt, his creator never directs the conversation to a point at which he says or does something comical. Instead, Luise Gottsched presents this merchant as a man who merits what he prizes so highly—the respect and friendship of other thinking, decent people.

Young Reinhart has at least as much formal education as his father, if his law degree may be taken as an accurate indication. Although he offers all of the filial devotion that a parent could ask, that career choice testifies to the same independence of thought that characterizes Lottchen. The young man has been attentive enough during his schooling to be able to quote an appropriate passage from the *Epistolae obscurorum virorum* from memory, and he retains an active interest in the muses that prompts him to read Pindar and Persius in the original (W, 28). His dialogue with Lottchen in the second scene reveals him to be equally appalled at the outrageous bearing and atrocious German that Vielwitz has brought through the front door. However, he also derives a great deal of pleasure from the posturings; it is he who has invited the two local know-it-alls for tea:

> *Jungfer Lottchen*: Ey was haben Sie gemacht? Sollt ich die poetische Cordegarde hier in meinem Zimmer haben?
> *Herr Reinhart*: Sie wird Ihnen tausend Lust machen! Und wer weis, wozu es gut seyn kann? (W, 16)

Although the young man has already expressed reluctance to speak with his father against the proposed match, he hints here that the tea may well work to Lottchen's advantage. His hope is that the fool will hang himself in a noose of his own making—which is of course precisely what happens. The junior Reinhart's attendance at the small affair is instrumental in achieving that result. He is a good friend to Lottchen under ticklish circumstances. The capacity of both Reinharts to form enduring friendships is contrasted with the rapidity with which the three "Witzlinge" first befriend one another and then fall out.

Both father and son are completely positive figures, and as such they constitute a first in this survey. However, it should be borne in mind that both are secondary characters; the playwright focuses attention on the fool and on the young woman whose happiness is at least mildly threatened. The reader must also respond to periodic reminders from the text that the play is a cannon blast in the literary artillery duel between J. C. Gottsched and his erstwhile followers. As to the merchant and his son, they do not take charge of the uncomfortable situation developing in their house; they are well intentioned but essentially passive. The older man has not sought out his house guest and spent time with him in order to develop an independent impression of the student's character. An overly prudent young Reinhart does not respond to the news of the envisioned match by taking direct action, i.e., by speaking candidly with his father.

Nevertheless, Luise Gottsched has advanced the status of the man of commerce and his family far beyond Borkenstein's Grobian and Agneta. To virtually any contemporary middle-class reader, regardless of profession, Reinhart and son would have seemed to be peers. No longer the coarse buffoon, the gullible and ineffectual father, or the man of highly limited competence and interests, the merchant has emerged as a worthy neighbor and a possible friend. The change in educational status is particularly apparent. Members of the merchant family in *Der Witzling* are able to run intellectual circles around young men who are attending the university. By extension, the Reinharts are the equals of real-world middle-class contemporaries whose formal education had made them physicians, attorneys, and municipal officials. Through the elder Reinhart, Luise Gottsched suggests that personal commitment to self-improvement is more efficacious than a host of professors. The resultant intellectual liveliness makes for an interesting person; small wonder that the character has so many friends. And he has taught his son to be a good friend, for such is young Reinhart to Lottchen. The older man's success as a parent stands in stark contrast to Grobian's ineptitude and indifference in the raising of his daughter.

In the development from Grobian through Germann, Wahrmund, and Sylvester to Reinhart, the comedies of the forties took a major step toward the rehabilitation of a suspect profession just as the importance of that profession's financial support was becoming clear. After all, by creating a merchant who has bought personal copies of *Die Deutsche Schaubühne*, Luise Gottsched is offering a fictive example to be followed by flesh-and-blood purchasers. However, the entrepreneur of the printed page is still not all that he might be. By the later 1740s, the time had come to replace prudence and passivity with active participation—and even heroism. What emerged was a stalwart, steadfast support for those in distress. In less than two decades, Haller's troubled and troubling presence became a savior of the downtrodden.

# IV. Virtue in the "Jewish Profession": Gellert

It is a fine irony, distilled from the cowardice of poets, the hatred of earlier centuries, the horror of our own, and—bathos. We see him huddled there, and we smile, painfully. There next to his horse; both covered with new-fallen snow. He has lost consciousness and lies dying of exposure in a remote corner of Siberia. He hails from Poland and is a merchant by trade, a Jew by confession.

Before his rescuer arrives on the scene, let us pause to note that this poor soul is the first Jew to play a significant, positive role in a German literary work, Christian Fürchtegott Gellert's *Das Leben der schwedischen Gräfin von G\*\*\** of 1747–48. Hence, the timing of the literary novum is as delayed as its manner is incongruous. Of course, basic to the Enlightenment in northern Germany was a challenging of the Lutheran orthodoxy; Hermann Hettner titled the first chapter of his literary history "Der Kampf gegen das engherzige lutherische Kirchentum."[1] The struggle was waged with foreign and domestic teachings. Descartes, Spinoza, and Locke provided the basis for a growth of empiricism and a reexamination of the old thesis that the highest form of human knowledge is achieved through faith, not reason. When the latter faculty was installed at the center of intellectual life, time-honored religious, governmental, and social institutions were opened to critical analysis. By mid-century, intellectual discussions could focus on the systematic segregation and discrimination practiced against Jews.

If rationalistic philosophy had jolted the orthodoxy from one side, Pietism confronted it from the other. Spener, Francke, and their followers did not seek to supplant faith as the cornerstone of human consciousness, but rather to channel it into vital new worldly institutions. The focus of Pietist concern was the individual within the small group of devoted Christians. Not dogma but the religiosity of the single being dominated an outlook directed beyond traditional and often stigmatizing labels. Richard Newald suggests another reason for this live-and-let-live posture when he observes that Pietists avoided confrontation in favor of accommodation in the quest for tolerance.[2] Like Rationalism, Pietism voiced a plea for the relaxation of previously rigid attitudes toward religion and its adherents. With the emergence of this stance, the literary tradition found itself in an intellectual epoch open to the possibility of the Jew as protagonist.

The appearance of our snow-covered figure was also made possible by Gellert's relationship with the audience for literature in the 1740s. It must be emphasized that that audience was tiny. Rudolf Schenda asserts that as of 1770 at most 15 percent of the German population could read its native language.[3] Publishers' expectations with regard to sales were proportionately humble. Helmuth Kiesel estimates that, in a country of approximately twenty-five million, only 0.1 percent of Germans read a given book and that 0.01 percent actually bought a copy.[4] The size of the literary market determined that a high premium was placed on the poet who could reach out to all potential readers. Such a figure was Gellert, the writer of fables, for as such he was known to prince and peasant alike. In the *Fabeln* (1746 and 1748) readers found a mixture of gentle moral instruction and mild teasing. By the time *Das Leben der schwedischen Gräfin von G\*\*\** appeared, Gellert had established both an unrivaled following within the small literate community and a reputation for perceptiveness, probity, and wit.

The "intellectual atmosphere" of the age was comparatively salubrious, the claim of orthodox Christianity to speak for all true believers had been rendered at least debatable, and the literary sphere was well disposed to Gellert. And yet, when his first novel found its way into print, it featured a plot so turbulent and so complex as to effectively camouflage the presence of the man from Poland. It is as if the author hoped that his reader would be too preoccupied with sensational twists and shocking relevations to pause overlong at the figure of an honorable Jew. Any pause that did occur can be attributed at least in part to the strength of historic anti-Semitism during the eighteenth century (p. 32). Gellert responded to the existence of the negative Jewish stereotype by exercising a large amount of caution and a modicum of courage. The Jew in question appears on only fifteen of the novel's one hundred fifty pages, and he is not one of the main characters. Nevertheless, the Pole does enhance the lives of those main characters to such an extent that he is finally admitted into their large "extended family." That literature of the early Enlightenment was not necessarily supportive of the struggling minority has already been demonstrated. How then does Gellert present the growth of a friendship between Christian and Jewish characters? To what extent does the Jew's career in commerce play a role? How does he compare with the novel's Christian merchants? The answers to such questions can be sobering to a latter-day student of German cultural history.

As a novel, *Das Leben der schwedischen Gräfin von G\*\*\** fails in the eyes of a modern reader because of the overburdened plot and the absence of character development. From beginning to end the several principal figures remain mouthpieces for ethical sermonizing, despite life histories that would normally enjoin reticence. Still, the work did enjoy considerable popularity during the eighteenth century. A second, slightly revised edition in 1750 provided the text that was reprinted several times during the writer's lifetime. English and French translations gave "the Countess" international renown during the 1750s. Modern scholarship has evinced greatest interest in the lady's contribution to genre history. To cite an example with high visibility, Dieter Kimpel's Metzler volume *Der Roman der Aufklärung* focuses its discussion of Gellert on narrative structure and theory of the novel.[5] The examination specifies the novelist's uses of picaresque traditions and of the adventurous and utopian Robinson novels even as he also manages to anticipate such figures as Blanckenburg and Wieland. Given the then impending spectacular surge in popularity experienced by the genre, given its approach toward acceptance as legitimate art by the end of the century, such examinations are of great importance.[6] However, here the topics of first concern are two elements of mid-eighteenth-century German society that any writer had to approach with all possible circumspection.

The novel's plot details the tangled destiny of a daughter of the rural nobility during the last quarter of the seventeenth and first quarter of the eighteenth centuries. The barest outlines of an overly elaborate plot are as follows: the girl's early marriage to the somewhat older Graf von G\*\*\* is interrupted when he is dispatched to military service. Soon she receives word that her husband has been lost during a counteroffensive mounted by the opposing Russian army. After nothing is heard from or about him for several years, the countess, now living in Amsterdam, marries the nobleman's best friend, the bourgeois Herr R. Of course, the count has not died but rather has been sent to a penal camp in Siberia, where he strikes up a close friendship with the prisoner Steeley. Once released, he is restored to his wife in part through the offices of the merchant Andreas. When the Graf von G\*\*\* actually appears in Holland, Herr R. withdraws from his now bigamous marriage back into friendship. The original marriage then resumes, and the couple's circle of friends grows to include the returning Steeley, his bride, and his father, an elderly London merchant. At the conclusion, the entire company is transplanted to old Steeley's estate not far from the English capital. It is there that they must endure the deaths of their host, the count, and Herr R.[7]

The Polish Jew's participation in this tale is related in two separate sections: first, in two letters written from the prisoner in Siberia to his wife, letters delivered only after the return of the count; and secondly, in the countess's narration of a visit paid by the Jew to the noble couple in Amsterdam. The friendship of Christian and Jew begins in the frozen wastes, where the count comes upon the dying man and helps "mit der größten Gefahr."[8] In so doing, he demonstrates an ancient ethical reflex: with no thought of reward, he acts to save a fellow creature. Later, when the Pole has had time to reflect, he seeks to return the favor. Gellert has him ignore the possible response consisting of a word of profound thanks followed by a farewell; the character takes quite a different course of action: "Dieser Mann ist auf die edelste Art dankbar gewesen und hat mir bewiesen, daß es auch unter dem Volke gute Herzen gibt, das sie am wenigsten zu haben scheint. Er hat nicht eher geruht, bis er mich vor den Gouverneur gebracht, bei dem er seines Reichtums wegen in Ansehen steht" (L, 221). Here, at the very beginning of the narrative sections involving the Jew, Gellert has the count establish in the reader's mind authorial awareness of the low esteem in which the minority is widely held; the historical, negative stereotype has been adumbrated at the outset. However, this is balanced by the simultaneous reflections that the particular Jew has advanced the speaker's cause and that such commendable instincts are common to a number of "gute Herzen" within the minority. The arrestingly unconscious comment that gratitude has been expressed in the most "noble" fashion provides a point of departure for the modern reader. How has a Jew been able to win the sort of praise that the nobleman would normally reserve for a peer? The process passes through three distinct stages.

The first stage is generosity. Gellert's count arrives at the work camp at Tobolskoy in rags. He is weak and sickly after a period of prolonged ill treatment while a prisoner in Moscow. Although active physical abuse ends, he is forced to join fellow inmates in the hunt for sable across hostile terrain, during the course of which activity he stumbles upon the Pole. The grateful new acquaintance is in a position to offer the prison superintendent a ransom for the soldier's release. When this is rejected, the Jew uses bribes to secure better clothes and living quarters for the count, to whom he also gives substantial sums of money on a regular basis. The largesse is then extended to Steeley and to another friend whom the count has met in prison. The Jew, who remains unnamed throughout the novel, visits his new acquaintance intermittently; but the content of their conversations is not revealed, except when the prisoner makes note of an expression of gratitude for a gift or sum of money. This is due in part to Gellert's consistent insensitivity to the demands of psychological character development. Few details concerning the merchant's personal circumstances emerge, and his extensive trading connections do not allow him to take part in the daily affairs of Tobolskoy. In its early stage, the personal relationship between the two men is a one-way street.

The great generosity displayed can be seen as a measure of the social gap between the two. If anything, the Jew gives too much in an attempt to communicate gratitude to a man from a totally different walk of life. Economic assistance is the one means of expression open to him, the one means of reciprocating an act that Gellert presents as prompted by the count's adherence to an age-old moral code and by his readiness as an army officer to take responsibility for the lives of others. That the count perceives the comfort bought for him as an effective bridge between two social levels reflects the novelist's optimistic, not to say utopistic, analysis of class relations. This perception makes possible the second stage of the Jew's passage to peer status.

Having demonstrated a capacity for generosity, the merchant jumps at the chance to prove his reliability. The count has come into possession of several jewels, with which he thinks to repay his benefactor. However, when the Jew assigns the stones a high value, he reveals his basic honesty and his commitment to a continuing relationship: he does not wish to be paid off. Instead, he volunteers to oversee the disposition of the new wealth to the nobleman's best advantage. This he means to do with the aid of two Jewish friends, one of whom will buy the jewels, while the other will use the funds accrued to bribe the superintendent at appropriate intervals.[9] In his reaction to the offer, the count speaks to a reversal of roles that now has him in the Jew's debt: "Ein Mann, der mir soviel Gutes erwiesen hat, wie Ihr, verdient das größte Vertrauen" (L, 232). The addition of a business arrangement to their relationship causes the two men to approach one another as equals for the first time. Previously, the act of mercy and the sense of indebtedness had formed a bond despite profound social and financial disparities. Now the condition of dependence has passed, replaced on the part of the noble by one of trust in a valued acquaintance who enjoys freedom of movement.

It is particularly revealing that the Pole involves other Jews in the care of the count; through this device Gellert prevents a contemporary reader from looking upon the Polish merchant as an anomaly. The Tobolskoy Jew who purchases leniency from the camp superintendent during his coreligionist's absences also stops in regularly to keep track of the count's condition. At one point he smuggles a letter to the prisoner at considerable personal risk. Then, when the nobleman has been told of his impending release, it is this Russian Jew who converts his Christian acquaintance's liquid assets into promissory notes that will be honored by the Jewish financial community in Moscow. This service is extended in addition to a cash gift intended to defray travel expenses. The count concludes his epistolary narration of the Russian Jew's kindnesses with the telling comment: "So ehrlich handelte dieser Mann an mir" (L, 240). Once he has arrived in Moscow, the notes are honored when presented. Only one small sum cannot be paid back immediately by a young Jew who has suffered serious financial reverses; however, his colleagues promise to produce the amount in question within a short time. Their high ethical standards are common to all Jews who appear in the novel; of course, that includes only men with significant financial assets and/or business connections. However, these men never use their freedom of movement to take even the slightest advantage of a Christian whose life in Russia is strictly controlled.

When the count and the Polish Jew have arrived at the second stage of their relationship, this very freedom of movement becomes the axis for Gellert's oblique analysis of anti-Semitism in his day. The urban German Jew of 1747 faced ghetto walls as formidable as those of a Russian prison. The novel presents an upright Christian character, a model of the virtues demanded by popular Enlightenment philosophy, suffering indignity at the hands of his intellectual and moral inferiors but finding aid and comfort in the person of a Jew who does not fit the negative stereotype but rather shows strong Enlightenment traits. Clearly, the challenge to Christian readers was to categorize themselves either with the Russian authorities or with the beneficent Jews when considering their own dealings with victims of real-world oppression. Through the imprisoned count, they could experience the treatment accorded denizens of the "Judengassen." It is revealing that the inverted image first comes into focus as Gellert's Pole takes on the role of financial adviser, or even banker. The novelist is aiming his plea for change at the commercial rather than the religious or philosophical reflexes of his middle-class audience. The great danger of such an approach is its inherent elitism. It avoids an opportunity to advocate the extension of basic human rights to those Jews less favored economically than these businessmen.

Reliability in money management is the chief prerequisite for the Polish Jew's admission into the circle of friends around the title figure, who continually reports on the splendid advance of her own investments. However, when the merchant chances to meet count and countess after the Siberian ordeal has ended, it is personal similarity that provides the final tie that binds. During a brief sojourn at their home in Holland, the now aging friend makes use of the same sentimental turns of expression common within the countess's circle. He demonstrates a piety equal to their own by kneeling in prayer for half an hour each day. Finally, his devotion to their welfare is such that he vows that he would gladly spend the rest of his life in their company but for the desire to be with his wife. The countess remarks: "Wir nahmen alle als von einem Vater Abschied von ihm" (L, 248).

Gellert takes pains to establish the former benefactor as a well-to-do bourgeois dedicated to the same ideals of reasoned behavior, virtuous social relationships, and tolerance so well known to the novelist's largely Christian audience. The old merchant's religiosity is emphasized, but not the nature of his faith—which is precisely the manner in which the author approaches the Christian beliefs of his other characters. This is due in part to the sensational plot line, in the midst of which any analysis of confession would be ludicrous. It is also true that Gellert's relatively small potential audience was divided between orthodox Protestants and Pietists and that the writer could not afford to alienate either group. The strategy of emphasizing general religiosity effectively neutralizes confessional differences; it is a strategy that enables Gellert to present his main Jewish character as the perfect peer—a more mature, wealthy bourgeois who finds a place for himself within a company of like-minded individuals. There he is at ease with patterns of family commerce, with a life-style identical to his own; so much so that he acquires the status of a patriarch in a second family unit.

Gellert's Pole has advanced to the head of an otherwise Christian table via generosity, then financial reliability, and then personal similarity. Each of these steps would have been unthinkable for the great majority of Jews in eighteenth-century Europe; quite simply, they would have lacked the requisite liquidity. Even at the presumable conclusion of the enfeebled old man's relationship with the countess and family, Gellert has him again cement the bond of affection with his great wealth. Just as he is about to leave, he presents the little daughter of the house with a Dutch bank account of some ten thousand talers and thereby ensures his family-member status after death and into a second generation. Exclaims the countess:

> Er ging darauf zu unserer Tochter und knüpfte ihr noch ein sehr kostbares Halsband um den Hals. . . . Der rechtschaffene Mann! Vielleicht würden viele von diesem Volke beßre Herzen haben, wenn wir sie nicht durch Verachtung und listige Gewalttätigkeiten niederträchtig und betrügerisch in ihren Handlungen machten und sie nicht oft durch unsere Aufführung nötigten, unsere Religion zu hassen. (L, 248)

Can Gellert be so naive as to equate a figure with jewelry at the ready and numerous sizable bank accounts on hand with any "Volk," let alone European Jewry at this point in history? Surely the merchant has paid an extraordinarily high price for his membership in this unique Christian family, for real and complete tolerance. Crucial to an understanding of such astounding optimism is a correct identification of the pronoun "wir." Gellert writes exclusively for those with whom he peoples his works: the educated upper middle class and lower nobility. Similarly, he presents a Jew who is typical only of the economic elite of his coreligionists.[10] The high-minded statement about tolerance must be understood in terms of the sentence concerning the necklace that precedes it. Because that elite was but a tiny fraction of the total Jewish population, it must be pointed out that the author charges a second and much higher price for tolerance. Perhaps unwittingly, he advocates its extension on a selective basis. Respect, understanding, and concern will be ready for those Jews who are able to rise above an ancient, entrenched pattern of discrimination and assume a middle-class life-style. It might be argued that even this humble degree of tolerance is a step forward: better some than none.

On the other hand, the basically passive attitude assumed by Gellert's Christians suggests that the burden of social change is to be borne by the victims of injustice; and how many members of the minority will be able to demonstrate generosity, financial reliability, and personal similarity? From such a passive posture, Christians might in fact come to look upon poor Jews with still greater disapproval. On balance then, Gellert is suggesting a standard for acceptance that is remote from demographic reality, a standard guaranteed to foster frustration and despair within the minority. From its point of view, the matter of requirements for tolerance is clear: better none than these.

It goes without saying that upper-middle-class merchants would have experienced waves of self-congratulation while reading a novel in which a business relationship makes possible the defeat of anti-

Semitism, a natural enemy of the Enlightenment. By 1747 the campaign against old superstitions, fears, and hatreds had been carried on in print for decades. Contemporary readers would have readily identified Gellert's plot as a continuation of that didactic thrust. In like fashion they would have observed that the implementation of theory has a solid financial basis each step of the way. The presence of positively drawn Jews actually argues for the merchant as a worthy participant in the Enlightenment, and more particularly, in Enlightenment literature. However, more direct argumentation is advanced in the writer's portrayals of Christian merchants.

The countess and Herr R. are taken in by one such man of trade at an early point in their travels. The master of the house runs his business from Amsterdam; he first extends his hospitality because his wife is a relative of Herr R.[11] However, the woman does not have to urge her husband to provide the two victims of court intrigue with a haven. The countess reports: "Sie nahm uns sehr gütig auf, und ihr Ehemann war ebenfalls ein vernünftiger und dienstfertiger Mann. . . . Mit einem Worte, diese Leute erwiesen mir, ehe ich sie noch kannte, mehr Hochachtung und Gefälligkeit, als ich fordern konnte. Sie gaben mir einen ganzen Teil von ihrem Hause zu meiner Wohnung ein; ich nahm aber nicht mehr als ein paar Zimmer" (L, 184). The couple remains unnamed. Periodic references are made to the generous "Wirt" and "Wirtin"; however, no details emerge concerning the course of their life together. That the "Wirt" is to be seen as a successful businessman is already evident in the fact that "a few rooms" constitute less than one section of his house, which therefore must be quite spacious, indeed. The host's sagacity in money matters is in fact the other form of aid which he extends to the countess and Herr R. during their marriage. It is he who manages their investments so skillfully until his death shortly before the count's return. The man's demise is all the more serious for the couple and their family since, as the countess readily admits, none of them knows anything about financial management (L, 206). Their response is a move to The Hague and to the household of Andreas, a second merchant-host. The pattern repeats itself again when old Steeley invites the company to join him in his native land. Although the three men of commerce differ strongly, each assumes responsibility for the physical well-being of the noblewoman and her steadily growing retinue. The image that is already emerging in Amsterdam is that of a caring steward, much in the manner of old Reinhart in Luise Gottsched's *Der Witzling*. However, here more wards are taken under the paternal wing; and, as adults, they have more and greater needs. In addition, these merchants do not have the right to exercise direct control over the lives of the countess and company; nor are they rewarded with the love of a child, such as the love of Lottchen for old Reinhart. In a sense, then, theirs is a more selfless generosity—all the more so since there is always the possibility that agents of the scheming Swedish court will find the countess, who assumes a false identity during her residence in Amsterdam. Her hosts, particularly the two in Holland, are risking the consequences of her discovery, consequences of a presumably unpleasant nature.

As a parallel to the "Wirt" in Amsterdam who comes to the aid of the countess in a moment of peril, Gellert presents an English merchant named Tompson who helps the count during his tense passage out of Russia. Tompson hears of Steeley's misfortune when the man is first sentenced to Siberian detention. The Moscow-based entrepreneur immediately sends word to those who would be concerned back in England. He then expedites communications between those friends and relatives and the English representatives to the court of the czar. Petitions on Steeley's behalf are filed with the parliament, and direct appeals are made to the regent. As a result of such negotiations, Moscow finally agrees to the release of the British captive. Once he has been assured that his friend will be released from Tobolskoy, the count asks Tompson's advice concerning the best means of leaving Russia. The merchant promptly arranges passage on a Dutch ship which his firm is loading in the port of Archangel, a ship in which Andreas has part ownership. The man in Moscow also promises to forward any correspondence that might be sent to the count in the Russian capital, in particular, any communication from Steeley.

Of the many merchants who appear in *Das Leben der schwedischen Gräfin von G\*\*\**, Tompson is doubtless the least clearly profiled. Only his actions are reported, not his personal characteristics; and his period of contact with the count is brief. Nevertheless, he is vital to Gellert's presentation of the merchant, and not simply as another helping hand for the main characters. Whereas the novelist's portrayals of other men of trade emphasize their great humanity in private contacts, through Tompson Gellert makes a case for the beneficial role that commerce as a profession plays in the larger world of competing national interests and disparate cultures. The writer offers no idealism concerning the fair distribution of the earth's resources. Instead, his delineation of Tompson suggests an evaluation of the international trader as a sort of unofficial diplomat who is in a position to intercede on an informal basis when unique problems concerning individuals arise, problems that threaten to strain official relations. That he acts as an international ombudsman is evident in Tompson's solution to the count's transportation needs: the English merchant puts a Swedish noble onto a Dutch ship in a Russian port. Originally, the count identifies Tompson as one member of a group of English merchants in Moscow who have been working for Steeley's release. Of course, this suggests that such mediation is not unique to one sterling individual but rather is common practice among merchants abroad. While old Steeley is an idealization of the merchant as the man of principle, Tompson is an idealization of the merchant as the man of affairs.

If Gellert provides any counterbalance to these two living monuments to commerce, it is in the person of Andreas, the brother of a member of the countess's extended family. He is worthy of special note since he is the character with whom a reader's empathy was and still is most possible. Far from being a breathing quintessence of strength and virtue, Andreas has his all-too-human ups and downs. And, while the noble couple and their close friends certainly experience many a trial and tribulation, their difficulties are assigned a different cause. They respond to hardship with passivity in the face of what are perceived as the unavoidable and immutable dictates of destiny. The following ruminations from the count illustrate an attitude that is totally foreign to a man such as Andreas: "Man sieht, wenn man den Betrachtungen über die Vorsehung nachhängt, die Unmöglichkeit, sich selbst zu helfen, deutlicher, als wenn man sich seinen Empfindungen überläßt; man sieht die Notwendigkeit, sich ihren Führungen zu überlassen, und man will doch zugleich nicht von dem Plane seiner eignen Wünsche abgehen" (L, 218). Because reason rules these people's actions, the posture indicated is enlightened resignation. The importance attached here to fate or providence meshes with both the pedagogic and the voyeuristic appeals of the novel. For centuries, sequences of events have been seen as "the workings of fate" when rulers and members of the ruling class are involved. Gellert's superfreighted plot enabled his middle-class peers to derive pleasure from observing the deleterious effects of a factor to which only their "betters" were answerable. Of course, the attitude of resignation would have struck a responsive chord among those with considerable education and/or commercial experience but without input into governmental decision-making.[12] However, Andreas's example certainly does not commend passivity in the managing of one's own business or family affairs.

The novelist does not have Andreas speculate as to the reasons for the hardship he has undergone; therefore, the reader is left to draw conclusions strongly suggested by the character's words and actions, and those conclusions have nothing to do with destiny. Quite simply, this merchant is a man of somewhat limited sensitivity and intellectual depth; the major reversal in his career presumably has been the result of poor decisions. His firm in The Hague went bankrupt years before the count's return from Russia, and Andreas himself journeyed to the East Indies in hope of restoring his losses. Before doing so, he committed to the care of a convent his niece, the count's illegitimate daughter. An illegitimate son is raised by the boy's mother, who believes the girl dead. In the midst of altered identities and a lack of parental awareness that sorely strains verisimilitude, brother marries sister, and the couple has a child. When Andreas returns to The Hague, his financial health restored, the circle of friends begins to suspect the awful truth. The countess reports the merchant's immediate reaction as follows: "Andreas, der der Philosophie wegen nicht nach Ostindien gereiset war, meinte, es läge schon in der Natur, daß ein paar so nahe Blutsfreunde einander nicht als Mann und Frau lieben könnten" (L, 194). Of course, the reasoning is faulty because it denies the existence of that which is known to exist, incest. As an isolated statement, the utterance could be passed off easily by understanding readers as attributable to the great anguish of the moment. However, the countess's sarcastic relative clause implies that the quality of thinking displayed here is typical of the man. Soon after this exchange of views, the friends decide to enlighten the young couple slowly and gently. But, upon first catching sight of the girl, Andreas blurts forth lamentations in which he assigns to himself all responsibility for the tragic state of affairs. Again the countess reacts with sarcasm and condescension. The man's actions are certainly imprudent to the point of insensitivity; however, the stressfulness of the situation fails to mitigate his behavior in the eyes of the others.

After his return from the East, Andreas receives courteous but distant treatment from the countess's circle because of a common perception of his severe limitations. However, Gellert offers several indications that such an assessment is flawed. After all, during the second half of the novel, Andreas rises from the ashes back to viability as an entrepreneur with a growing clientele and a staffed office. The man is not stupid and doomed to failure; in fact, he is ultimately successful. Furthermore, he repeatedly offers food and shelter to those in need: first to his infant niece and then to a group of rather unappreciative adults when the countess's original "Wirt" dies in

Amsterdam. He is equally generous in putting his business connections at their service, not only by taking charge of selected investments but also by giving employment to a youth to whom the circle has given emotional support in the midst of personal adversity. Andreas is not fundamentally insensitive; in fact, he is as compassionate as any of the others. He remains an "outsider" who is, nevertheless, a credit to his profession. Through him, Gellert extends his campaign for approval of that profession beyond what some readers might have looked upon as exclusive, not to say elitist, criteria for peer status with the countess and friends. Though obviously a man of less formal education, less cultural refinement, the merchant is productively involved in the world around him even as he is free of serious character deficiencies. The reader's final impression is that of a happy, fulfilled man. His presence in the work ensures that such readers will not reserve their approval of merchants for such "insiders" as old Steeley, a man possessed of education to a degree unknown to most German traders of Gellert's day. And, if any of those traders picked up the novel, Andreas would have been for them the character deserving of sympathy because of his hard-won success and his unfailing humanity.

By contrast, the elder Steeley is welcomed as a peer from the moment he first sets foot on the countess's doorstep and inquires in French as to the whereabouts of his son. Gellert specifies the language in order to establish the speaker's learning and civility. He is comfortable using the common tongue of well-educated Europe. In conversations with his new acquaintances, he proves himself to be both plain-spoken and sensitive, both personally modest and solicitous about the welfare of others. At age seventy-nine, he is healthy and physically active; still, the fact that he has undertaken a journey abroad at an advanced age testifies to his great love for his child. When he later recalls his dead wife with great affection, it becomes apparent that theirs must have been a close-knit household. The countess and her friends are particularly struck by their white-haired visitor's perpetual cheerfulness and liveliness. In response to their inquiries, old Steeley gives voice to Gellert's strongest and most direct statement on commerce as a sphere of human activity:

"Daß ich noch so munter bin," sprach er, "das ist eine Gabe von Gott und eine Wirkung eines ordentlichen Lebens, zu dem ich von den ersten Jahren an gewöhnet worden bin. Und warum sollte ich mich vor dem Tode fürchten? Ich bin ein Kaufmann; ich habe meine Pflicht in acht genommen, und Gott weiß, daß ich niemanden mit Willen um einen Pfennig betrogen habe. Ich bin gegen die Notleidenden gütig gewesen, und Gott wird es auch gegen mich sein. Die Welt ist schön; aber jene wird noch besser sein." (L, 271)

A large house in London and an extensive estate in the country indicate just how effectively he has made use of his abilities, abilities given freer rein in his native land than would have been the case in the mercantilist nations of Europe. In fact, the main action of the novel transpires in England and Holland, the principal trading countries of the era. Andreas and old Steeley remain virtuous in nations whose laissez-faire commercial policies left the door open for the sort of avarice and dishonesty old Steeley is proud to have avoided. On his very deathbed, he reasserts his professional integrity by swearing to his son that no part of his inheritance results from improper dealings (L, 273). It is clear from the quotation above that this posture results from simple, deep religious faith and from an adherence to common decency in daily affairs. That decency includes regular acts of charity. As the old merchant delivers what amounts to a credo for his profession, he does not know he is close to death. And yet it is apparent that his professional activity causes him no trepidation when he contemplates his mortality. The man has accomplished what long tradition deemed impossible: he has earned both a profit on earth and a place in heaven.

In the attempt to arrive at a believable, positive image of the merchant, the crux of the problem for Gellert, as a disciple of the Enlightenment, was the reconciliation of wealth and virtue. After all, the pursuit of one's self-interest was clearly compatible with an ethics founded in part on the free operation of reason. The potential stumbling block for a figure such as old Steeley was that other great support of an increasingly secular morality—virtue. The writer's solution to this problem is twofold. First, none of his characters—notably old Steeley, his son's wife, and the countess—cultivate a luxurious or pseudoaristocratic life-style. To the contrary, moderation in consumption is a guiding principle. Gellert carefully omits any mention of the quality of food, clothing, and accommodations enjoyed by these people. Secondly, old Steeley does address the question of wealth, although he does so indirectly. Upon reuniting with his long-absent son, he learns that the younger man has recently married. The bride Amalie has brought into the marriage a large case containing a fabulous treasure in precious jewels. Her father-in-law's reaction is predictably sober: "Er bezeigte über das große Vermögen, das Amalie besaß, keine besondere Freude. 'Mein Sohn,' sprach er, 'du hast ein Glück mehr als andre Leute; aber du hast auch eine Last mehr, wenn du dein Glück recht gebrauchen willst' " (L, 271). Wealth can be harmful if it is not properly managed. That is to say, the couple's life together will be less fulfilling if they use the money improperly (by luxuriating) or if they do not manage it at all (by vegetating at their present status quo). Old Steeley is suggesting that wealth tends to be an ethical burden. Only constant vigilance and a strong will can force it to follow the path of virtue, a path that he believes he has kept ever in view despite a wide profit margin.

To carry the writer's train of logic one step further: the presence of wealth actually provides the opportunity for a demonstration of exceptional dedication to high moral ideals. The rich man begins his pursuit of inner worth under an onus unknown to the man of modest means. That old Steeley feels no fondness for an abundance of assets is emphasized by the countess when she describes the accidental loss of Amalie's treasure chest; the old servant Christian has dropped it into the sea: "Der alte Steeley, so wenig er das Geld liebte, konnte doch den Zufall nicht vergessen. Er hielt dem alten Christian eine lange Strafpredigt" (L, 272). Gellert has the merchant incorporate the age-old distrust of wealth as an indication of immorality into a philosophy of life that is beyond reproach. Money in itself is surely worthy of such distrust; it is dangerous since it so easily becomes an ethical burden. However, it can serve just as easily as the ultimate test for virtue. The novelist has his title figure state this position in the following terms: "Mußte man einen solchen Mann nicht lieben, der von Jugend auf mit dem Gewinn umgegangen war und doch ein so edelmütiges Herz hatte?" (L, 271). He is the most pristine figure in the novel; in fact, the countess's characterization is strongly reminiscent of the emerging concept of the "schöne Seele," which the German tradition borrowed from Shaftesbury.[13] Old Steeley is the third and last father-figure to sit at the head of the countess's table. Early in the action, the count's father serves as a supportive companion to his daughter-in-law during the first stage of the count's absence, the younger man's active participation in the war.[14] Later, the Polish Jew enters the circle of friends through the process detailed above. However, old Steeley is in a sense the best father to the group since his life is an example that all can follow. When they move to his estate, it is as though long-lost children finally have found their way home.

Such is Gellert's presentation of the merchant: a virtuous man, whether Christian or Jew. The positive treatment of the Pole in particular is fully in line with the novel's championing of the moneyed bourgeoisie. Part of the shakiness of the merchant's reputation in the eighteenth century resulted from the activity of the Jewish elite in German commerce. To put it in stark terms, the ill repute of the Jew cast a dark shadow on the Christian merchant. That species of bigotry had surfaced in German literature just a few years before the appearance of Gellert's novel.

Toward the end of his exhaustive analysis of the legal and social condition of Jews in medieval Germany, Guido Kisch notes that throughout the period Jews were always at the forefront in the development of previously dormant categories of economic activity. They frequently found themselves consigned to services needed by but abhorrent to the Christian majority: "This need existed as long as the majority of the population had either no interest in, or no ability for, such economic services. As soon as they learned to satisfy this need themselves, the mission of the Jew was finished."[15] The rise of the middle class in society and in the arts during the Age of Enlightenment was based to a large extent upon the growth of commerce. Hence, that class found itself expanding into a realm of activity that had long engaged members of the small Jewish middle and upper classes.

Gellert realized that, as it now began to satisfy its own economic needs, the religious majority would also be in a better position to support the literary tradition, and more broadly, literary life. He attempted to further the developing trend and win the favor of merchants for letters by moving against an obstacle in their path to high esteem in the eyes of their fellow citizens. In his novel, the means of "finishing the mission of the Jew" is the granting of peer status on the basis of personality—that is to say, on the basis of Jewish recognition of supraconfessional, Enlightenment ideals. The man from Poland is himself a product of "reeducation."

The novel attempts to complete Kisch's cycle in an "enlightened" fashion. The Polish Jew is completely at home among Christians who hold to the century's great philosophical impetus. However, even the famous Gellert could not put to rest the suspicion of commerce, the animosity toward Jews, and the interrelationship of the two attitudes. That much is apparent in a contemporary reaction to the *Schwedische Gräfin* and to Lessing's comedy *Die Juden* (1754), which features a Jewish hero. The hostile review in the *Göttingische Anzeigen von gelehrten Sachen* has been attributed to Johann David Michaelis. Concerning the two fictional Jews he writes:

Aber auch die mittelmäßige Tugend und Redlichkeit findet sich unter diesem Volcke so selten, daß die wenigen Beyspiele davon den Haß gegen dasselbe nicht so sehr mindern, als man wünschen möchte. Bey den Grund-Sätzen der Sittenlehre, welche zum wenigsten der große Theil desselben angenommen hat, ist auch eine allgemeine Redlichkeit kaum möglich, sonderlich da fast das gantze Volck von der Handlung leben muß, die mehr Gelegenheit und Versuchung zum Betruge giebt, als andere Lebens-Arten.[16]

Michaelis's blatant animosity toward the minority also colors his attitude toward those Christians who engage in what is described here as *the* Jewish profession. He suggests that they have made a decision to distance themselves from Enlightenment ethics. Not only does the reviewer deny the likelihood of such a phenomenon as an honest Jew but, in the final portion of the second sentence, he also draws an equality that points to the less immediately apparent reason for the inclusion of the count's Jewish friend.

Gellert uses the Jew to counter the ambivalence felt by other members of the educated, Christian middle class with regard to their merchant brother. The preaching of tolerance is therefore in part an attempt to solidify the position of the merchant by revealing the benign nature of a trading partner cursed with a negative stereotype. Hence, *Das Leben der schwedischen Gräfin von G\*\*\** makes two appeals for tolerance, one stated and one implied. In itself, this is no mean accomplishment, an accomplishment doubtless facilitated by the genre's uncertain status at this point in literary history. The reading audience brought less clearly defined expectations to the novel than it did, for example, to comedy. Therefore, a writer shouldered the burden of establishing expectations within his or her novel. On the other hand, a generous measure of freedom in form and content was also offered.[17]

For readily understandable historical reasons, it is the stated appeal for tolerance that has attracted scholarly interest. However, close attention to the text supports the contention that, far from directly assaulting the bastions of anti-Semitism, Gellert is only probing a distant perimeter. No broad extrapolations should be drawn from relationships dominated by the tending of personal fortunes. Gellert's presentation of European Jewry is too narrow to allow an interpretation of the count's benefactor as the focus of a first major appeal for religious tolerance. In fact, the primary appeal is for professional tolerance, an unstated appeal to civil servants and professionals not to shun a figure so essential to the survival of German letters as the Christian merchant.

And this is the ultimate irony for modern readers: much as we would like to see the snowy rescue of Gellert's Jew as a heroic early blow struck for freedom of religion, we can only conclude that the novelist had other ends in view. His direct appeal for tolerance in matters of faith is of secondary importance and of dangerously limited scope.

On the other hand, Gellert's adulation of the Christian merchant old Steeley knows no limits. The latter is a sage at whose feet both the novel's characters and the novel's readers hear lessons in how to live and how to die. In him the merchant finally sheds the status of a black sheep within the middle class and steps forth as first among equals.

# V. The Merchant as Hero: Lessing

Even as Gotthold Ephraim Lessing (1729-81) was serving his apprenticeship as a man of letters during the late 1740s and early 1750s, the merchant was entering a third decade of representation in literature of the German Enlightenment.[1] In Kamenz and Meißen the schoolboy had experimented with correspondence and occasional writings.[2] However, his first sustained dedication to a major genre allied him with Borkenstein, J.E. Schlegel, and Luise Gottsched as a writer of comedies. When he withdrew from the university in 1748, Lessing had already produced one comedy, *Der junge Gelehrte* (first published in 1754), and he was anxious to try his hand at journalism as well.[3] Of the many and varied fruits of the resultant activity, two plays raise the man of commerce to previously uncharted heights. Both are short, one-act comedies, and, although neither directly identifies its central figure as a merchant, each suggests that occupation while parading the character's exemplary humanity and genuine heroism. These early attempts to reconcile heroic humanity and commerce were later overshadowed by the commanding figure of Nathan the Wise. Taken together, the three plays constitute the final stage in the evolution of the merchant into a subject worthy of literary treatment.

Lessing wrote *Der Schatz* in 1750, his second complete year of residence in the capital of Prussia. The plot is built around the reunion of a long-absent father, Anselmo, and his irresponsible, wastrel son, Lelio. In the first scene, the upright young Leander asks his guardian, Staleno, for permission to marry Lelio's sister. Staleno must refuse because Lelio's extravagances have cost Kamilla her dowry. Later, Staleno rebukes his old friend Philto for the latter's alleged contribution to the young couple's frustration. To all appearances, Philto has abrogated his responsibility as guardian to the brother and sister by purchasing the family home from a financially strapped Lelio, thereby enabling the errant ward to further squander his family's remaining assets. Upon hearing the accusation, Philto confides to Staleno that their old comrade Anselmo revealed to him alone the hiding place of a secret cache of money, the "treasure" of the play's title, just before leaving for parts unknown. The sum was intended either as a form of insurance or as a dowry for the daughter of the house. When, blissfully unaware of the hidden funds, Lelio put the building up for sale, Philto felt compelled to buy it in order to keep both home and cache secure until Anselmo's return. Together, Philto and Staleno conceive a plan for producing the dowry without further injury to Philto's reputation and without danger of intervention by Lelio. They hire a local to masquerade as Anselmo's friend from abroad, whom the absent father has supposedly asked to convey a sum of money home. The counterfeit friend is to describe the amount as a dowry for the girl, whose matrimonial status is to be in Philto's control. The two old schemers also agree to support Leander's intentions. Of course, the first person whom the "friend" encounters is none other than Anselmo, who has just concluded his journeys. After no small confusion and comic sparring comes the revelation. The betrothal wins final approval; father and son are reconciled.

Scholarship has been slow to warm to *Der Schatz*, a state of affairs due in large measure to the play's status as an adaptation, but also to its length and its categorization as a "Jugenddrama" that precedes the canonical oeuvre. The early biographer Theodor Wilhelm Danzel, whose five-hundred-page volume on the years 1729 through 1764 first appeared in 1850, refers to the play only once and with no analysis at all.[4] The well-known study by Erich Schmidt does take up the one-acter, and in so doing it established a pattern that has been followed by subsequent scholars.[5] The great bulk of Schmidt's treatment consists of a plot comparison of the German play and its Latin progenitor, Plautus's *Trinummus* (ca. 194 B.C.). Not that Lessing deserves a charge of relative lack of creativity: in his "Prologus," the Roman cites the subsequently lost *Thesauros* of the Greek Philemon as the source of *his* play.[6] In the course of detailed recapitulations, Schmidt points to alterations made by Lessing. Among the more noteworthy are the elimination of the five-act structure, the merging of two old cohorts of the wandering paterfamilias into one (Staleno), and the embellishing of Leander and his interests. However, the underlying negative evaluation pervades the analysis and finally surfaces with punning sarcasm at its conclusion.[7] Three and a half decades later, another noteworthy biographer repeated the formula: a brief analysis, concentration on plot comparison, and words of praise for Lessing's attempts to streamline the piece and add a psychological dimension—all of which fails to counterbalance the superficiality of the Latin original and the "painful" inability of the German playwright to blend entertainment and instruction.[8] Waldemar Oehlke's charge of a lack of moral profundity is all the more serious given the

Enlightenment's expectation that the audience at a comedy should learn as it laughs. If this scholar is to be believed, the one-acter was out of step with contemporary literary life. If his predecessor Erich Schmidt is to be believed, the play was out of touch with contemporary everyday life. More recent studies have evinced the by now traditional discomfort: any positive comments have a distinctly apologetic ring.[9]

However weak its other claims to literary immortality may be, *Der Schatz* does constitute a significant advance in the presentation of the merchant on stage. That advance rests squarely on the shoulders of three old friends: Philto, Staleno, and Anselmo. Although their professional activities are not described in so many words, the text does provide ample indication, particularly in its presentation of Anselmo. The man left his home and two children nine years before the action of the play commences; for the past four years, no communication has been received from him. Soon after he first sets foot on stage, the play's central character delivers a brief soliloquy that indicates the nature of his mysterious doings:

> Ich [darf] die Augen nicht sehr von meinem Koffer verwenden. Ich dächte, ich setzte mich darauf. – – Bald, bald werde ich nun wohl ruhiger sitzen können. Ich habe mir es sauer genug werden lassen, und Gefahr genug ausgestanden, daß ich mir schon, mit gutem Gewissen, meine letzten Tage zu Rast- und Freudentagen machen kann. – – Ja gewiß, das sollen sie werden. Und wer wird mir es verdenken? Wenn ich es nur ganz obenhin überschlage, so besitze ich doch – (er spricht die letzten Worte immer sachter und sachter, bis er zuletzt in bloßen Gedanken an Fingern zählt.)[10]

He is just beginning to allow himself to relax after withstanding enough emotional stress and danger to last the remainder of his lifetime. The third sentence reveals that the price he has paid in risks taken has in fact purchased Anselmo a peaceful retirement. The final, incomplete sentence and the stage direction leave no doubt as to the form of his guarantee: the profits he is reckoning mean financial security. The mild defensiveness ("Und wer wird mir es verdenken?") is directed against any of his old friends and neighbors who may think ill of him for enjoying the fruits of his labors. The weary, happy, successful businessman has reached a long-sought goal. The nature of that business emerges from several isolated comments.

The first townsman to recognize Anselmo and speak with him is Lelio's cheeky servant Maskarill. The sale of the family house is soon made known, but the understandably unmanned bearer of these tidings is loathe to reveal the reason behind Lelio's action. When mystification fails to check a barrage of questions from the concerned father, Maskarill changes the subject even as he shares a private joke with the audience:

> *Maskarill*: . . . So viel werden Sie doch wohl erfahren haben, daß er ein großer Handelsmann geworden ist?
> *Anselmo*: Mein Sohn ein großer Handelsmann?
> *Maskarill*: Ein sehr großer! Er lebt, schon seit mehr als einem Jahre, von nichts als vom Verkaufen.
> *Anselmo*: Was sagst du? So wird er vielleicht zur Niederlage für seine Waaren ein großes Haus gebraucht haben?
> *Maskarill*: Ganz recht, ganz recht.
> *Anselmo*: Das ist vortreflich! Ich bringe auch Waaren mit; kostbare Indische Waaren. (S, 155)

Instead of reacting to the fictitious news of his son's commercial success as Maskarill hopes, by allowing himself to be distracted from the sale of the family homestead, Anselmo immediately reconciles the two changes in the image of his son as a merchant. It makes sense to him that more space would have been required as business and inventory grew. The celerity with which the returning father can summon forth this particular cause and effect as well as the image itself suggest personal experience in the activity under discussion. Then follows the revelation that Anselmo has brought trade goods of his own, colonial wares from India. His travels are thereby explained as involvement in the international wholesale trade. The attributive "kostbar" suggests that the old fellow has made quite a "killing."

While the text does not provide adequate grounds for the inference that Anselmo has actually journeyed to the other side of the earth, direct reference *is* made to travel abroad, travel to a land blessed with a flourishing commercial life. This occurs just as Anselmo is informed of the tentative betrothal of his daughter; the following words are addressed to Staleno, who has arranged the prospective nuptials:

> *Anselmo*: . . . Ohne ihn [the bridegroom] zu kennen, würde ich, bloß in Ansehung Ihrer, Ja dazu sagen, wenn ich meine Tochter nicht bereits versprochen hätte; und zwar an den Sohn eines guten Freundes, der vor kurzen in Engeland verstorben ist. Ich habe ihm noch auf seinem Todbette mein Wort geben müssen, daß ich seinen Sohn, welcher sich hier aufhalten soll, auch zu dem Meinigen machen wolle. Er hat mir sein Verlangen so gar schrift-

lich hinterlassen, und es muß eine von meinen ersten Verrichtungen seyn, daß ich den jungen Leander aufsuche, und ihm davon Nachricht gebe.
*Staleno*: Wen? den jungen Leander? Je! das ist ja eben mein Mündel.
*Anselmo*: Leander ist Ihr Mündel? des alten Pandolfo Sohn?
*Staleno*: Leander, des alten Pandolfo Sohn ist mein Mündel.
*Anselmo*: Und eben diesen Leander sollte meine Tochter haben?
*Philto*: Eben diesen.
*Anselmo*: Was für ein glücklicher Zufall! (S, 167–68)

By this late point in the play, the audience understands why Anselmo has been away from home so long. Either to breathe new life into a fading business or to dramatically raise profit levels (possibly with a view to the uncertainties of old age), he has dedicated a significant span of years to mercantile endeavor. It is only natural for that audience to assume that those designs took him to England. Personal contacts made in the island kingdom would have resulted from the traveler's business concerns; which is to say, in all likelihood old Pandolfo was himself a merchant. The latter conclusion is further supported by the obvious parallels with Anselmo: Pandolfo also left a child with a trusted coeval in order to live and work elsewhere.

In an otherwise perceptive study of social structure in Lessing's plays, Ariane Neuhaus-Koch asserts that Anselmo does not pursue mercantile goals in the betrothal of his daughter to the son of a friend.[11] The thinking suggested would certainly be inconsistent with the portrayal of the central character as a highly successful businessman. But if Pandolfo was in fact a merchant, there is no inconsistency. Pandolfo has just died. His son stands to inherit a legacy that would insure two futures: the son's and the son's bride's. If that bride happened to be Anselmo's daughter, the old merchant would not have to concern himself with starting a new son-in-law in business; both capital and contacts would devolve from Pandolfo. Significantly, the stay in England is the single episode of his long absence to be related by Anselmo. Until this point in the action, the audience has been led to assume that he has returned because of weariness or homesickness or the desire to see his children.

The young playwright has a surprise in store for spectators: Anselmo has actually come home at this particular time to seal the betrothal before either of the partners is tied to a third person. He is acting in accordance with both long tradition and personal self-interest. And his haste is warranted: as guardian, Philto has been about to consent to the girl's marriage. In a happy final twist, Lessing makes Leander and the third person feared by Anselmo one and the same. From his initial appearance until the final resolution of all conflict, Anselmo pursues mercantile goals.

In similar fashion, his two friends' sharp financial reflexes guide the action, particularly in the course of the eight scenes that precede the father's arrival. Neither man refers directly to his profession. However, both *are* Anselmo's close friends; and, by virtue of often tenuous relationships with other members of their social class, businessmen and merchants in eighteenth-century Germany were constrained to look upon their colleagues as the largest pool of potential friends. During the course of the play, behavior associated with the popular stereotype of Anselmo's merchant colleagues is linked to Staleno and Philto. When Staleno is approached by his ward for permission to wed, his single concern is the size of the girl's dowry. News that no such bridal gift is forthcoming prompts him to inform young Leander that in all probability he will not give his consent to the match. This stance results not only from a determination to follow custom but also from the older man's somewhat exaggerated respect for liquidity. In a scene with Philto, he declares that he loves money even more than friendship (S, 134). Through the words of a disinterested outside observer, Lessing makes clear that the same attitude in Philto has been observed by other townsmen for a long time. The observer is an unnamed porter whom Anselmo engages as the man passes him on the street. According to the "Träger," no one has been unduly surprised at Philto's apparent decision to put profit before honor in the purchase of the house from the dissolute Lelio: "Er ist alle sein Lebtage für einen eigennützigen Mann gehalten worden, und was ein Rabe ist, das bleibt wohl ein Rabe" (S, 164). The implicit charge is thievery—and not just the one instance but chronic, lifelong thievery. Of course, it is understood that Philto's profit-seeking has transpired within legal bounds. The simple laborer's evaluation of the man who loves money above all things squares with the old prejudice against commerce. As Lessing reveals the true motivations behind the actions of the three men, he explodes that prejudice. But first, the playwright makes clear that the general populace sees Anselmo in the same light. Unaware that the man to whom he is speaking is the long-absent businessman, the same porter says of Lelio: "Sein Vater war der alte Anselmo. Das war ein garstiger, geiziger Mann, der nie genug kriegen konnte" (S, 163). Although Lessing does not identify the calling followed by Staleno and Philto, he consistently presents the two and their returned friend as three of a kind—three of a kind in the eyes of the public, in their estimation of the role of money in human affairs, and in their shared ethical reflexes. As the writer illuminates those reflexes, he reconciles the three characters with the popular philosophy of the Enlightenment.

Staleno's insistence upon an adequate dowry from his ward's bride results from a well-developed sense of responsibility. That Leander is a model of courtesy, candor, and obedience is a tribute to Staleno's attentiveness to the duties of a surrogate father. The older man's pique is aroused because he thinks that Philto has not kept faith with the absent friend. Under Philto's care, Lelio's behavior has been lamentable, and both brother and sister face destitution as a result. Clearly, Staleno sets high standards for the ethical component of relationships with family and friends. However, it is Philto who finally emerges as a martyr to high ideals. He has willingly subjected himself to public censure and condemnation in order to protect the secret treasure; even Staleno calls him "ein alter Betrieger" (S, 131). Later, when the reason for his purchase of the house is understood by all concerned, Philto comments as follows on the insults he has borne: "Was wollen Verleumdungen sagen, wenn man bey sich überzeugt ist, daß man sie nicht verdient habe?" (S, 167). Rather than take the path of expediency, he has followed the dictates of his conscience—this in spite of the damage a deteriorating reputation has done to his personal and professional life. Philto satisfies the highest of expectations with regard to decency and personal honor. It also becomes clear that he has in fact made every effort to discharge his duty to oversee Lelio's activities, and that the young rake was stirring up trouble well before his father's departure.[12] Just before play's end, when the wayward son contemplates the inevitable confrontation with his father, he casts about for an intercessor who might plead for mercy. His guardian is not considered a possibility: "An den alten Philto darf ich mich nicht wenden. Ich habe seine Lehren, seine Warnungen, seinen Rath allzu oft verachtet, als daß ich auf sein gutes Wort einigen Anspruch machen könnte" (S, 166). In the final scene, however, Philto does in fact speak for Lelio and thereby displays the extent of his magnanimity. Both he and Staleno demonstrate that a profound commitment to virtuous behavior can coexist with an equally determined pursuit of financial strength.

Lest Anselmo's interest in arranging an advantageous match for his daughter seem overly calculating, it should be recalled that a contemporary audience would have viewed his actions as laudable.

He has placed a traditional paternal responsibility before whatever business activities have been commanding his attention. Of course, his mysterious and possibly exotic commercial affairs will ultimately benefit not only himself but also the other members of his family; his toils have not been for himself alone. And they have cost him nine years of separation from the comforts of home, years of uncertainty and physical hazard for a man well beyond his prime. He returns to find not a joyous, warm, peaceful reception but confusion, trickery, and bitter disappointment. The disappointment sets in when he must learn that his son is known to the whole city as "der lüderliche Lelio" (S, 163). Later, when his daughter's future with Leander has been settled, Anselmo cannot suppress a sigh of regret: "Ach! wenn ich den ungerathnen Sohn nicht hätte, was für ein beneidenswürdiger Mann könnte ich seyn!" (S, 168). The clemency extended to Lelio in the final scene is conditional: if the young man does not mend his ways, his father will take stern measures. This means ongoing responsibility for a man who desires a tranquil retirement. If Anselmo's heroism is diluted by the presence of the profit motive, it is that very dilution that lends him credibility. He is neither one-dimensional nor larger-than-life, but rather a believable central character who brings concern and selflessness to bear on a chaotic situation and thereby creates order. At long last a German playwright had produced a well-developed merchant-hero whose attitudes and actions were not just worthy of emulation but susceptible of it as well. Plautus's contribution to the effort cannot be denied, but the final three scenes in *Der Schatz*, which decide the fates of Leander, his beloved, and the errant Lelio, are Lessing's creation.[13] The German playwright has embellished Anselmo's function as the one who dissolves complications, and with that the merchant had come into his own on the stage of the Enlightenment.

The one who dissolves complications in the one-acter *Die Juden* (written in 1749, published in 1754) also comes from afar, but his very identity remains mysterious until the climactic final scenes. As the play opens, his act of heroism is reviled by the villains, Michael Stich and Martin Krumm. The two are employed as the "Vogt" and "Schulze" of an estate owned by a local baron. With a coachman's connivance, they have attempted to waylay the landowner as he returned homeward on the evening before the action of the drama commences. Michael Metzger has observed that, although the appearance of such rustics was rare for Enlightenment theater, a contemporary audience would have been ready with a prejudice against them as members of the lowest social class, a prejudice with intellectual and ethical components.[14] The would-be highwaymen *were* clever enough to disguise themselves with false beards; at this point in German history, a man with a long dark beard was assumed to be a Jew. However, the scheme was foiled by the fortuitous arrival of an armed stranger and his servant, who sent Stich and Krumm scurrying into the bordering forest and the gathering dusk. The ill-tempered conversation begun after the curtain rises is interrupted when the two miscreants spot the stranger approaching. Stich slinks off in the face of the one cryptically identified in the *dramatis personae* as "der Reisende." "The Traveler" has yet to set foot on stage, but Lessing has already focused his audience's attention on two points: the identity of the unlucky thieves and the identity of their nemesis. What will the other characters learn? What can the audience discover about the stranger? Any information relevant to either question will stand in sharp relief as the plot unfolds.

Martin Krumm cannot fawn enough on the one whom he identifies as his master's fearless savior. The other man demonstrates his innate modesty by responding that his was the only decent course of action and that no accolades are necessary. He describes the attackers as disguised, and notes that, because of the beards, the baron believes the pair to have been Jews. At that, Krumm lets forth a stream of invective directed against all Jews, sentiments later repeated by the baron in the course of discussions with his newfound friend. The Traveler consents to spend first the night of the incident and then, reluctantly, the following day at the residence of a nobleman drawn to him not only out of gratitude but also because of the stranger's keen mind, dignified bearing, and transparent moral rectitude. For his part, the Traveler takes gentle exception to blanket condemnations of any people even as he questions the easy assumption concerning the assailants. He seems ill at ease when asked for any personal information, so the baron sends his sharp-tongued maid to quiz the Traveler's servant. It has been asserted that the scenes between Lisette and Christoph constitute a harsh contrast to the idealistic thrust of the main action.[15] Through their off-color, mendacious, self-aggrandizing exchanges, the maid comes around to the opinion that Christoph's master is actually a nobleman. In the meantime, the Traveler chances to see a false beard spill from Krumm's pocket, and the malefactors are soon revealed. Now doubly indebted to his guest, the baron offers his daughter's hand in marriage and the status of sole heir. The Traveler replies that he must refuse; for he is not the baron's peer but in fact a Jew. When the stunned noble offers a large reward, the other man replies that the God of his fathers has amply provided for his financial needs. Each asserts that if the other were typical of his coreligionists, they would be an extraordinary people indeed.

Lessing's debt to the English tradition, specifically to Vanbrugh and Farquhar, has been well established.[16] However, Harvey I. Dunkle, while recognizing the playwright's sources and the one-acter's limitations as drama, argues that the underlying idea was original.[17] The intent to write a didactic play is apparent from the plot alone. If the writer is to be faulted, it is not for slavish imitation of gifted foreign predecessors but for uninspired plotting elements and negligible character development. Although the central figure says little about himself, speculation has focused on the Berlin physician and scholar Aron Emmerich Gumpertz as Lessing's model.[18] However, if the text itself is consulted, the question still cries out for an answer: who is the Traveler? More specifically, who was he in the eyes of eighteenth-century audiences? To reiterate: Lessing has so constructed the play as to spur such speculation. The man's name is never given, his occupation never revealed. But a number of hints are dropped.

Doubtless the most telling is the character's wealth. He is journeying by horse with a servant who reports to the baron's inquisitive maid that the two have enjoyed a comfortable passage.[19] The Traveler is accustomed to indulging not only a need for pleasant accommodations and good food but also a craving for intellectual stimulation. One of Christoph's responsibilities, a heavy bundle of books, testifies to that (J, 391–92); such items were quite expensive at mid-century. When he thinks a solid silver snuff-box is either lost or stolen, the Jew, although mildly agitated, can still refer to it as a "Kleinigkeit" (J, 399). Clearly, the audience is to understand that this is a very wealthy man. As such he must hail from that razor-thin highest level of Jewish society, a level dominated by merchants, bankers, and financial advisers (p. 33). Because the baron quickly seizes upon the notion of arranging a marriage with his teenage daughter, it is reasonable to assume that the character is in early middle age at the oldest and therefore that the great wealth is in all likelihood at least in part the result of activity by one or more earlier generations. Such an assumption would also account for the fact that the Traveler has had the time and the financial support to acquire the education evident in his speech and in his fondness for books.

At first reading, the geographic location of the baron's residence may well seem unclear. There is no direct reference to it as a part of a larger sovereign state. Because of the presence of two members of the peasant class, a search for telltale regional usages is clearly in order. However, concerning the speeches of Stich and Krumm, Michael M. Metzger reports: "In its phonology, syntax, and content, this is surely not a realistic rendering of any 'Bauernsprache.' It is merely the common colloquial language associated with the lower social levels in Lessing's plays with a few dialect forms added."[20] Nevertheless, if how the two speak is not revealing, what they say is. In the following speech, Martin Krumm uses the Traveler as a sounding board for a rant against the Jews:

> Mein Herr, zum Exempel: ich bin einmal auf der Messe gewesen – ja! wenn ich an die Messe gedenke, so möchte ich gleich die verdammten Juden alle auf einmal mit Gifte vergeben, wenn ich nur könnte. Dem einen hatten sie im Gedrenge das Schnupftuch, dem andern die Tabacksdose, dem dritten die Uhr, und ich weiß nicht was sonst mehr, wegstipitzt. Geschwind sind sie, ochsenmäßig geschwind, wenn es aufs Stehlen ankömmt. So behende, als unser Schulmeister nimmermehr auf der Orgel ist. Zum Exempel, mein Herr: erstlich drengen sie sich an einen heran, so wie ich mich ungefähr jetzo an Sie – (J, 379)

A person of Krumm's social estate knew very little mobility in the eighteenth century. Therefore, when he speaks of "the fair" with its crowds of people and its sizable component of Jewish participants, he is describing a major event that takes place in a city that is reasonably close and probably in the same country. One of that nation's internal policies is mentioned by the Traveler himself as he expresses reservations concerning the belief that the highwaymen were Jews: "Denn ich begreife nicht, wie die Juden die Straßen sollten können unsicher machen, da doch in diesem Lande so wenige geduldet werden" (J, 378). Of course, during this era Germany's great fair took place at Leipzig in Electoral Saxony, a state that only permitted members of the minority within its borders during the event. The other fair of international significance took place in Frankfurt, a city that allowed Jews permanent residence in a ghetto. Numbers of Jews with their foreign dress and accented German would certainly have made a strong impression on a peasant unaccustomed to seeing such people during the balance of the year. In addition, the young playwright's biography suggests that the selection of this location and its concomitant hostile ambience for *Die Juden* was inevitable. Lessing completed work on the play late in 1749, at the end of his first year of residence in Berlin.[21] He had sought a home outside of his native

Saxony for the first time in November of 1748, when he withdrew from a university career of two and a half years in Leipzig. The changes wrought in that city when the participants in the fair began to arrive must have made a strong impression on the youth from rural Kamenz and Meißen.

Although the Traveler's destination is not specified, his point of origin is mentioned twice—Hamburg. No other place-name is linked to the main characters. The text does not identify the Hanseatic town as the man's home; however, the journey with Christoph did begin there after the Traveler rescued his new servant from a scrape of some kind. The northern city is first mentioned as an amorous Christoph recounts to Lisette just how much he knows about his companion. An audience's natural inclination would be to juxtapose its mental picture of the metropolis on the Elbe with the wealthy, well-spoken figure on stage. Then as now, Hamburg was the harbor, and the harbor was Hamburg. It would have been very tempting to conclude that the character is involved in commercial dealings.[22] The second reference to the city occurs immediately after the Traveler's great revelation. Christoph expresses disgust at hearing that he has served a Jew, whereupon the Traveler recalls the miserable circumstances endured by the thankless wretch when they first met in Hamburg. Suddenly, the reader/spectator must summon forth a personal image of that city once more and this time confront it with any impressions of Jews in general and this Jew in particular. Because of the port's comparatively large Jewish population, one would almost have to assume that the protagonist has at least a strong affiliation with and probably resides in the trading center. The man's sophistication and his ability to conceal his religious affiliation easily from Christian eyes constantly searching for a particular physical archetype, a phenotype (J, 386!)—both might have suggested membership in Hamburg's old Sephardic community, a community long renowned for its international trade connections.

Several details suggest that the appellation "der Reisende" is particularly appropriate for Lessing's hero. The presence of a "Reisebibliothek" indicates an ability to relax and enjoy intellectual pleasures while on the road. On the other hand, weaponry immediately at the ready bespeaks the wariness of experience. The man is quite modest, not at all given to the strong assertion of firmly held opinions. Nevertheless, he does offer both observations and fixed conclusions which result from extensive travel when the baron laments his daughter's somewhat uncivilized behavior:

*Der Baron*: . . . Es ist alles bey ihr noch die sich selbst gelaßne Natur.

*Der Reisende*: Und diese ist desto liebenswürdiger, je weniger man sie in den Städten antrifft. Alles ist da verstellt, gezwungen und erlernt. Ja, man ist schon so weit darinnen gekommen, daß man Dummheit, Grobheit und Natur für gleichviel bedeutende Worte hält. (J, 384)

The normally reserved speaker is so confident in his opinions concerning urban life that he allows himself a strongly condemnatory expatiation. Echoes of Haller's "Die Alpen" are clearly audible. Like the young Swiss poet, Lessing's comedic hero is a city-dweller who yearns for the more "natural," more honest ways of the countryside. The choice of "in den Städten" as opposed to "in der Stadt" suggests firsthand experience and the ability to draw comparisons among a number of urban areas known to the speaker. The "alles" is both sweeping and vague; precisely which aspects of everyday life in town are so artificial remains unspoken. The fact that the character has spent an appreciable portion of time passing from city to city would have been critical to the determination of his probable calling in the view of a contemporary reader. More than likely he is not a rabbi or physician, for such professionals had to remain among those to whose needs they ministered.

The objection might be raised that Lessing's hero could have undertaken the journey with Christoph as a pleasure jaunt. Perhaps he is the scion of a fabulously wealthy Court Jew and has a budget for recreation that is larger than most. Irreconcilable with such a hypothesis is the transparent textual implication that this is a man on a tight schedule. In the eighteenth century, Germany's roadways were not safe after dark, and yet night has nearly fallen when the baron is attacked. That attack is carried out at a secluded, heavily forested, remote point. The noble lives in the vicinity and so presumably is going no great distance. But his rescuer *is* far from home. If he were an idle tourist, the Traveler would have been ensconced securely in a comfortable inn by this time. After all, he is presented as a man who knows how to journey between points in comfort. In addition, why should he choose to spend leisure time in a country that tolerates very few Jews? If his identity were discovered, he would be at considerable peril. And would Saxony or any other such country allow him within its borders without specification of a reason acceptable to its officialdom? Finally, the Traveler has to be pleaded with before he will spend first the night of the failed robbery and then the following day at the baron's estate. Early that day, the noble is surprised to hear from his daughter that the brave guest has given his servant orders to prepare for departure:

*Der Baron*: Was? wer? sein Diener?
*Der Reisende*: Ja, mein Herr, ich hab es ihm befohlen. Meine Verrichtungen und die Besorgniß, Ihnen beschwerlich zu fallen – (J, 387)

Of the two reasons given, one testifies anew to the speaker's great civility. The other, "meine Verrichtungen," points to work-related responsibilities to be met in the course of the trip. Clearly, those responsibilities must be discharged in the near future.

Taken together, the passages cited would have suggested to an eighteenth-century audience expecting verisimilitude in drama that the Traveler might well be a merchant. In fact, *Die Juden* contains enough clues to support a fairly detailed composite portrait: the hero is the youthful (if not young) son of a wealthy, cultured family of Hamburg merchants (possibly Sephardim) who is traveling through Saxony to attend the fair at Leipzig. He is reticent about his identity in order to spare himself unpleasant encounters with anti-Semites. This policy is shown to be well founded; representatives of three different levels of society—the aristocracy, the urban servant class (Christoph), and the peasantry—are consumed with bigotry. Unlike the Jewish professional, who could spend an entire career within the walls of his own community, the successful merchant had to pass beyond the gates of the ghetto and come to terms with the kind of unthinking hatred voiced by the one-acter's Christian characters. By way of contrast, Gellert's Polish Jew does not encounter such attitudes in the course of his appearances in the *Schwedische Gräfin*. The tentative identification as a merchant does tally with the Traveler's movements and demeanor.

Whereas Gellert attempts to slip a Jewish character into his plot as unobtrusively as possible, the device of the bearded highwaymen immediately reinforces the title and focuses an audience's attention on the reputation and condition of Jews for Lessing's entire play. At the same time, the playwright takes steps that would have made a Jewish businessman more attractive. As Erich Schmidt noted a century ago, this is the first educated Jew in German literature.[23] Both the sentiments he expresses and the language he uses bespeak not only a solid fundamental education but also a thorough acquaintance with the basic tenets of the Enlightenment. In addition, he is German not Polish, youthful not old, and far more open with opinions that are invariably rooted in transparent common sense. He is in fact just the man that the Enlightenment wanted the Christian merchant to be; his marital status was designed to appeal to the growing population of female readers. Clearly, he has managed to develop a lifestyle that is both comfortable and humane; and any reader's initial evaluation must be that this is a man of great character. Gellert's Jew is benign, fatherly, and passive; Lessing's is forthcoming, affable, and active. His ability to dominate his environment in a nonconfrontational manner is a hallmark of the successful businessman. The Traveler's personality has been molded not only by formal education but also by his presumably considerable experience at reconciling his own needs with those of a far-flung network of contacts. The total image is far more engaging and, for the eighteenth century, far more provocative. The step beyond Gellert is a long one indeed. However, as Waldemar Oehlke has intimated, one element is still lacking, an element that, if present, would have caused the figure to startle and then deeply trouble contemporary audiences—poverty.[24] Without that element, the Traveler is, like the Pole, credible as a regularly observed type—the wealthy Jewish merchant. And, while his personality contravenes stereotypes of the Jew, it also contravenes stereotypes of the merchant.

Lessing has his aristocrat state the perceived connection between the confession and the profession in these terms:

> Ein Volk, das auf den Gewinnst so erpicht ist, fragt wenig darnach, ob es ihn mit Recht oder Unrecht, mit List oder Gewaltsamkeit erhält – – Es scheinet auch zur Handelschaft, oder deutsch zu reden, zur Betrügerey gemacht zu seyn. Höflich, frey, unternehmend, verschwiegen, sind Eigenschaften die es schätzbar machen würden, wenn es sie nicht allzusehr zu unserm Unglück anwendete. – (er hält etwas inne.) – – Die Juden haben mir sonst schon nicht wenig Schaden und Verdruß gemacht. Als ich noch in Kriegsdiensten war, ließ ich mich bereden, einen Wechsel für einen meiner Bekannten mit zu unterschreiben; und der Jude, an den er ausgestellet war, brachte mich nicht allein dahin, daß ich ihn bezahlen, sondern, daß ich ihn so gar zweymal bezahlen mußte – – O! es sind die allerboshaftesten, und niederträchtigsten Leute – Was sagen Sie dazu? Sie scheinen ganz niedergeschlagen. (J, 386)

It is a triple equation: "Handelschaft" equals "Betrügerey" equals "die Juden." Lessing is so confident of his ability to strike a blow against that equation that he has the audacity to present it in such brutally simple lines. The virtues cited in adjectival form—"höflich, frey, unternehmend, verschwiegen"—apply in context to merchants as well as Jews, and these are perverted virtues. The profit motive is again assailed as a direct contributor to injustice, treachery, and violence. At no time earlier in the century, not even in Schnabel and Haller, did a career in commerce receive such a furious pummeling. The catch is that the expressions come from a character whose perspective on the equation is shown to be false even as he speaks. Even the account of the earlier episode with the Jewish loan shark does not quite ring true. A man of such inordinate inherited wealth could not have been badly harmed in such a transaction, and, in the final analysis, it was *his* decision to stand security for the acquaintance. Yet, this is obviously the worst experience the man has had with a minority that he nevertheless villifies in the strongest terms, terms patently at odds with a lone instance of (partially misdirected) aggravation. Of course, if the Traveler had been "auf den Gewinnst so erpicht," he would not have disrupted his schedule in order to help the baron—nor would he have allowed himself to be persuaded to extend his stay at the estate. In fact, he embodies precisely the virtues supposedly corrupted, but in their original, pure form. Even as a spectator's attitudes toward Jews were to be altered by *Die Juden* so, too, could hostility toward merchants be lessened.

The previously cited review by Michaelis (see p. 107) demonstrates that precisely the opposite responses characterized the reader who could not shed anti-Semitic attitudes. To repeat the salient sentence: "Bey den Grund-Sätzen der Sittenlehre, welche zum wenigsten der große Theil desselben angenommen hat, ist auch eine allgemeine Redlichkeit kaum möglich, sonderlich da fast das gantze Volck von der Handlung leben muß, die mehr Gelegenheit und Versuchung zum Betruge giebt, als andere Lebens-Arten." Michaelis is merely restating the baron's position in learned terminology. The same three-part equation is constructed: "Handlung" equals "Betrug" equals "fast das gantze [Jewish] Volck." The same charge of moral perversion is made, albeit indirectly and subtly: the portion of the sentence before the first comma immediately recalls to a literate contemporary those fundamental precepts of morality that the Enlightenment has been propagating for years. But by the middle of the sentence it is clear that the Jewish version of this code does not admit of common decency. It is a code of immorality. The final portion of the sentence then asserts that commerce must bear the great brunt ("fast das gantze Volck") of responsibility for the situation. He may be using qualifiers, and he may be exercising rhetorical circumspection, but the critic's basic stance is that of the baron before the Traveler's revelation. Michaelis remains unmoved. His antipathy toward commerce indicates that the great change in the merchant's image wrought during the 1740s had yet to be accepted by at least one significant participant in the world of letters anno 1754, the *Göttingische Anzeigen von gelehrten Sachen*. Support for its position soon appeared in a number of the *Jenaische gelehrte Zeitungen*.[25]

Lessing responded immediately in the first issue of his periodical, the *Theatralische Bibliothek* (1754–58). The sixth and final article is entitled "Ueber das Lustspiel die Juden, im vierten Theile der Leßingschen Schriften." The young writer begins by making direct reference to the review from Göttingen, which he actually quotes at length. He then asserts that his critic has made two points: first, that a decent Jew is an improbable phenomenon in everyday life, and also, that presentation of such a figure in the play renders it less believable. Of these two points distilled from the review, Lessing replies only to the second. As an antidote to the perception that an honest, upright Jew is a rarity, he offers a letter written from one unidentified Jewish acquaintance to another. The letter is now known to have been from Moses Mendelssohn to A. S. Gumpertz; in it Mendelssohn gives eloquent expression to the minority's anger that such attitudes exist among educated Christians.

Lessing confines his own comments to a defense of the play. He summarizes the arguments of his "Gegner" with these words:

> Er giebt zur Ursache der Unwahrscheinlichkeit eines solchen Juden die Verachtung und Unterdrückung, in welcher dieses Volk seufzet, und die Nothwendigkeit an, in welcher es sich befindet, blos und allein von der Handlung zu leben. Es sey; folgt aber also nicht nothwendig, daß die Unwahrscheinlichkeit wegfalle, so bald diese Umstände sie zu verursachen aufhören? Wenn hören sie aber auf, dieses zu thun? Ohne Zweifel alsdann, wenn sie von andern Umständen vernichtet werden, das ist, wenn sich ein Jude im Stande befindet, die Verachtung und Unterdrückung der Christen weniger zu fühlen, und sich nicht gezwungen sieht, durch die Vortheile eines kleinen nichtswürdigen Handels ein elendes Leben zu unterhalten. Was aber wird mehr hierzu erfordert, als Reichthum? Doch ja, auch die richtige Anwendung dieses Reichthums wird dazu erfordert.[26]

The passage is a study in slippery rhetoric. His "Es sey . . ." constitutes a means of avoiding direct confrontation with the train of logic in the first sentence. He might have counterpunched with praise for commerce and those who practice it or else with stout denials that the Traveler necessarily is or has to be a merchant. Since the reviewer mentions Gellert's *Schwedische Gräfin*, Lessing might have pointed to old Steeley and asked rhetorically whether this character is either improbable or given to treachery and deceit. Instead, he backpedals into his own corner, the play itself.

There he is relatively safe, since details about the main character must be inferred. He reasons that the whole question of verisimilitude would be obviated if a Jew were to find himself in different circumstances, i.e., circumstances other than those which Michaelis would term "normal." The circumstances Lessing proposes would have a hypothetical Jew in a position to feel the effects of anti-Semitism less by removing him from the sphere of hawkers and peddlers, which is to say, from the sphere of small-scale retailing. It soon becomes clear that, with this hypothetical figure, he actually has the Traveler in mind. But surely that character has suffered from anti-Semitism; after all, he does not feel free to divulge his identity. He is an honest man who is forced into mildly misleading silences. As Oehlke has pointed out, the Traveler's act of engaging a Christian as his servant was actually illegal.[27] The man's difficulties continue during the play when he must listen to bigoted rantings against his people from several different characters. Finally, the standard happy ending of an Enlightenment comedy, a betrothal, is denied him solely because of his membership in the minority. The other attribute of Lessing's hypothetical Jew is nonparticipation in subsistence-level merchandising. Here he is reacting to Michaelis's attack on commerce by setting up a straw man. The critic questions the morality of commerce in general; the playwright distances his creation from one particular type of business activity, a type of activity that has nothing to do with the play.

In other words, Lessing is employing obfuscation. Why? Five years after writing the one-acter, he may have realized—with the "aid" of some contemporary reception—that he could not strike a blow for both Jews and merchants. The resistance within the small literary public was too great. Lessing's response to Michaelis represents a tactical retreat; he is withdrawing from that offensive to which the text of the play does not clearly commit him. As of 1754, the image of the merchant presented in literature has developed far beyond the image still strong within the reading population.

In the absence of attention to the series of implications regarding the background, occupation, and destination of the Traveler, the play does take on a less timely, more strongly utopian aspect. For instance, Karl S. Guthke asserts that the central character is a futuristic demonstrative paradigm rather than a *dramatis persona*.[28] Here, a hypothesis that the Traveler had counterparts in the real world of 1750 has been used to examine the text. Although the author aborted his campaign on behalf of the merchant five years later, he could not call back the play. During the brief interval between publication of the one-acter and publication of his response to Michaelis, Lessing saw a storm brew up and therefore was ready to strike his sails before its fury. His original decision to publish the piece earlier than plays that were written after *Die Juden*, such as *Der Schatz*, testifies to an eagerness to set his challenging work before the public. Armed with the arrogance of youth, he positioned himself to reeducate the audience concerning two related antipathies—that is, if his point of reference was not an envisioned better world but the very nonutopian, very prejudiced world of Leipzig and Berlin at mid-century.

Just as an attentive audience would have identified the man from Hamburg as a traveling businessman, so, too, would it have accorded him hero status not once but twice. The initial act of bravery is not presented on stage but reported in the first scene as yesterday's news. It is in fact the second rescue of the baron that supplies the plot. The Traveler's active curiosity, his powers of observation and ratiocination, and a self-confidence that enables him to broach a sensitive topic with a new acquaintance—these are the qualities that put him in a position to help the nobleman extricate himself from the midst of treacherous, even homicidal servants. The first instance of heroism is pure physical courage, action to save another regardless of danger to one's person. But the second instance, impressed upon the audience as it is by functioning as the solution to the drama's complication, results from attributes critical to success in business. Perspicacity and poise mark the Traveler's every action during a situation made still more delicate by the obvious romantic interest evinced by his host's young and uninhibited daughter. It is this sophistication that also allows the Traveler to complete the microcosm of society gathered at the baron's estate—by representing the middle class.

The mysterious man of the highway is the only character with whom most contemporary readers could have identified. The other members of the cast are of either higher or lower estate. From the outset of the action, it would have been apparent that the Traveler is well-to-do; yet nothing about him suggests the sort of external display or "representation" closely associated with wealthy aristocrats.

To the contrary, the text fairly bristles with suggestions that he is a professional man, and one of whose personality and accomplishments real-world businessmen could be proud. As a representative of their middle class, he actually appears in a better light than does the member of the ruling class. The Traveler is more intelligent, better spoken, more broad-minded, and better able to deal with emergencies. Throughout the play his nobleman host responds to him as to one who is more worthy. He repeatedly craves the guest's friendship and finally offers his daughter's hand in order to form a permanent bond with the man he so reveres. Scholarship has been divided as to whether the baron is a positive figure or a flawed, laughable fool of the kind so popular in comedies of the earlier 1740s.[29] What is undeniable is that he is presented as the Traveler's inferior from beginning to end. In other words, Lessing has created a microcosm of society and in the process has put forth a representative of the middle class as the problem-solver, the esteemed model, the natural leader. Enlightenment comedy had already cast the nobleman as a degenerate and a roadblock to the progress of the virtuous civil servant.[30] Here, the aristocrat is basically decent, albeit ineffectual (both at protecting himself and at raising his daughter) and parochial.

Meanwhile, the bourgeois has stepped forth in heroic fashion. Audience members who would cavil either at his confession or at his likely calling risk appearing mean-spirited, even ridiculous. Doubly so, since they have heard both the baron's anti-Semitic, anticommercial fulminations and then his expressions of acceptance at the play's end. The Traveler is a man who readily takes charge of situations even as he takes care of those less able than himself, regardless of social station. He has saved not only the baron but also the lowly Christoph. It falls to the servant to indicate what Lessing hopes to receive in return for his efforts on behalf of the middle class, the business community, and the Jews. The contents of the Traveler's book bag are described by his flippant servant in the following terms: "Es ist meines Herrn Reisebibliothek. Sie besteht aus Lustspielen, die zum Weinen, und aus Trauerspielen, die zum Lachen bewegen; aus zärtlichen Heldengedichten; aus tiefsinnigen Trinkliedern, und was dergleichen neue Siebensachen mehr sind" (S, 392). During their journey, the Traveler has talked to his companion about recent developments in literature, among them the "comédie larmoyante." Contained in the servant's comic litany is the revelation that his employer supports contemporary literary life by buying books and then by discussing the latest with whoever shows the slightest interest. The playwright has incorporated his commitment to an expansion of the literary public into his main character. That character is one who belongs to the literary public and who challenges it to acknowledge his membership—the membership of a man who is a heroic Jew and, quite possibly, a literate businessman.

While prudence dictates that an identification of the Traveler as a merchant be tentative, no such caution is required in the case of *Nathan der Weise* (1779). The play does not fall within the period of greatest change in the literary portrayal of the man of commerce; however, not only its prominence in the high canon of Enlightenment literature but also its status as the last, greatest work of the man who more than any other was the "Aufklärung"—both factors commend attention to the sagacious old interlocutor par excellence. Nathan is the most prominent merchant in Germany's eighteenth-century tradition, a circumstance that has doubtless fostered recent scholarly interest in the play's hero as a businessman.[31]

The central character in Lessing's "dramatic poem" is hardly a struggling peddler whose business suffers because of the constant turmoil that the Crusades have brought to the Middle East. When Saladin asks after this fellow inhabitant of Jerusalem, the ruler's sister describes Nathan in glowing terms:

*Saladin*: Denn er handelt; wie ich hörte.
*Sittah*: Sein Saumthier treibt auf allen Straßen, zieht
Durch alle Wüsten; seine Schiffe liegen
In allen Häfen.[32]

Earlier in the play, the governess and companion of Nathan's daughter announces her employer's arrival with the following lines:

*Daja*: Er kömmt von Babylon;
Mit zwanzig hochbeladenen Kameelen,
Und allem, was an edeln Specereyen,
An Steinen und an Stoffen, Indien
Und Persien und Syrien, gar Sina,
Kostbares nur gewähren. (N, 36)

However modest the man's personal bearing may be, Nathan is to be perceived as the owner and operator of an extensive international trading entity. That his interests include luxury items in large quantities suggests extraordinary income levels. Since he has only two household dependents and eschews opulence, personal circumstances do not constitute a significant financial drain. In fact, this is one old man who has not chosen to devote his final years to family concerns. He has continued to travel on business even though he is clearly in a position to delegate authority to the best agents money can buy. Whether because of strong feelings of personal responsibility or because of simple love of calling, Nathan's occupation has continued to dominate not only his daily routine but also his attitude toward life in general. It has been noted that the language he uses in conducting his personal affairs bristles with expressions common to the trading world he knows so well.[33]

In his seminal treatment of Nathan qua merchant, Paul Hernadi finds the central character's personality to be equally determined by "innere Menschlichkeit" and by the "vita activa" of a burgher with professional commitments.[34] The dichotomy proposed puts into perspective Nathan's responses to a crisis. As the action begins, he has just returned from a business trip which has provided him with cash receipts on debts called in as well as with goods for the retail trade. Hence, his financial condition is so rosy that he can meet even the needs of a Saladin who is dangerously short on liquid assets. On the other hand, this professional activity has involved an extended absence, which has complicated the relationship of his daughter Recha and the Templar in the wake of the nearly fatal fire. Prompt application of "wise humanity" would have spared much misunderstanding and emotional wounding. The feelings of the two young people could have been guided into more appropriate channels had Nathan been present from the outset and therefore able to identify them as siblings at an earlier point. And yet, it is not love of money or the accumulation of wealth that has kept Nathan far from his hearth. No miser would dream of offering all of his treasures *after* a service has been performed, but such is the merchant's response when he hears of the bravery of his daughter's rescuer (N, 7). The man is neither obsessive about the profit motive nor defensive about his profession. In fact, his professional status occasions little judgmental comment in the play: the low profile accorded commerce goes far to explain why prominent literary histories fail to mention, let alone consider, the impact it has on the course of the plot.[35] Hernadi goes so far as to cast Nathan as an embodiment of the "Protestant ethic," which, the scholar believes, Lessing accepted.[36] The thesis is attractive in light of the transformation of the merchant in literature as traced in these pages. Healthy balance sheets could then testify to divine favor; material gain would no longer constitute a stumbling block to complete acceptance into the "virtuous" middle class and into the society of letters.

Nathan's identity as a merchant is subsumed within his identity as a burgher, a middle-class subject who has cause to view his prince with feelings as mixed as those held by contemporaries of the playwright. It has been customary to cite Saladin's intelligence, tolerance, and compassion; he has been found to rival the old merchant in wisdom.[37] But the bright picture darkens when the prince's attitude toward his subject as a businessman is taken into account. After all, it is only when the flow of tribute moneys is interrupted during a particularly expensive governmental function—war—that the ruler summons his wealthy subject. The royal treasurer Al-Hafi tries to warn his friend Nathan of the dangers inherent in establishing a financial link with Saladin:

> Ich sollt es wohl
> Mit ansehn, wie er Euch von Tag zu Tag
> Aushöhlen wird bis auf die Zehen? Sollt'
> Es wohl mit ansehn, daß Verschwendung aus
> Der weisen Milde sonst nie leeren Scheuern
> So lange borgt, und borgt, und borgt, bis auch
> Die armen eingebornen Mäuschen drinn
> Verhungern? – Bildet Ihr vielleicht Euch ein,
> Wer Euers Gelds bedürftig sey, der werde
> Doch Euerm Rathe wohl auch folgen? – Ja;
> Er Rathe folgen! Wenn hat Saladin
> Sich rathen lassen? (N, 70)

In his recent article, Wolf Wucherpfennig argues convincingly that Saladin is actually seeking a Court Jew whom he can exploit when necessary.[38] As the speech above indicates, that perception of necessity equates the personal and the governmental. Furthermore, the perception is insulated against the advice of a mere merchant by layers of noblesse oblige. It is clear that any hopes of rationalizing state finances that a banker to the prince might harbor, that any such hopes are doomed to frustration. Wucherpfennig points out that it is a deux ex machina in the form of the tribute caravan from Egypt that replenishes the potentate's coffers and saves the merchant from paving the road to insolvency with loans to a client who is ultimately responsible to no one.[39]

However, before the caravan arrives, the old Jew has managed to make such a positive impression on the ruler that the latter asks to be considered Nathan's friend (N, 95) and that he is concerned about the merchant's opinion of him (N, 130). The depth of the relationship suggests that, even in the absence of the funds from Egypt, Saladin would treat Nathan with far greater concern than Al-Hafi expects. Of course, it is the play's structural climax, the meeting of Nathan and Saladin, that renders such expectations less applicable. The prince has summoned a wealthy subject to an audience with the secret agenda of throwing him off balance and then suggesting a loan. In order to accomplish the first objective, the sultan not only surprises his guest by not mentioning finances but confronts him with the high esteem in which the Jew is held.

> *Saladin*: Du nennst dich Nathan?
> *Nathan*: Ja.
> *Saladin*: Den weisen Nathan?
> *Nathan*: Nein.
> *Saladin*: Wohl! nennst du dich nicht; nennt dich das Volk.
> *Nathan*: Kann seyn; das Volk!
> *Saladin*: Du glaubst doch nicht, daß ich
> Verächtlich von des Volkes Stimme denke? –
> Ich habe längst gewünscht, den Mann zu kennen,
> Den es den Weisen nennt. (N, 86)

The title of the play arouses expectations in the audience that the central character will demonstrate the merit of the attribution of sage status. Thus, what is initially only a tactical feint from the sultan's perspective constitutes the playwright's major thrust from the audience's perspective. Not only is Lessing able to merge the two but he then has Nathan parry the feint and leave the secret agenda behind. The astonished sultan must concede that "der Weise" is an apt description of the man who tells the parable of the three rings.

But what precisely is the description, and does it relate to the man's profession? The adjective "weise" and the substantive "der Weise" account for thirty-three columns in the Grimm dictionary.[40] Of the many meanings and shades of meaning offered, the words of Lessing's Saladin are cited for one particular definition of the noun. The passage in question appears just after the initial meeting reproduced above. At the conclusion of that scene, the potentate leaves to give Nathan a moment to think. In a soliloquy, the old merchant conceives the idea of a story. At the beginning of the next scene, the sultan reappears, urges Nathan to speak, and observes that they are after all quite alone.

> *Saladin*: Es hört uns keine Seele.
> *Nathan*: Möcht auch doch
> Die ganze Welt uns hören.

*Saladin:* So gewiß
Ist Nathan seiner Sache? Ha! das nenn'
Ich einen Weisen! Nie die Wahrheit zu
Verhehlen! für sie alles auf das Spiel
Zu setzen! Leib und Leben! Gut und Blut! (N, 89-90)

The definition tied to this passage reads as follows: ". . . der im sein und handeln reife und maszvolle (gelegentlich fast gleichbedeutend mit 'der edle, gütige')."[41] The sultan describes wisdom as the assertion of truth regardless of the consequences to life and property. The "alles" that Nathan is about to put at hazard includes what he is as a man and what he has worked for as a merchant. The dictionary definition combines personal morality and ethics. The presence of "handeln" suggests that wisdom is partially dependent upon the nature of an individual's contact with the society around him. Moderation and maturity are also frequently associated with experience in interpersonal relationships. In the case of Nathan, such qualities make for a valuable, honored subject.

With the old Jewish merchant, Lessing illustrates that the intelligence prized by his own increasingly meritocratic society can be had not only through the university but also through the "school of experience." Here at long last was a frontal assault on the common bourgeois perception that the merchant was intellectually inferior. Far from being drained of sensitivity and creativity by the quest for commercial success, Nathan has learned to act in a "mature and moderate," even "noble" fashion through interpersonal contacts, many of which have been trading contacts. This demeanor is evident in his private role as father and in his public role as counselor/philosopher. The definition cited above suggests a model worthy of emulation; a somewhat different perspective is evident in the related definition of the adjective. There "weise" is presented as the attribute of a somewhat more active individual: "'wissend, einsichtig im sittlichen sein und handeln.'"[42] "Einsichtig" in particular suggests a guide in ethical matters. An eighteenth-century audience would have been jarred in its expectations to observe Nathan the Jew acting as a guide to the Christian Recha even as Nathan the merchant—not Nathan the lawyer or Nathan the privy councillor—acts as a guide to the prince. And yet, because of the nature of the concept "wisdom" as a highly honored quality of mind not necessarily tied to formal schooling, Lessing has not strained the requirement for verisimilitude. Here the "long ago and far away" setting is helpful. Members of a theater audience are asked to accept a rather vaguely defined type of intelligence in a man who does business by camel. Of course, just as it was possible that such spectators would learn a lesson in tolerance of use in their lives, so, too, was it possible that they might gain a new, more appreciative perspective on a professional identity rooted in the worldliness and acumen of a successful entrepreneur.

By 1779 little is left of the outright hostility to trade evident in the literature of earlier decades. Still, at the beginning of the climactic audience, Saladin does intimate some mild contempt for the old man's calling. When Nathan inquires as to whether the ruler is interested in his wares, the reply is as follows:

> Wo von sprichst du? doch wohl nicht
> Von deinen Waaren? – Schachern wird mit dir
> Schon meine Schwester. (Das der Horcherinn!) –
> Ich habe mit dem Kaufmann nichts zu thun. (N, 87)

The aside is of course for Sittah, who is eavesdropping unbeknownst to Nathan. That Saladin assigns the role of customer to a woman constitutes vertical distancing which is then reinforced by the last sentence, a sentence with the specific referent Nathan in his role as merchant, but also with the general referent—any merchant. In addition, the verb "schachern" has pejorative force. Although haggling is an old Middle Eastern custom, this sultan is not accustomed to dealing with subjects on such a basis. The lines are heavy with sarcasm.

Nevertheless, the nature of the play dictates that little more of the prince's response to commerce per se emerges. The profession is neither praised nor pilloried. Lessing's presentation of this arena of human activity is subordinate to his presentation of the one merchant in the piece. It is instructive to compare that presentation with the playwright's earlier heroes. *Die Juden* has been cited as a preliminary study for Lessing's masterpiece.[43] Certainly the most apparent tie is the attack on religious intolerance by means of strong, positively drawn Jews as central characters. In both instances, a victim of hatred rises above the hostility of others and the potential for hostility within himself to teach a lesson in acceptance. It should also be noted that in both instances personal wealth serves as an entrée for relations with the non-Jewish ruling nobility. This is more readily apparent in *Nathan der Weise*; however, it is capital earned or inherited that has educated the Traveler to such an extent that the baron finds him at least an equal as a conversation partner. In addition, the text of *Die Juden* suggests that the Jew found himself on the road at the time of the attack because of business commitments. Both heroes have considerable experience in journeying among a variety of locations well known to them, a circumstance that goes far toward explaining sophistication in dealings with their fellow man. Finally, if the identification of the Traveler as a merchant is accepted, then it can be argued that both the problem-solving ability demonstrated by each character and their adaptability to new, potentially hostile environments would have lent dignity to commerce in the estimation of Lessing's contemporaries.

Still, the sharp contrasts between the two characters are so numerous as to render highly suspect the view that the Traveler is a forerunner of Nathan. At the center of the one-acter is a man whose identity is a matter for speculation by the other characters; only his public identity is so much as partially known. Nathan, on the other hand, is a man with deep roots in his community. Throughout the piece his guiding concern is for the welfare of his family, that is, for his adopted daughter. As a man of hearth and home, Nathan resembles Anselmo of *Der Schatz* in several respects. Both are active old men returning home from successful commercial dealings abroad. Each finds his family in a state of confusion and drift, and each takes effective steps to restore order. Anselmo's professional activity has put him in a position to right the family's financial condition; his success makes possible a resolution to the quandary confronting his marriageable daughter. The stewardship of Lelio is not directly related to commerce; if anything, the father's long absence has set the stage for the son's irresponsible behavior. However, that the man has finally made his fortune means that he can now devote large amounts of time and attention to the wayward child.

In one sense, Nathan's occupation is less directly related to the eventual resolution of the conflict that has enveloped Recha, the Templar, and the sultan. After all, he must first be summoned to court, and then he is allowed to contribute to the search for truth and happiness. This passive posture is dictated by the presence of the ruling class, which is absent in *Der Schatz*. However, in another sense, the esteem that the old merchant garners for himself in conversation with Saladin is indirectly attributable to a businessman's instincts. Wucherpfennig asserts that the parable of the rings is presented as a problem in the legal title to property.[44] The nature of truth and revealed faith is approached through the concept of ownership. When the equally valid claims of three sons make public recognition of legal title impractical, the father in the parable recasts ownership as a private, even secret claim. The controlling factor of practicality also informs the future for the three ring-wearers. In his daily life, each is to confirm the genuineness of his ring; truth has become a function of human activity. Similarly, Nathan's response to the sultan's unsettling question is suggested by his life as a man who deals in property, while the Jew's life and moral stature constitute a concrete realization of the essence of that response.

One other character deserves mention as a Christian counterpart to Nathan—the paterfamilias of the countess's circle of friends in *Das Leben der schwedischen Gräfin von G\*\*\**. Old Steeley's mildly defensive credo for the man of commerce is no longer necessary by 1779; Nathan offers no direct, self-conscious evaluation of his calling. The striking similarity between the two is that each mediates in both the public and the private lives of their dependents. Gellert's wealthy Englishman provides a final home in Britain for the noblewoman and her large retinue, a home that guarantees generous shelter and sustenance for life. Contact with the Swedish court is of course the great threat that hangs over the noble couple throughout the novel's tumultuous plot. However, at the conclusion, the count and countess are able to face the designing courtier Prince S\*\*\* secure in the knowledge that the geographic base and the financial and familial solidity provided by old Steeley have removed them from the reach of the dangerous rulers of their homeland. They have been afforded the opportunity to withdraw from public life, an opportunity they seize upon.

Each comparison of *Nathan der Weise* with a work from mid-century has its flaws. Gellert's old Steeley is after all a minor character who dies within a few pages. His act of generosity involves no risk to himself or to his immediate family, and he does not deal directly with the countess's status vis-á-vis Sweden. Still, Nathan's heroic diplomacy boasts a pedigree that reaches back to a time at which the merchant could not openly lead others in public and private affairs—at least, not in literature. Although the image of the businessman was indeed undergoing change, rapid change, such a character would have been received as a violation of verisimilitude. Michaelis and his supporters were waiting. Nevertheless, beginning in the late 1740s, the man of commerce is consistently presented as the one who knows how to solve problems and who tries to do so. In the space of half a century, he has become a pillar of society and the master of any situation.

# Conclusion

Ask a Germanist to comment on the image of the merchant presented in literature of the eighteenth century, and in all probability the first work cited will be an English drama—George Lillo's *The London Merchant, or The History of George Barnwell* (1731). It comes to mind so quickly on the strength of its well-established status as a major precursor of one of the Enlightenment's great gifts to German theater, the bourgeois tragedy. Marxist literary histories also discuss Lillo in conjunction with a development in genre first manifest in Germany with the appearance of Lessing's *Miß Sara Sampson* in 1755.[1] However, questions of genre history aside, it should be apparent that in 1731 the two national traditions were diametrically opposed with regard to their attitudes toward commerce. A member of Lillo's audience is taken into the merchant Thorowgood's London home and office as though that spectator belonged to the firm. On the other hand, Haller's reader gazes over the poet's shoulder and down upon the urban civilization beneath their feet and, almost, beneath their notice. By the same token, assertions of a long divergence between the two literatures in their response to the business world do not stand up to close scrutiny. Dieter Borchmeyer states that the professional pride radiating from Thorowgood is nowhere to be found in Germany's sentimental family tragedies.[2] But it *is* to be found, and at an earlier time, in the Enlightenment comedy and in Gellert's highly popular sentimentalist novel.

The complete turnabout in German literature's presentation of the merchant in the course of just a quarter century has been the topic of this study. Its survey of seven key writers is bounded by two strikingly similar figures. Both Albrecht von Haller and Gotthold Ephraim Lessing infuse their early works with youthful self-assurance and a determination to improve the human condition. Both subscribed to the ideals of the Enlightenment, and both hoped for greater participation by the general public in cultural and intellectual life. However, they differed strongly concerning the nature of such participation within their own class. Haller's appeal reaches for those with whose intellectual training and interests he is comfortable. It is a highly focused attempt to limit rather than to expand. The poet wishes to convince his readers that the city around them is replete with dangers, many of which find personification in particular denizens of his own hometown. Those readers are to insulate themselves against materialism, luxury, pretentiousness, hypocrisy, greed, and spite—against vices supposedly introduced into society by the need to have more. The acquisitive urge institutionalized as the profit motive was of course one of the more blatant evils when the world below the Alpine highland was viewed from such a perspective. No businessman could possibly know happiness since ambition and suspicion would rob him of all repose and all peace of mind. Not only was such a man a danger to others, but his professional activities constituted self-destructive behavior as well. For Haller, he was the living symbol of a civilization whose priorities were diametrically opposed to the idealism of the intellectual elite. Twenty-five years later, Lessing sends his man of credit and debit onto the stage for comedy as the hero. That character has joined the educational, experiential, and economic stratum then assuming responsibility for the further development of the literary tradition. Lessing's merchant is modest in demeanor, solicitous of family and friends, and desirous of new contacts with interesting people and fresh ideas. His personal ethics are unassailable, and he acts to safeguard those in his environment whose positions are weak because of youth, gender, level of education or sophistication—even because of actual physical attack. The former pariah has assumed a leadership role.

Enlightenment literature steadily develops into a promoter of the bourgeois business world. Significantly, aristocratic entrepreneurs do not occupy prominent positions in works from the period. That they did exist but are not included points to the advocacy function assumed by writers such as Lessing and Gellert. The latter's novel features characters from both classes, but the merchants are all bourgeois. They are the active, productive members of society; they solve problems and disentangle complications created by their social "betters." Such is the case in *Das Leben der schwedischen Gräfin von G\*\*\**; even there, members of the first estate can hardly be said to direct the course of events. And, in comedies of the 1740s and '50s that present men of trade as characters, the aristocracy is more often than not completely absent. Although the audience for literature draws from both classes, the promotional effort is so structured as to address only one.

The entire middle class benefits from the advocacy of the merchant since he has the lowest status within that social level. If their least-respected peer is elevated, the professionals and civil servants can only benefit. That is precisely the logic behind the earliest positive portrayals of Jews in works by Gellert and Lessing. The reputation of the business world had labored long under the onus of close association with the oppressed and reviled minority. First as a secondary character and then as the hero, the Jewish businessman is granted peer status with the bourgeoisie on the basis of mutual commitment to Enlightenment ideals. As is readily apparent in the writings of Luise Gottsched and Johann David Michaelis, such tolerance could not claim any supportive consensus. However, it was one more logical step to take, a step that brought Gellert and Lessing to the forefront of a trend that had been developing ever since Haller and Schnabel first highlighted commercial activity by flailing it.

The literature of the mid-eighteenth century softens the image of the merchant in clearly recognizable stages. First, the threatening, dangerous element so noticeable in works from the thirties is replaced by the farcical in a play such as *Der Bookesbeutel*. The merchant may still be a lamentable specimen of humanity, but he is no longer ethically bankrupt, much less depraved. His foolishness presents virtuous characters with an obstacle, but hardly one of insurmountable dimensions. That very foolishness is then sharply reduced in Luise Gottsched's *Die Hausfranzösinn*. There the commercially active paterfamilias dithers his way into a chaotic situation that has the security of his children at hazard. However, under the guidance of a wiser brother, he is able to participate in the untangling of the complication. Although humbled and more than a bit ridiculous, the merchant has begun to emerge from under a very large and very old dark cloud. Both J. E. Schlegel and an older Luise Gottsched offer pragmatic, upright, innocuous men of commerce as secondary characters in comedies from the mid-1740s. These earliest positive businessmen are hustled on and off stage before the audience has time to put together what is said with who is saying it. Gellert's *Schwedische Gräfin* carries the trend further with its profusion of secondary mercantile figures. From the somewhat limited Andreas to the saintly old Steeley, representatives of the world of trade supply the central characters with food, clothing, shelter, money, encouragement, and advice—all according to need. It is as though this social level had been charged with the nurturing of those wounded by destiny. The count and countess actually proceed from one merchant to the next in their search for happiness. However, it is young Lessing who commits two works to the promotion of the businessman to such an extent that the once lowly capitalist can actually become the hero. In fact, he is presented as a natural leader, a trustworthy counselor, a generous benefactor. There is nothing mean or deceitful in any of the merchants in the works written by Gellert and Lessing. To the contrary, their common posture suggests that they are successful, sophisticated, and self-possessed members of the "arriving" class. The merchant has become a shining representative of the bourgeoisie.

Through their advocacy of the businessman, Enlightenment writers stood to gain more than an acceptance of commerce by the balance of the middle class and more than an expansion of the market for literature to include real-world merchants. It was also an opportunity to flex their muscles, to show what a writer could accomplish in an effort to effect change. By recognizing the merchant as an essential figure in literature, they established theirs as a solidly middle-class tradition. No longer was art to be produced for the upper class by its servants, for it now had begun to become art for and by the one vital social level. At least, such was the hope of Gellert and Lessing as it shines forth from their works. Their merchants stand ready to shoulder a heavy share of a rapidly growing burden, for, in 1755, German letters stood at a threshold. Literary activity increased at a rapid rate during the quarter century that followed. The cultivation of an informed, sympathetic public for that artistic production can be traced in part to the efforts of writers who resisted the temptation to mount a traditional attack on many of their readers. By embracing the merchant, such writers completed the formation of the audience for a great literary revival.

# Notes

## I. The Merchant in Society

1. Leo Balet, *Die Verbürgerlichung der deutschen Kunst, Literatur und Musik im 18. Jahrhundert* (Strasbourg: Heitz, 1936).
2. See the following: Franklin Kopitzsch, "Einleitung: Die Sozialgeschichte der deutschen Aufklärung als Forschungsaufgabe," in *Aufklärung, Absolutismus und Bürgertum in Deutschland*, ed. Franklin Kopitzsch (Munich: Nymphenburg, 1976); Thomas P. Saine, "Scholarship on the German Enlightenment as Cultural History," *Lessing Yearbook* 6 (1974): 139–49; and Gerhard Sauder, "Sozialgeschichtliche Aspekte der Literatur im 18. Jahrhundert," *Internationales Archiv für Sozialgeschichte der deutschen Literatur* 4 (1979): 197–241.
3. For example, Wilfried Barner, Gunter Grimm, Helmuth Kiesel, and Martin Kramer, *Lessing: Epoche – Werk – Wirkung*, (Munich: Beck, 1975), esp. pp. 37–75, and Helmuth Kiesel and Paul Münch, *Gesellschaft und Literatur im 18. Jahrhundert: Voraussetzungen und Entstehung des literarischen Markts in Deutschland* (Munich: Beck, 1977), esp. pp. 13–76.
4. Balet, p. 13.
5. Friedrich Lütge, *Deutsche Sozial- und Wirtschaftsgeschichte: Ein Überblick*, 3d ed. (Berlin: Springer, 1966), p. 378.
6. Rolf Engelsing, *Sozial- und Wirtschaftsgeschichte Deutschlands*, 2d ed. (Göttingen: Vandenhoeck und Ruprecht, 1976), p. 82.
7. For example, Sauder, p. 198, and Kopitzsch, pp. 14–16.
8. Compare Wolfgang Zorn, "Sozialgeschichte 1648–1800," in *Handbuch der deutschen Wirtschafts- und Sozialgeschichte*, ed. Hermann Aubin and Wolfgang Zorn (Stuttgart: Union, 1971), 1: 574–83.
9. Balet, pp. 45–53.
10. Alan Menhennet, *Order and Freedom: Literature and Society in Germany from 1720 to 1805* (London: Weidenfeld and Nicolson, 1973), p. 26.
11. Zorn, p. 577.
12. Norbert Elias, *Die höfische Gesellschaft: Untersuchungen zur Soziologie des Königtums und der höfischen Aristokratie mit einer Einleitung: Soziologie und Geschichtswissenschaft* (Neuwied and Berlin: Luchterhand, 1969), p. 107.
13. Wolfgang Zorn, "Schwerpunkte der deutschen Ausfuhrindustrie im 18. Jahrhundert," *Jahrbücher für Nationalökonomie und Statistik* 173, no. 5 (1961): 447.
14. For a brief overview of standard absolutist economic policy, see Kiesel and Münch, pp. 31–42. For an example of the manner in which one German state treated beggars, see Reinhold August Dorwart, *The Prussian Welfare*

*State before 1740* (Cambridge, Mass.: Harvard University Press, 1971), pp. 94–111.

15. Rudolf Vierhaus, "Deutschland im 18. Jahrhundert: Soziales Gefüge, politische Verfassung, geistige Bewegung," in *Aufklärung, Absolutismus und Bürgertum in Deutschland*, ed. Franklin Kopitzsch (Munich: Nymphenburg, 1976), p. 177.

16. Hans Rudolf Rytz, *Geistliche des alten Bern zwischen Merkantilismus und Physiokratie: Ein Beitrag zur Schweizer Sozialgeschichte des 18. Jahrhunderts* (Basle and Stuttgart: Helbing und Lichtenhahn, 1971), pp. 1–6. Also, see below, p. 144, n. 65.

17. Engelsing, p. 92.

18. Barner et al., p. 48. Kiesel and Münch, p. 47.

19. Compare Rolf Engelsing, *Analphabetentum und Lektüre: Zur Sozialgeschichte des Lesens in Deutschland zwischen feudaler und industrieller Gesellschaft* (Stuttgart: Metzler, 1973), p. 87.

20. See Menhennet, p. 42.

21. Engelsing, *Analphabetentum*, p. 51.

22. Kiesel and Münch, p. 53.

23. See Lütge, pp. 373–74.

24. Lütge, p. 373.

25. Hans Mottek, *Wirtschaftsgeschichte Deutschlands: Ein Grundriß* (Berlin: VEB Deutscher Verlag der Wissenschaften, 1964), 1: 299.

26. Lütge, p. 373.

27. Wolfgang Martens cites further examples of middle-class hostility to sloth in *Die Botschaft der Tugend: Die Aufklärung im Spiegel der deutschen moralischen Wochenschriften* (Stuttgart: Metzler, 1968), pp. 318–21. The sentiment was well entrenched well before "the last decades of the eighteenth century" (Lütge, p. 374).

28. See Lutz Graf Schwerin von Krosigk, *Alles auf Wagnis: Der Kaufmann gestern, heute und morgen* (Tübingen: Wunderlich, 1963), pp. 149–55.

29. Krosigk, p. 154.

30. Erwin Wiskemann, *Hamburg und die Welthandelspolitik von den Anfängen bis zur Gegenwart* (Hamburg: Friederichsen und de Gruyter, 1929), p. 108.

31. Karl Biedermann, *Deutschland im achtzehnten Jahrhundert*, 2d ed. (Leipzig: Weber, 1880), 1: 292–93.

32. Johann Michael Hudtwalcker, "Elternhaus und Jugendjahre eines Hamburger Kaufmanns in der Mitte des 18. Jahrhunderts," in *Kaufleute zu Haus und über See: Hamburgische Zeugnisse des 17., 18. und 19. Jahrhunderts*, ed. Percy Ernst Schramm (Hamburg: Hoffmann und Campe, 1949), p. 188.

33. Zorn, "Schwerpunkte," p. 426.

34. Hudtwalcker, pp. 196–97.

35. See, for example, John Walter Van Cleve, *Harlequin Besieged: The Reception of Comedy in Germany during the Early Enlightenment* (Berne: Lang, 1980), pp. 77–78.

36. Werner Kohlschmidt, *Geschichte der deutschen Literatur vom Barock bis zur Klassik* (Stuttgart: Reclam, 1965), p. 256.

37. See Pamela Currie, "Moral Weeklies and the Reading Public in Germany, 1711–1750," *Oxford German Studies* 3 (1968): 79.
38. For a brief overview of Hamburg's participation in eighteenth-century music, see Hans-Heinrich Reuter and Werner Rieck, *Geschichte der deutschen Literatur: Vom Ausgang des 17. Jahrhunderts bis 1789* (Berlin: Volk und Wissen Volkseigener Verlag, 1979), pp. 48–49.
39. For a description of the scene at a typical fair, see Albert Ward, *Book Production, Fiction and the German Reading Public, 1740–1800* (Oxford: Clarendon, 1974), pp. 37–40.
40. Georg Witkowski, *Geschichte des literarischen Lebens in Leipzig* (Leipzig and Berlin: Teubner, 1909), p. 168.
41. Compare Reuter and Rieck, p. 50.
42. See Ernst Kroker, *Handelsgeschichte der Stadt Leipzig: Die Entwicklung des Leipziger Handels und der Leipziger Messen von der Gründung der Stadt bis auf die Gegenwart* (Leipzig: Bielefeld, 1925), p. 131.
43. Zorn, "Schwerpunkte," pp. 425–26.
44. For a discussion of the French and Italian "colonies" in Leipzig, see Kroker, pp. 153–56.
45. Kroker offers short biographies of these and other merchants, pp. 141–50.
46. Balet, p. 52.
47. Kroker, p. 164.
48. Kiesel and Münch, p. 15.
49. Compare Stefi Jersch-Wenzel, "Der Einfluß zugewanderter Minoritäten als Wirtschaftsgruppen auf die Berliner Wirtschaft in vor- und frühindustrieller Zeit," in *Untersuchungen zur Geschichte der frühen Industrialisierung vornehmlich im Wirtschaftsraum Berlin/Brandenburg*, ed. Otto Büsch (Berlin: Colloquium, 1971), p. 201.
50. Jersch-Wenzel, p. 202.
51. For two authoritative voices, see, on the "pro" side, Biedermann, pp. 303–6. For the "con" side, see Ludwig Geiger, *Berlin 1688–1840: Geschichte des geistigen Lebens der preußischen Hauptstadt* (Berlin: Paetel, 1892), 1: 278–81. More recently, Dorwart has clearly documented Friedrich Wilhelm's commitment to effective policing of Berlin's various markets (pp. 67–74), especially with regard to merchants from foreign parts (p. 69).
52. For more about the "Lagerhaus," see Geiger, pp. 280–81.
53. Zorn, "Schwerpunkte," p. 437.
54. For a detailed study of Splitgerber and Daum, see W. O. Henderson, *Studies in the Economic Policy of Frederick the Great* (London: Cass, 1963), pp. 1–16.
55. Balet, p. 22.
56. For details of Gotzkowsky's career up to the Seven Years' War, see Henderson, pp. 17–28.
57. For a brief description of periodicals at this time, see Van Cleve, pp. 33–44.
58. The relationship of the two fairs is treated in Zorn, "Schwerpunkte,"

pp. 426–27. The figures on population can be found in Kiesel and Münch, p. 15.
59. Zorn, "Sozialgeschichte," p. 564.
60. Kiesel and Münch, p. 57.
61. Kiesel and Münch, p. 58.
62. Biedermann, pp. 292–93.
63. For further information about trade patterns in northern coastal cities other than Hamburg, see Zorn, "Sozialgeschichte," pp. 561–64.
64. Currie, pp. 79–80.
65. For a brief history of Berne during the period 1690–1750, see E. Bonjour, H. S. Offler, and G. R. Potter, *A Short History of Switzerland* (Oxford: University Press, 1952), pp. 200–203.
66. Rytz, pp. 3–5.
67. Rytz, pp. 11–12.
68. See Lütge, p. 378.
69. Wolfgang Martens, "Bürgerlichkeit in der frühen Aufklärung," in *Aufklärung, Absolutismus und Bürgertum in Deutschland*, ed. Franklin Kopitzsch (Munich: Nymphenburg, 1976), pp. 353–55.
70. Cited in Martens, "Bürgerlichkeit," p. 353.
71. Rolf Engelsing, *Der Bürger als Leser: Lesergeschichte in Deutschland 1500–1800* (Stuttgart: Metzler, 1974), pp. 138–39.
72. Engelsing, *Bürger*, pp. 138–39.
73. Engelsing, *Bürger*, p. 148.
74. Cited in Engelsing, *Bürger*, pp. 140–41.
75. Hudtwalcker, p. 185.
76. Hudtwalcker, p. 186.
77. Hudtwalcker, pp. 186–87.
78. Hudtwalcker, p. 192.
79. Hudtwalcker, p. 193.
80. Hudtwalcker, p. 209.
81. Hudtwalcker, p. 209.
82. Compare Gerhard von Glinski, *Die Königsberger Kaufmannschaft des 17. und 18. Jahrhunderts* (Marburg/L: Herder-Institut, 1964), pp. 58–59.
83. See Krosigk, p. 156.
84. Martens, "Bürgerlichkeit," pp. 354–55.
85. Curt Gebauer, "Studien zur Geschichte der bürgerlichen Sittenreform des 18. Jahrhunderts," *Archiv für Kulturgeschichte* 15 (1923): 101.
86. Engelsing, *Analphabetentum*, p. 69.
87. Hudtwalcker, p. 198.
88. Hudtwalcker, p. 198.
89. Hudtwalcker, p. 198.
90. For a discussion of the woman's role in an eighteenth-century family, see Ingeborg Weber-Kellermann, *Die deutsche Familie: Versuch einer Sozialgeschichte* (Frankfurt/M: Suhrkamp, 1974), pp. 74–81.
91. For what follows, compare, in addition to Weber-Kellermann, Gebauer.

92. Hudtwalcker, p. 198.
93. Hudtwalcker, pp. 207–8.
94. For what follows, see Hudtwalcker, pp. 193–94.
95. Currie, p. 74.
96. See Barner et al., pp. 64–65. See also Paul Raabe, "Buchproduktion und Lesepublikum in Deutschland 1770–1780," *Philobiblon* 21, no. 1 (1977): 3.
97. Compare Herbert G. Göpfert, "Lesegesellschaften im 18. Jahrhundert," in *Dichtung Sprache Gesellschaft: Akten des IV. Internationalen Germanisten-Kongresses 1970 in Princeton*, ed. Victor Lange and Hans-Gert Roloff (Frankfurt/M: Athenäum, 1971), p. 325.
98. The organizational and philosophical principles of early German freemasonry are discussed in Heinrich Schneider, *Quest for Mysteries: The Masonic Background for Literature in Eighteenth-Century Germany* (Ithaca, New York: Cornell University Press, 1947), esp. pp. 56–66. See also Jacob Katz, "Echte und imaginäre Beziehungen zwischen Freimaurerei und Judentum," in *Geheime Gesellschaften*, ed. Peter Christian Ludz (Heidelberg: Schneider, 1979).
99. For that list, see Günter Wicke, *Die Struktur des deutschen Lustspiels der Aufklärung: Versuch einer Typologie* (Bonn: Bouvier, 1965), pp. 135–36.
100. Hudtwalcker, p. 210.
101. Karl S. Guthke, *Literarisches Leben im achtzehnten Jahrhundert in Deutschland und in der Schweiz* (Berne and Munich: Francke, 1975), p. 11.
102. George L. Mosse, *Germans and Jews* (New York: Grosset and Dunlap, 1970), p. 41.
103. For an overview of the legal status of the German Jew at the end of the Middle Ages, see Guido Kisch, *The Jews in Medieval Germany: A Study of Their Legal and Social Status*, 2d ed. (New York: Ktav, 1970), pp. 342–64. A brief description of the legal situation and the economic condition of Jews during the eighteenth century can be found in Zorn, "Sozialgeschichte," pp. 601–3. For details about dress and ghetto life, see Herman Pollack, *Jewish Folkways in Germanic Lands (1648–1806): Studies in Aspects of Daily Life* (Cambridge, Mass.: M.I.T. Press, 1971), esp. pp. 1–14.
104. H. G. Adler, *The Jews in Germany: From the Enlightenment to National Socialism* (Notre Dame, Indiana: Notre Dame Press, 1969), p. 17.
105. Zorn, "Sozialgeschichte," p. 603.
106. Cited by Mosse, p. 46. Text from Johann Wolfgang von Goethe, *Aus meinem Leben: Dichtung und Wahrheit*, in *Werke*, ed. Erich Trunz, 10th ed. (Munich: Beck, 1981), 9: 149.
107. Compare Karl Heinrich Rengstorf, "Judentum im Zeitalter der Aufklärung: Geschichtliche Voraussetzungen und einige zentrale Probleme," in *Judentum im Zeitalter der Aufklärung*, ed. Günter Schulz (Bremen and Wolfenbüttel: Jacobi, 1977), pp. 14–15. See also Julius H. Schoeps, "Aufklärung, Judentum und Emanzipation," in *Judentum im Zeitalter der Aufklärung*, ed. Günter Schulz (Bremen and Wolfenbüttel: Jacobi, 1977), p. 81.
108. The social stratification of Jewish society is discussed in Zorn, "Sozi-

algeschichte," p. 603.

109. For an outline of Jewish involvement in German trade through the early eighteenth century, see Lütge, pp. 379–81.

110. Perhaps the most famous example is Joseph Süß-Oppenheimer, immortalized in Lion Feuchtwanger's *Jud Süß*. See below, p. 82.

111. For further information, see Hermann Kellenbenz, *Sephardim an der unteren Elbe: Ihre wirtschaftliche und politische Bedeutung vom Ende des 16. bis zum Beginn des 18. Jahrhunderts* (Wiesbaden: Steiner, 1958), esp. pp. 54–57 and 182–85. See also Alfred Feilchenfeld, "Hamburg," *The Jewish Encyclopedia*, 1912 ed., and Adolf Kober, "Hamburg," *The Universal Jewish Encyclopedia*, 1941 ed.

112. Glückel of Hameln, *Memoirs*, trans. Marvin Lowenthal (1932; rpt., New York: Schocken, 1977), p. 179.

113. See Salo W. Baron and Arcadius Kahan, *Economic History of the Jews* (New York: Schocken, 1975), p. 248, and Lütge, p. 380.

114. Baron and Kahan, p. 247.

115. For specifics concerning the fee structure, see Kroker, pp. 133–35. Concerning the function of the scales house, see Jacob Grimm and Wilhelm Grimm, *Deutsches Wörterbuch* (Leipzig: Hirzel, 1854–1961), 13: col. 364–65 and 370.

116. Glückel of Hameln, pp. 126–27.

117. See Selma Stern, *The Court Jew: A Contribution to the Period of Absolutism in Central Europe*, trans. Ralph Weiman (Philadelphia: Jewish Publication Society of America, 1950), pp. 144–45.

118. For an excellent, well-documented survey of official policy from the Great Elector to Friedrich II, see Peter Baumgart, "Absoluter Staat und Judenemanzipation in Brandenburg-Preußen," *Jahrbuch für die Geschichte Mittel- und Ostdeutschlands* 13–14 (1965): 60–87.

119. Baumgart, p. 71.

120. Geiger, p. 222.

121. Stern, p. 146. For detailed examinations of Prussian Jewry under the two kings, see Selma Stern, *Der preußische Staat und die Juden: Zweiter Teil: Die Zeit Friedrich Wilhelms I.* (Tübingen: Mohr, 1962) and *Der preußische Staat und die Juden: Dritter Teil: Die Zeit Friedrichs des Großen* (Tübingen: Mohr, 1971).

122. Cited in Baumgart, p. 80.

123. Stern, *Dritter Teil*, pp. 321–23.

124. Stern, *Dritter Teil*, p. 323.

125. Werner Sombart, *Die Juden und das Wirtschaftsleben* (Leipzig: Duncker und Humblot, 1911). Sombart's famous nemesis in the analysis of the interaction of religion and capitalism was Max Weber. See *Die protestantische Ethik und der Geist des Kapitalismus*, in Weber, *Gesammelte Aufsätze zur Religionssoziologie* (Tübingen: Mohr, 1920), 1: 17–19. The classic study points to a historical link between profitable business and Protestant faith. The guiding "spirit" is Calvinistic asceticism. Weber notes that a commonly recognized characteristic of Pietism is the combination of deep religiosity and business acumen (pp. 28–29).

126. Jersch-Wenzel, pp. 198–99.

127. "Quae bona sunt fiduciam faciunt, divitiae audaciam. Quae bona sunt magnitudinem animi dant, divitiae insolentiam. Nihil autem aliud est insolentia quam species magnitudinis falsa." Lucius Annaeus Seneca, *Ad Lucilium epistulae morales*, ed. and trans. Richard M. Gummere (Cambridge, Mass.: Harvard University Press, 1970), pp. 340 and 342.

128. "Secunda [commutatio] autem juste vituperatur, quia, quantum est de se, deservit cupiditati lucri, quae terminum nescit, sed in infinitum tendit." St. Thomas Aquinas, *Summa Theologiae* (New York and London: McGraw-Hill, Blackfriars, and Eyre and Spottiswoode, 1975), pp. 228–29.

129. For a discussion of medieval attitudes toward wealth, see R. H. Tawney, *Religion and the Rise of Capitalism: A Historical Study* (New York: Harcourt and Brace, 1926), esp. pp. 34–35.

130. Martin Luther, "Von Kaufshandlung und Wucher: 1524," in *Werke*, ed. Otto Clemen and Albert Leitzmann, 5th ed. (Berlin: de Gruyter, 1959), 3: 2–3. At the time "fynantzen" implied usury and fraud; see Grimm and Grimm, 3: col. 1639–40.

131. Lütge, pp. 368–69.

132. Compare Georg Steinhausen, *Der Kaufmann in der deutschen Vergangenheit* (Leipzig: Diederichs, 1899), p. 125.

133. Steinhausen, p. 126. See also Engelsing, *Bürger als Leser*, pp. 139–40.

134. Rytz, p. 6.

135. Cited in Henderson, p. 7.

136. Wolfgang Schaer's unsupported assertion to the contrary is incorrect. Wolfgang Schaer, *Die Gesellschaft im deutschen bürgerlichen Drama des 18. Jahrhunderts: Grundlagen und Bedrohung im Spiegel der dramatischen Literatur* (Bonn: Bouvier, 1963), p. 64.

137. For an example of confusion in the face of the merchant-in-literature constellation, see Ernst Baasch, "Der Kaufmann in der deutschen Romanliteratur des 18. Jahrhunderts," in *Aus Sozial- und Wirtschaftsgeschichte: Gedächtnisschrift für Georg von Below* (Stuttgart: Kohlhammer, 1928), pp. 279–98. The period 1815–1914 is stressed in Wolfgang Kockjoy, *Der deutsche Kaufmannsroman: Versuch einer kultur- und geistesgeschichtlichen genetischen Darstellung* (Strasbourg: Heitz, 1933).

138. Peter Szondi, *Die Theorie des bürgerlichen Trauerspiels im 18. Jahrhundert: Der Kaufmann, der Hausvater und der Hofmeister* (Frankfurt/M: Suhrkamp, 1974), pp. 59–60.

139. Szondi, p. 60.

140. Martens, *Botschaft*, pp. 304–15.

## II. Menace and Menaced: Haller, Schnabel

1. See Christoph Siegrist, *Albrecht von Haller* (Stuttgart: Metzler, 1967), pp. 5–17. For greatest detail, see the biography in Ludwig Hirzel, ed., *Albrecht von Hallers Gedichte* (Frauenfeld: Huber, 1882).

2. Albrecht von Haller, "Die Alpen," in *Vorboten der bürgerlichen Kultur:*

*Johann Gottfried Schnabel und Albrecht von Haller,* ed. Fritz Brüggemann (Darmstadt: Wissenschaftliche Buchgesellschaft, 1964), p. 310. This stanza appeared for the first time in the second edition of 1734, the earliest to supply its author's name. Otherwise, Brüggemann follows the first edition of 1732. Hereafter, references to pages from Brüggemann are given in parentheses after a prefixed "A."

3. See Werner Kohlschmidt, "Hallers Gedichte und die Tradition," in his *Dichter, Tradition und Zeitgeist: Gesammelte Studien zur Literaturgeschichte* (Berne and Munich: Francke, 1965), pp. 206–21.

4. For example, Herman Meyer, "Hütte und Palast in der Dichtung des 18. Jahrhunderts," in *Formenwandel: Festschrift zum 65. Geburtstag von Paul Böckmann,* ed. Walter Müller-Seidel (Hamburg: Hoffmann und Campe, 1964), pp. 138–42. Also, Andreas Müller, *Landschaftserlebnis und Landschaftsbild: Studien zur deutschen Dichtung des 18. Jahrhunderts und der Romantik* (Hechingen: Kohlhammer, 1955), pp. 30–31.

5. See Paul Böckmann, "Anfänge der Naturlyrik bei Brockes, Haller und Günther," in *Literatur und Geistesgeschichte: Festgabe für Heinz Otto Bürger,* ed. Reinhold Grimm and Conrad Wiedemann (Berlin: Schmidt, 1968), pp. 119–20.

6. Böckmann, pp. 119–20.

7. Meyer, p. 142.

8. Müller, p. 30.

9. Karl S. Guthke has provided an extraordinarily thorough documentation of Haller's career in print through numerous articles and books, notably *Haller und die Literatur* (Göttingen: Vandenhoeck und Ruprecht, 1962) and *Hallers Literaturkritik* (Tübingen: Niemeyer, 1970).

10. See Johann Gottfried Schnabel, *Insel Felsenburg,* ed. Wilhelm Voßkamp (Reinbek: Rowohlt, 1969), pp. 257–58. See also Johann Gottfried Schnabel, *Insel Felsenburg,* ed. Volker Meid and Ingeborg Springer-Strand (Stuttgart: Reclam, 1979), pp. 585–86. References to pages from Voßkamp are given in parentheses after a prefixed "F." The text follows the 1731 edition.

11. For a treatment of Robinson literature with an eye to *Insel Felsenburg,* see Wilhelm Voßkamp, "Theorie und Praxis der literarischen Fiktion in Johann Gottfried Schnabels Roman 'Die Insel Felsenburg,' " *Germanisch-Romanische Monatsschrift* 18, no. 2 (1968): 131–36.

12. An analysis of the utopian landscape is offered in Rosemarie Haas, "Die Landschaft auf der Insel Felsenburg," *Zeitschrift für deutsches Altertum und deutsche Literatur* 91, no. 1 (1961): 63–84.

13. Dietrich Naumann, *Politik und Moral: Studien zur Utopie der deutschen Aufklärung* (Heidelberg: Winter, 1977), pp. 97 and 102. For a similarly structured treatment, see Jürgen Jacobs, *Prosa der Aufklärung: Moralische Wochenschriften, Autobiographie, Satire, Roman: Kommentar zu einer Epoche* (Munich: Winkler, 1976), pp. 139–43.

14. Schnabel, *Felsenburg,* ed. Meid and Springer-Strand, p. 567.

15. Rolf Allerdissen, *Die Reise als Flucht: Zu Schnabels "Insel Felsenburg" und Thümmels "Reise in die mittäglichen Provinzen von Frankreich"* (Berne: Lang, 1975), p. 29.

16. See Roland Haas, *Lesend wird sich der Bürger seiner Welt bewußt: Der Schriftsteller Johann Gottfried Schnabel und die deutsche Entwicklung des Bürgertums in der ersten Hälfte des 18. Jahrhunderts* (Frankfurt/M, Berne, Las Vegas: Lang, 1977), pp. 46–49.

17. The absolutist nature of governance on the island is indicated in Jan Knopf, *Frühzeit des Bürgers: Erfahrene und verleugnete Realität in den Romanen Wickrams, Grimmelshausens, Schnabels* (Stuttgart: Metzler, 1978), p. 92.

18. Horst Brunner notes the ongoing relationship between the island and the continent in *Die poetische Insel: Inseln und Inselvorstellungen in der deutschen Literatur* (Stuttgart: Metzler, 1967), p. 111.

## III. From Fool to Friend: Borkenstein, L. A. V. Gottsched, J. E. Schlegel

1. Most notably by Werner Rieck, *Johann Christoph Gottsched: Eine kritische Würdigung seines Werkes* (Berlin: Akademie-Verlag, 1972), and by Hans Freier, *Kritische Poetik: Legitimation und Kritik in Gottscheds Dichtkunst* (Stuttgart: Metzler, 1973).

2. The last two decades have supplied a plethora of studies treating the Enlightenment comedy. Among them are Walter Hinck, *Das deutsche Lustspiel des 17. und 18. Jahrhunderts und die italienische Komödie: Commedia dell' Arte und Théâtre Italien* (Stuttgart: Metzler, 1965); Günter Wicke, *Die Struktur des deutschen Lustspiels der Aufklärung: Versuch einer Typologie* (Bonn: Bouvier, 1965); Hans Steffen, ed., *Das deutsche Lustspiel* (Göttingen: Vandenhoeck und Ruprecht, 1968), vol. 1; Diethelm Brüggemann, *Die sächsische Komödie: Studien zum Sprachstil* (Cologne: Böhlau, 1970); Horst Steinmetz, *Die Komödie der Aufklärung*, 2d ed., (Stuttgart: Metzler, 1971); Fritz Martini, *Lustspiele – und das Lustspiel* (Stuttgart: Klett, 1974). The old standard work for comedy is Karl Holl, *Geschichte des deutschen Lustspiels* (1923; rpt. Darmstadt: Wissenschaftliche Buchgesellschaft, 1964). For a more recent general survey, see Walter Hinck, ed., *Die deutsche Komödie: Vom Mittelalter bis zur Gegenwart* (Düsseldorf: Bagel, 1977).

3. Further biographical details are furnished by Franz Ferdinand Heitmüller in his editor's preface to the text used here: Hinrich Borkenstein, *Der Bookesbeutel* (1896; rpt. Nendeln, Liechtenstein: Kraus, 1968). References to the text are given in parentheses after a prefixed "B." Heitmüller follows the original edition of 1742.

4. See Jacob and Wilhelm Grimm, *Deutsches Wörterbuch* (Leipzig: Hirzel, 1860), 2: col. 206. See also Alfred Götze, ed., *Trübners Deutsches Wörterbuch* (Berlin: de Gruyter, 1939), I: 379.

5. Hans Friederici discusses the divergence of tradition with regard to the education of women in *Das deutsche bürgerliche Lustspiel der Frühaufklärung (1736–1750) unter besonderer Berücksichtigung seiner Anschauungen von der Gesellschaft* (Halle/Saale: Niemeyer, 1957), p. 122. This orthodox Marxist monograph has long stood unique as a sociological analysis of the Enlightenment comedy.

150  Notes to Pages 74–85

6. For a discussion of greed as motivation in *Der Bookesbeutel*, see Jochen Schulte-Sasse, "Drama," in *Deutsche Aufklärung bis zur französischen Revolution 1680–1789*, ed. Rolf Grimminger (Munich: Hanser, 1980), pp. 439–41. Schulte-Sasse asserts that the middle class felt particular aversion for the miser as one who does not allow his money to circulate as a part of the money- and credit-supply of a nation; such a figure would not be contributing to the economic growth of his class.

7. Of Grobian, Günter Wicke comments in passing: "Überhaupt ist ihm das Geld Ziel und Maßstab aller Dinge. Er ist der Typ des asozialen, vorbürgerlichen Menschen, der nur auf den eigenen Nutzen bedacht ist" (Wicke, p. 14).

8. See Veronica C. Richel, *Luise Gottsched: A Reconsideration* (Berne: Lang, 1973), and Paul Schlenther, *Frau Gottsched und die bürgerliche Komödie: Ein Kulturbild aus der Zopfzeit* (Berlin: Hertz, 1886).

9. See Eckehard Catholy on the famous "Ständeklausel" in his "Die deutsche Komödie vor Lessing," in Hinck, ed., *Die deutsche Komödie*, pp. 42–47.

10. It has been pointed out that the critique of francophilia is compromised by the casting of the primary exponents as felons (Steinmetz, p. 33).

11. Luise Gottsched, *Die Hausfranzösinn, oder die Mammsell*, in *Die Deutsche Schaubühne, nach den Regeln und Mustern der Alten*, ed. Johann Christoph Gottsched, 2d ed. (Leipzig: Breitkopf, 1749), 5: 107. References to this text are given in parentheses after a prefixed "H."

12. "Den heftigsten Angriff gegen den Einfluß französischer Sitten führt die Gottschedin in ihrem Lustspiel 'Die Hausfranzösinn,' in dem sie das Bild einer französischer Erzieherin bis zum Kriminellen einschwärzt." Walter Hinck, "Das deutsche Lustspiel im 18. Jahrhundert," in Steffen, ed., p. 15.

13. For a brief discussion of the life of Joseph Süß-Oppenheimer, see Rengstorf, pp. 24–25.

14. For a study of J. E. Schlegel that emphasizes his dramas, see Peter Wolf, *Die Dramen Johann Elias Schlegels: Ein Beitrag zur Geschichte des Dramas im 18. Jahrhundert* (Zurich: Atlantis, 1964).

15. Schlegel's earlier, strict observance of Gottsched's dictates is evident in Günter Wicke's description of *Müßiggänger* as "das 'gottschedischste' aller Lustspiele" (Wicke, p. 18).

16. Johann Elias Schlegel, *Der Geschäfftige Müßiggänger*, in his *Werke*, ed. Johann Heinrich Schlegel (Copenhagen and Leipzig: Proft und Rothen, 1773), 2: 140. References to this text are given in parentheses after a prefixed "M."

17. Luise Gottsched, *Der Witzling*, ed. Wolfgang Hecht (Berlin: de Gruyter, 1962), p. 8. Hecht follows the edition in *Die Deutsche Schaubühne, nach den Regeln und Mustern der Alten*, ed. Johann Christoph Gottsched, 2d ed. (Leipzig: Breitkopf, 1750), vol. 6. References to Hecht's edition are given in parentheses after a prefixed "W."

18. See Richel, pp. 46–47, and Van Cleve, *Harlequin Besieged*, pp. 158–60.

## IV. Virtue in the "Jewish Profession": Gellert

1. Hermann Hettner, *Geschichte der deutschen Literatur im 18. Jahrhundert* (Leipzig: List, 1928), p. 23.
2. Richard Newald, *Die deutsche Literatur vom Späthumanismus zur Empfindsamkeit*, 6th ed., vol. 5 of Helmut de Boor and Richard Newald, *Geschichte der deutschen Literatur von den Anfängen bis zur Gegenwart* (Munich: Beck, 1967), p. 437. Newald's emphasis.
3. Rudolf Schenda, *Volk ohne Buch: Studien zur Sozialgeschichte der populären Lesestoffe 1770–1910* (Frankfurt/M: Klostermann, 1970), p. 445.
4. Kiesel and Münch, p. 160.
5. Dieter Kimpel, *Der Roman der Aufklärung* (Stuttgart: Metzler, 1967), pp. 72–87.
6. For a still more detailed structural consideration, see Eckhardt Meyer-Krentler, *Der andere Roman: Gellerts "Schwedische Gräfin": Von der aufklärerischen Propaganda gegen den "Roman" zur empfindsamen Erlebnisdichtung* (Göppingen: Kümmerle, 1974). No significant analysis is offered of the novel's presentation of eighteenth-century society.
7. In his book *Gellert: Eine literarhistorische Revision* (Bad Homburg: Gehlen, 1967), pp. 140–46, Carsten Schlingmann concentrates on the relationship between the complex plot briefly outlined here and genre history. His formalistic analysis may be somewhat disjointed, but then again, many would charge that the novel is just that. Schlingmann's method precludes anything more than passing mention of the positively drawn Jew. For a Victorian savaging of the *Schwedische Gräfin*, see Hettner, pp. 244–45.
8. Christian Fürchtegott Gellert, *Das Leben der schwedischen Gräfin von G\*\*\**, in *Deutsche Literatur in Entwicklungsreihen*, Series: "Aufklärung," vol. 5, *Die bürgerliche Gemeinschaftskultur der vierziger Jahre*, ed. Fritz Brüggemann (Leipzig: Reclam, 1933), p. 221. References to this text are given in parentheses after a prefixed "L."
9. In his article, "Some Unspoken Assumptions in Gellert's 'Schwedische Gräfin,'" *Orbis Litterarum* 28 (1973), D. M. Van Abbé finds this sufficient grounds to write of Gellert's "open-eyed philo-Semitism" (p. 120) without analyzing motivation on either side; he is too fascinated by a plot that he recapitulates too thoroughly. Incredibly, no "unspoken assumptions" about Christians and Jews are discussed.
10. For a discussion of this Jewish elite, see Schoeps.
11. That the cast of characters is inbred has a decidedly deleterious effect on the novel; in this context, Ferdinand Josef Schneider's unkind evaluation of the work as a "seltsamer literarischer Wechselbalg" is understandable. Schneider, *Die deutsche Dichtung der Aufklärungszeit 1700–1775*, 2d ed. (Stuttgart: Metzler, 1948), p. 308.
12. Fritz Brüggemann argues that Gellert presents resignation as a high virtue, as a mechanism for inner control of strong feelings. Brüggemann, "Einführung" to Gellert, *Gräfin*, ed. Brüggemann, p. 20. He does not take

into account the complete absence of such a posture in all of the novel's merchant characters.

13. For an examination of the novel that emphasizes Shaftesbury as well as the Pietist influence, see Kohlschmidt, *Geschichte der deutschen Literatur*, pp. 365–69.

14. This brief companionship and the still briefer "second marriage" of the count and countess are the only episodes in the action of the novel in which membership in the aristocracy is of central importance. The nobleman and his wife most often live incognito. Werner Rieck's reference to the novel's setting "in adligem, teilweise höfischem Milieu" is without foundation (Reuter and Rieck, *Geschichte der deutschen Literatur*, p. 229). Rieck's treatment is superficial and disappointing.

15. Kisch, p. 332.

16. Review of *Lessings Schrifften*, T. 4, *Göttingische Anzeigen von gelehrten Sachen*, no. 70, 13 June 1754, pp. 621–22.

17. Kimpel, pp. 73–75.

## V. The Merchant as Hero: Lessing

1. For Lessing scholarship from its beginnings through August 1971, see: Siegfried Seifert, *Lessing-Bibliographie* (Berlin and Weimar: Aufbau-Verlag, 1973). See also the bibliographic volume in the "Sammlung Metzler": Karl S. Guthke, *Gotthold Ephraim Lessing*, 3d ed. (Stuttgart: Metzler, 1979).

2. For a study of this earliest period in Lessing's literary career, see Klaus Briegleb, *Lessings Anfänge 1742–1746: Zur Grundlegung kritischer Sprachdemokratie* (Frankfurt/M: Athenäum, 1971).

3. The early comedies and particularly *Der junge Gelehrte* are examined in Hans-Ulrich Lappert, *G. E. Lessings Jugendlustspiele und die Komödientheorie der frühen Aufklärung* (Zurich: Juris, 1968). For a study of the young journalist in Berlin, see Bernd Peschken, "Lessings Anfang in Berlin im sozialgeschichtlichen Zusammenhang," in *Analecta Helvetica et Germanica: Eine Festschrift zu Ehren von Hermann Boeschenstein*, ed. A. Arnold, H. Eichner, E. Heier, S. Hoefert (Bonn: Bouvier, 1979).

4. Theodor Wilhelm Danzel, *Gotthold Ephraim Lessing: Sein Leben und seine Werke*, ed. Robert Boxberger and Wendelin von Maltzahn, 2d ed. (Berlin: Hoffmann, 1880), 1:115.

5. Erich Schmidt, *Lessing: Geschichte seines Lebens und seiner Schriften* (Berlin: Weidmann, 1884), 1:161–65.

6. Titus Maccius Plautus, *Trinummus*, in *Plautus*, with an English translation by Paul Nixon (London and Cambridge, Mass.: Heinemann and Harvard University Press, 1938), p. 102:

> huic Graece nomen est Thesauro fabulae:
> Philemo scripsit, Plautus vertit barbare,
> nomen Trinummo fecit, nunc hoc vos rogat
> ut liceat possidere hanc nomen fabulam.

7. Schmidt, pp. 164–65: "Man hat die Bearbeitung wegen ihrer unläugbaren technischen und dialogischen Gewandtheit fast allenthalben stark überschätzt. Halb antik, halb modern, verdient sie nur den Namen eines Tragelaphen und ist allmählich aus dem Repertoire des deutschen Theaters dahin gewandert, wo antikisierende Anachronismen am leichtesten ertragen werden, auf die Gelegenheitsbühne von Gymnasiasten und Studenten."

8. Waldemar Oehlke, *Lessing und seine Zeit* (Munich: Beck, 1919), p. 129: "Nicht ganz gelang es ihm, ein Lustspiel zu schaffen, dem Ewigkeitswert zuzusprechen wäre. Plautinische Komödien widerstehen dem Gedanken sittlicher Vertiefung zu stark. So stoßen lustiges und sittliches Empfinden einmal heftig aufeinander und wirken peinlich."

9. For example: Michael M. Metzger, *Lessing and the Language of Comedy* (The Hague: Mouton, 1966), p. 142: "Considered in its totality, *Der Schatz* shows too much interest in virtuosity and sprightliness of form and the movement of scenes and relatively little creative use of the devices of language at Lessing's disposal. This is a temporary imbalance and one which Lessing will have overcome at the height of his powers." Otto Mann and Rotraut Straube-Mann, *Lessing-Kommentar* (Munich: Winkler, 1971), 1: 53: "Dieses letzte der Jugendlustspiele Lessings, 1750 geschrieben, ist nur eine Bearbeitung und Modernisierung des *Trinummus* von Plautus, zeigt aber Lessings originale dramatische Kraft gerade bei der Zueignung schon vorgebildeter Stoffe und Motive." The already cited *Lessing: Epoche – Werk – Wirkung* (1977), with its emphasis on historical and sociological determinants, makes no mention of *Der Schatz*. Finally, the previously cited *Geschichte der deutschen Literatur* (1979) by the GDR scholars Reuter and Rieck, p. 301: "Ungeachtet der Übernahme tradierter komischer Effekte aus der römischen und europäischen Komödienliteratur und der durch komische Handlungsschemata vorgegebenen Fabelführung, spürt man die Lebensnähe der gezeigten Welt, da die Gestalten, ihre Auffassungen und ihre Sprache der Wirklichkeit abgelauscht sind. Das bezeugt auch die 1750 entstandene Komödie 'Der Schatz,' in der auf die in bürgerlichen Häusern anzutreffende Jagd nach einer reichen Mitgift satirisch angespielt wird."

10. Gotthold Ephraim Lessing, *Der Schatz*, in *Gotthold Ephraim Lessings sämtliche Schriften*, ed. Karl Lachmann, 3d ed. reedited by Franz Muncker (Stuttgart: Göschen, 1886), 2: 156. Subsequent references to this text are given in parentheses after a prefixed "S." Lachmann and Muncker follow an edition from 1770; variants found in the *editio princeps* of 1755 are indicated in footnotes. In this study, only that first edition is cited.

11. Ariane Neuhaus-Koch, *G. E. Lessing: Die Sozialstrukturen in seinen Dramen* (Bonn: Bouvier, 1977), p. 164.

12. See Volker Riedel, *Lessing und die römische Literatur* (Weimar: Böhlau, 1976), p. 164.

13. Metzger, p. 137.

14. Metzger, pp. 89–90.

15. Robert Rentschler, "Lisette, the Laugher," *Lessing Yearbook* 10 (1978): 55–56.

16. See Paul P. Kies, "The Sources of Lessing's *Die Juden*," *Philological*

*Quarterly* 6, no. 4 (1927), pp. 406-10. See also Karl S. Guthke, "Kommentar," in Gotthold Ephraim Lessing, *Werke* (Munich: Hanser, 1971), 2: 144-45.

17. Harvey I. Dunkle, "Lessing's 'Die Juden': An Original Experiment," *Monatshefte* 49, no. 6 (1957), pp. 323-29. A needed correction is made by Hendrik Birus, *Poetische Namengebung: Zur Bedeutung der Namen in Lessings "Nathan der Weise"* (Göttingen: Vandenhoeck und Ruprecht, 1978), pp. 84-85.

18. See for example E. J. Engel, "Young Lessing as Literary Critic (1749-1755)," *Lessing Yearbook* 11 (1979): 73.

19. Lessing, *Die Juden*, in *Gotthold Ephraim Lessings sämtliche Schriften*, ed. Karl Lachmann, 3d ed. reedited by Franz Muncker (Stuttgart: Göschen, 1886), 1: 398. Subsequent references to this text are given in parentheses after a prefixed "J." Lachmann and Muncker follow an edition from 1770; variants found in the *editio princeps* of 1754 are indicated in footnotes. In this study, only that first edition is cited.

20. Metzger, p. 91.

21. See Gerd Hillen, *Lessing Chronik: Daten zu Leben und Werk* (Munich and Vienna: Hanser, 1979), p. 22.

22. Neuhaus-Koch states that each of Lessing's early comedies features a merchant with the sole exception of *Die alte Jungfer* (pp. 162-63). Inexplicably, she does not expand upon the statement with reference to *Die Juden*.

23. Schmidt, p. 135.

24. Oehlke, p. 124.

25. Review of *Lessings Schrifften*, T. 4, *Jenaische gelehrte Zeitungen*, no. 66, 24 August 1754, p. 526.

26. Gotthold Ephraim Lessing, "Ueber das Lustspiel die Juden, im vierten Theile der Leßingschen Schriften," *Theatralische Bibliothek*, no. 1 (1754); cited in *Gotthold Ephraim Lessings sämtliche Schriften*, ed. Karl Lachmann, 3d ed. reedited by Franz Muncker (Stuttgart: Göschen, 1890), 6: 161.

27. Oehlke, p. 123.

28. Karl S. Guthke, "Lessing und das Judentum: Rezeption. Dramatik und Kritik. Krypto-Spinozismus," in *Wolfenbütteler Studien zur Aufklärung*, vol. 4, *Judentum im Zeitalter der Aufklärung*, ed. Günter Schulz (Bremen: Jacobi, 1977), p. 244.

29. For a discussion of the positions, see Wolfgang Trautwein, "Zwischen Typenlustspiel und ernster Komödie: Zur produktiven Verletzung von Gattungsmustern in Lessings 'Die Juden,'" *Jahrbuch der deutschen Schillergesellschaft* 24 (1980): 5-6.

30. See John W. Van Cleve, "Social Climbing during the Age of Absolutism: Personality Distortion and Career Advancement in J. C. Krüger's *Die Candidaten*," *Orbis Litterarum* 35 (1980): 318-26.

31. See Paul Hernadi, "Nathan der Bürger: Lessings Mythos vom aufgeklärten Kaufmann," *Lessing Yearbook* 3 (1971), pp. 151-59; Dominik von König, *Natürlichkeit und Wirklichkeit: Studien zu Lessings "Nathan der Weise"* (Bonn: Bouvier, 1976), esp. pp. 93-102; Wolf Wucherpfennig, "Nathan, der weise Händler," in *Akten des VI. Internationalen Germanisten-Kongresses Basel 1980*, ed. Hans-Gert Roloff and Heinz Rupp (Berne: Lang, 1980).

32. Lessing, *Nathan der Weise*, in *Gotthold Ephraim Lessings sämtliche Schriften*, ed. Karl Lachmann, 3d ed. reedited by Franz Muncker (Stuttgart: Göschen, 1887), 3: 84. Subsequent references to this text are given in parentheses after a prefixed "N."
33. Hernadi, p. 152; Neuhaus-Koch, pp. 167–68.
34. Hernadi, p. 156. The point is also touched briefly by Helmuth Kiesel in Barner et al., pp. 293–94.
35. Kohlschmidt, pp. 417–23; Newald, pp. 70–72.
36. Hernadi, pp. 155–56.
37. Kohlschmidt, p. 418; Newald, p. 70.
38. Wucherpfennig, pp. 57–58.
39. Wucherpfennig, p. 58.
40. Jacob Grimm and Wilhelm Grimm, *Deutsches Wörterbuch* (Leipzig: Hirzel, 1854–1961), vol. 14, section 1, part 1, cols. 1012–1045.
41. Grimm and Grimm, 14: col. 1042.
42. Grimm and Grimm, 14: col. 1030.
43. For example, Kohlschmidt, p. 411.
44. Wucherpfennig, pp. 58–60.

## Conclusion

1. Reuter and Rieck, *Geschichte der deutschen Literatur*, p. 311.
2. Dieter Borchmeyer, "Lessing und sein Umkreis," in *Geschichte der deutschen Literatur vom 18. Jahrhundert bis zur Gegenwart*, ed. Viktor Žmegač (Königstein: Athenäum, 1978), I, 1, 118.

# Bibliography

Adler, H. G. *The Jews in Germany: From the Enlightenment to National Socialism.* Notre Dame, Indiana: Notre Dame Press, 1969.
Allerdissen, Rolf. *Die Reise als Flucht: Zu Schnabels "Insel Felsenburg" und Thümmels "Reise in die mittäglichen Provinzen von Frankreich."* Berne: Lang, 1975.
Aquinas, Saint Thomas. *Summa Theologiae.* New York and London: McGraw-Hill, Blackfriars, and Eyre and Spottiswoode, 1975.
Arntzen, Helmut. *Die ernste Komödie: Das deutsche Lustspiel von Lessing bis Kleist.* Munich: Nymphenburg, 1968.
Baasch, Ernst. "Der Kaufmann in der deutschen Romanliteratur des 18. Jahrhunderts." In *Aus Sozial- und Wirtschaftsgeschichte: Gedächtnisschrift für Georg von Below.* Stuttgart: Kohlhammer, 1928.
Balet, Leo. *Die Verbürgerlichung der deutschen Kunst, Literatur und Musik im 18. Jahrhundert.* Strasbourg: Heitz, 1936.
Barner, Wilfried, Gunter Grimm, Helmuth Kiesel, and Martin Kramer. *Lessing: Epoche – Werk – Wirkung.* Munich: Beck, 1975.
Baron, Salo W., and Arcadius Kahan. *Economic History of the Jews.* New York: Schocken, 1975.
Baumgart, Peter. "Absoluter Staat und Judenemanzipation in Brandenburg-Preußen." *Jahrbuch für die Geschichte Mittel- und Ostdeutschlands* 13–14 (1965), pp. 60-87.
Biedermann, Karl. *Deutschland im achtzehnten Jahrhundert.* 2d ed. Leipzig: Weber, 1880.
Birus, Hendrik. *Poetische Namengebung: Zur Bedeutung der Namen in Lessings "Nathan der Weise."* Göttingen: Vandenhoeck und Ruprecht, 1978.
Blackall, Eric H. *The Emergence of German as a Literary Language 1700–75.* Cambridge: University Press, 1959.
Böckmann, Paul. "Anfänge der Naturlyrik bei Brockes, Haller und Günther." In *Literatur und Geistesgeschichte: Festgabe für Heinz Otto Bürger.* Ed. Reinhold Grimm and Conrad Wiedemann. Berlin: Schmidt, 1968.
Bonjour, E., H. S. Offler, and G. R. Potter. *A Short History of Switzerland.* Oxford: University Press, 1952.
Borchmeyer, Dieter. "Lessing und sein Umkreis." In *Geschichte der deutschen Literatur vom 18. Jahrhundert bis zur Gegenwart.* Ed. Viktor Žmegač. Königstein: Athenäum, 1978.
Borkenstein, Hinrich. *Der Bookesbeutel.* Ed. Franz Ferdinand Heitmüller. 1896; rpt. Nendeln, Liechtenstein: Kraus, 1968.
Briegleb, Klaus. *Lessings Anfänge 1742–1746: Zur Grundlegung kritischer Sprachdemokratie.* Frankfurt/M: Athenäum, 1971.

Brüggemann, Diethelm. *Die sächsische Komödie: Studien zum Sprachstil.* Cologne: Böhlau, 1970.

Brüggemann, Fritz. "Einführung" to *Das Leben der schwedischen Gräfin von G\*\*\** by Christian Fürchtegott Gellert. In *Deutsche Literatur in Entwicklungsreihen.* Series: "Aufklärung." Vol. 5, *Die bürgerliche Gemeinschaftskultur der vierziger Jahre.* Ed. Fritz Brüggemann. Leipzig: Reclam, 1933.

Bruford, Walter Horace. *Germany in the Eighteenth Century: The Social Background of the Literary Revival.* Cambridge: University Press, 1965.

Brunner, Horst. *Die poetische Insel: Inseln und Inselvorstellungen in der deutschen Literatur.* Stuttgart: Metzler, 1967.

Campe, Joachim Heinrich. *Wörterbuch der Deutschen Sprache.* 1807; rpt. Hildesheim: Olms, 1969.

Catholy, Eckehard. "Die deutsche Komödie vor Lessing." In *Die deutsche Komödie: Vom Mittelalter bis zur Gegenwart.* Ed. Walter Hinck. Düsseldorf: Bagel, 1977.

Currie, Pamela. "Moral Weeklies and the Reading Public in Germany, 1711-1750." *Oxford German Studies* 3 (1968), pp. 69-86.

Danzel, Theodor Wilhelm. *Gotthold Ephraim Lessing: Sein Leben und seine Werke.* Ed. Robert Boxberger and Wendelin von Maltzahn. 2d ed. Vol. 1. Berlin: Hofmann, 1880.

Dorwart, Reinhold August. *The Prussian Welfare State before 1740.* Cambridge, Mass.: Harvard University Press, 1971.

Dunkle, Harvey I. "Lessing's 'Die Juden': An Original Experiment." *Monatshefte* 49, no. 6 (1957), pp. 323-29.

Elias, Norbert. *Die höfische Gesellschaft: Untersuchungen zur Soziologie des Königtums und der höfischen Aristokratie mit einer Einleitung: Soziologie und Geschichtswissenschaft.* Neuwied and Berlin: Luchterhand, 1969.

Engel, E. J. "Young Lessing as Literary Critic (1749-1755)." *Lessing Yearbook* 11 (1979), pp. 69-82.

Engelsing, Rolf. *Analphabetentum und Lektüre: Zur Sozialgeschichte des Lesers in Deutschland zwischen feudaler und industrieller Gesellschaft.* Stuttgart: Metzler, 1973.

———. *Der Bürger als Leser: Lesergeschichte in Deutschland 1500-1800.* Stuttgart: Metzler, 1974.

———. *Sozial- und Wirtschaftsgeschichte Deutschlands.* 2d ed. Göttingen: Vandenhoeck und Ruprecht, 1976.

Feilchenfeld, Alfred. "Hamburg." *The Jewish Encyclopedia.* New York and London: Funk and Wagnalls, 1912.

Freier, Hans. *Kritische Poetik: Legitimation und Kritik in Gottscheds Dichtkunst.* Stuttgart: Metzler, 1973.

Friederici, Hans. *Das deutsche bürgerliche Lustspiel der Frühaufklärung (1736-1750) unter besonderer Berücksichtigung seiner Anschauungen von der Gesellschaft.* Halle/Saale: Niemeyer, 1957.

Gebauer, Curt. "Studien zur Geschichte der bürgerlichen Sittenreform des 18. Jahrhunderts." *Archiv für Kulturgeschichte* 15 (1923), pp. 97-116.

Geiger, Ludwig. *Berlin 1688–1840: Geschichte des geistigen Lebens der preußischen Hauptstadt.* Berlin: Paetel, 1892.
Gellert, Christian Fürchtegott. *Das Leben der schwedischen Gräfin von G\*\*\*.* In *Deutsche Literatur in Entwicklungsreihen.* Series: "Aufklärung." Vol. 5, *Die bürgerliche Gemeinschaftskultur der vierziger Jahre.* Ed. Fritz Brüggemann. Leipzig: Reclam, 1933.
Glinski, Gerhard von. *Die Königsberger Kaufmannschaft des 17. und 18. Jahrhunderts.* Marburg/L: Herder-Institut, 1964.
Glückel of Hameln. *Memoirs.* Trans. Marvin Lowenthal. 1932; rpt. New York: Schocken, 1977.
Göpfert, Herbert G. "Lesegesellschaften im 18. Jahrhundert." In *Dichtung Sprache Gesellschaft: Akten des IV. Internationalen Germanisten-Kongresses 1970 in Princeton.* Ed. Victor Lange and Hans-Gert Roloff. Frankfurt/M: Athenäum, 1971.
Goethe, Johann Wolfgang von. *Werke: Hamburger Ausgabe in 14 Bänden.* Ed. Erich Trunz. 10th ed. Munich: Beck, 1981.
Götze, Alfred, ed. *Trübners Deutsches Wörterbuch.* Berlin: de Gruyter, 1939.
Gottsched, Luise Adelgunde Viktoria. *Die Hausfranzösinn, oder die Mammsell.* In *Die Deutsche Schaubühne, nach den Regeln und Mustern der Alten.* Ed. Johann Christoph Gottsched. 2d. ed. Vol. 5. Leipzig: Breitkopf, 1749.
———. *Der Witzling.* Ed. Wolfgang Hecht. Berlin: de Gruyter, 1962.
Grimm, Jacob, and Wilhelm Grimm. *Deutsches Wörterbuch.* Leipzig: Hirzel, 1854–1961.
Guthke, Karl S. *Haller und die Literatur.* Göttingen: Vandenhoeck und Ruprecht, 1962.
———, ed. *Hallers Literaturkritik.* Tübingen: Niemeyer, 1970.
———. "Kommentar." In *Werke* by Gotthold Ephraim Lessing. Ed. Herbert G. Göpfert. Vol. 2. Munich: Hanser, 1971.
———. *Literarisches Leben im achtzehnten Jahrhundert in Deutschland und in der Schweiz.* Berne and Munich: Francke, 1975.
———. "Lessing und das Judentum: Rezeption. Dramatik und Kritik. Krypto-Spinozismus." In *Wolfenbütteler Studien zur Aufklärung.* Vol. 4, *Judentum im Zeitalter der Aufklärung.* Ed. Günter Schulz. Bremen: Jacobi, 1977.
———. *Gotthold Ephraim Lessing.* 3d. ed. Stuttgart: Metzler, 1979.
Haas, Roland. *Lesend wird sich der Bürger seiner Welt bewußt: Der Schriftsteller Johann Gottfried Schnabel und die deutsche Entwicklung des Bürgertums in der ersten Hälfte des 18. Jahrhunderts.* Frankfurt/M, Berne, and Las Vegas: Lang, 1977.
Haas, Rosemarie. "Die Landschaft auf der Insel Felsenburg." *Zeitschrift für deutsches Altertum und deutsche Literatur* 91, no. 1 (1961), pp. 63–84.
Haller, Albrecht von. *Albrecht von Hallers Gedichte.* Ed. Ludwig Hirzel. Frauenfeld: Huber, 1882.
———. "Die Alpen." In *Vorboten der bürgerlichen Kultur: Johann Gottfried Schnabel und Albrecht von Haller.* Ed. Fritz Brüggemann. Darmstadt:

Wissenschaftliche Buchgesellschaft, 1964.
Hauser, Arnold. *Soziologie der Kunst*. Munich: Beck, 1974.
Henderson, W. O. *Studies in the Economic Policy of Frederick the Great*. London: Cass, 1963.
Hernadi, Paul. "Nathan der Bürger: Lessings Mythos vom aufgeklärten Kaufmann." *Lessing Yearbook* 3 (1971), pp. 151–59.
Hettner, Hermann. *Geschichte der deutschen Literatur im 18. Jahrhundert*. Vol. 1. Leipzig: List, 1928.
Hillen, Gerd. *Lessing Chronik: Daten zu Leben und Werk*. Munich and Vienna: Hanser, 1979.
Hinck, Walter. *Das deutsche Lustspiel des 17. und 18. Jahrhunderts und die italienische Komödie: Commedia dell' Arte und Théâtre Italien*. Stuttgart: Metzler, 1965.
―――, ed. *Die deutsche Komödie: Vom Mittelalter bis zur Gegenwart*. Düsseldorf: Bagel, 1977.
Holl, Karl. *Geschichte des deutschen Lustspiels*. 1923; rpt. Darmstadt: Wissenschaftliche Buchgesellschaft, 1964.
Hudtwalcker, Johann Michael. "Elternhaus und Jugendjahre eines Hamburger Kaufmanns in der Mitte des 18. Jahrhunderts." In *Kaufleute zu Haus und über See: Hamburgische Zeugnisse des 17., 18. und 19. Jahrhunderts*. Ed. Percy Ernst Schramm. Hamburg: Hoffmann und Campe, 1949.
Jacobs, Jürgen. *Prosa der Aufklärung: Moralische Wochenschriften, Autobiographie, Satire, Roman: Kommentar zu einer Epoche*. Munich: Winkler, 1976.
Jersch-Wenzel, Stefi. "Der Einfluß zugewanderter Minoritäten als Wirtschaftsgruppen auf die Berliner Wirtschaft in vor- und frühindustrieller Zeit." In *Untersuchungen zur Geschichte der frühen Industrialisierung vornehmlich im Wirtschaftsraum Berlin/Brandenburg*. Ed. Otto Büsch. Berlin: Colloquium, 1971.
Katz, Jacob. "Echte und imaginäre Beziehungen zwischen Freimaurerei und Judentum." In *Geheime Gesellschaften*. Ed. Peter Christian Ludz. Heidelberg: Schneider, 1979.
Kellenbenz, Hermann. *Sephardim an der unteren Elbe: Ihre wirtschaftliche und politische Bedeutung vom Ende des 16. bis zum Beginn des 18. Jahrhunderts*. Wiesbaden: Steiner, 1958.
Kies, Paul P. "The Sources of Lessing's *Die Juden*." *Philological Quarterly* 6, no. 4 (1927), pp. 406–10.
Kiesel, Helmuth, and Paul Münch. *Gesellschaft und Literatur im 18. Jahrhundert: Voraussetzungen und Entstehung des literarischen Markts in Deutschland*. Munich: Beck, 1977.
Kimpel, Dieter. *Der Roman der Aufklärung*. Stuttgart: Metzler, 1967.
Kisch, Guido. *The Jews in Medieval Germany: A Study of Their Legal and Social Status*. 2d ed. New York: Ktav, 1970.
Knopf, Jan. *Frühzeit des Bürgers: Erfahrene und verleugnete Realität in den Romanen Wickrams, Grimmelshausens, Schnabels*. Stuttgart: Metzler, 1978.
Kober, Adolf. "Hamburg." *The Universal Jewish Encyclopedia*. New York: Universal Jewish Encyclopedia, 1941.

Kockjoy, Wolfgang. *Der deutsche Kaufmannsroman: Versuch einer kultur- und geistesgeschichtlichen genetischen Darstellung.* Strasbourg: Heitz, 1933.

König, Dominik von. *Natürlichkeit und Wirklichkeit: Studien zu Lessings "Nathan der Weise."* Bonn: Bouvier, 1976.

Kohlschmidt, Werner. *Dichter, Tradition und Zeitgeist: Gesammelte Studien zur Literaturgeschichte.* Berne and Munich: Francke, 1965.

———. *Geschichte der deutschen Literatur vom Barock bis zur Klassik.* Stuttgart: Reclam, 1965.

Kopitzsch, Franklin. "Einleitung: Die Sozialgeschichte der deutschen Aufklärung als Forschungsaufgabe." In *Aufklärung, Absolutismus und Bürgertum in Deutschland.* Ed. Franklin Kopitzsch. Munich: Nymphenburg, 1976.

Kroker, Ernst. *Handelsgeschichte der Stadt Leipzig: Die Entwicklung des Leipziger Handels und der Leipziger Messen von der Gründung der Stadt bis auf die Gegenwart.* Leipzig: Bielefeld, 1925.

Krosigk, Lutz Graf Schwerin von. *Alles auf Wagnis: Der Kaufmann gestern, heute und morgen.* Tübingen: Wunderlich, 1963.

Lappert, Hans-Ulrich. *G. E. Lessings Jugendlustspiele und die Komödientheorie der frühen Aufklärung.* Zurich: Juris, 1968.

Lessing, Gotthold Ephraim. *Gotthold Ephraim Lessings sämtliche Schriften.* Ed. Karl Lachmann. 3d ed. reedited by Franz Muncker. Vols. 1 and 2. Stuttgart: Göschen, 1886.

Lütge, Friedrich. *Deutsche Sozial- und Wirtschaftsgeschichte: Ein Überblick.* 3d ed. Berlin: Springer, 1966.

Luther, Martin. "Von Kaufshandlung und Wucher: 1524." In *Martin Luther, Werke.* Ed. Otto Clemen and Albert Leitzmann. 5th ed. Vol. 3. Berlin: de Gruyter, 1959.

Mann, Otto, and Rotraut Straube-Mann. *Lessing-Kommentar.* Munich: Winkler, 1971.

Martens, Wolfgang. *Die Botschaft der Tugend: Die Aufklärung im Spiegel der deutschen moralischen Wochenschriften.* Stuttgart: Metzler, 1968.

———. "Bürgerlichkeit in der frühen Aufklärung." In *Aufklärung, Absolutismus und Bürgertum in Deutschland.* Ed. Franklin Kopitzsch. Munich: Nymphenburg, 1976.

Martini, Fritz. *Lustspiele – und das Lustspiel.* Stuttgart: Klett, 1974.

Menhennet, Alan. *Order and Freedom: Literature and Society in Germany from 1720 to 1805.* London: Weidenfeld and Nicolson, 1973.

Metzger, Michael M. *Lessing and the Language of Comedy.* The Hague: Mouton, 1966.

Meyer, Herman. "Hütte und Palast in der Dichtung des 18. Jahrhunderts." In *Formenwandel: Festschrift zum 65. Geburtstag von Paul Böckmann.* Ed. Walter Müller-Seidel. Hamburg: Hoffmann und Campe, 1964.

Meyer-Krentler, Eckhardt. *Der andere Roman: Gellerts "Schwedische Gräfin": Von der aufklärerischen Propaganda gegen den "Roman" zur empfindsamen Erlebnisdichtung.* Göppingen: Kümmerle, 1974.

Mosse, George L. *Germans and Jews.* New York: Grosset and Dunlap, 1970.

Mottek, Hans. *Wirtschaftsgeschichte Deutschlands: Ein Grundriß.* Berlin: VEB

## Bibliography

Deutscher Verlag der Wissenschaften, 1964.
Müller, Andreas. *Landschaftserlebnis und Landschaftsbild: Studien zur deutschen Dichtung des 18. Jahrhunderts und der Romantik.* Hechingen: Kohlhammer, 1955.
Naumann, Dietrich. *Politik und Moral: Studien zur Utopie der deutschen Aufklärung.* Heidelberg: Winter, 1977.
Neuhaus-Koch, Ariane. *G. E. Lessing: Die Sozialstrukturen in seinen Dramen.* Bonn: Bouvier, 1977.
Newald, Richard. *Die deutsche Literatur vom Späthumanismus zur Empfindsamkeit.* 6th ed. Vol. 5 of *Geschichte der deutschen Literatur von den Anfängen bis zur Gegenwart* by Helmut de Boor and Richard Newald. Munich: Beck, 1967.
Oehlke, Waldemar. *Lessing und seine Zeit.* Munich: Beck, 1919.
Peschken, Bernd. "Lessings Anfang in Berlin im sozialgeschichtlichen Zusammenhang." In *Analecta Helvetica et Germanica: Eine Festschrift zu Ehren von Hermann Boeschenstein.* Ed. A. Arnold, H. Eichner, E. Heier, and S. Hoefert. Bonn: Bouvier, 1979.
Plautus, Titus Maccius. *Trinummus.* In *Plautus.* Edited and translated by Paul Nixon. London and Cambridge, Mass.: Heinemann and Harvard University Press, 1938.
Pollack, Herman. *Jewish Folkways in Germanic Lands (1648–1806): Studies in Aspects of Daily Life.* Cambridge, Mass.: M.I.T. Press, 1971.
Raabe, Paul. "Buchproduktion und Lesepublikum in Deutschland 1770–1780." *Philobiblon* 21, no. 1 (1977), pp. 2–16.
Rengstorf, Karl Heinrich. "Judentum im Zeitalter der Aufklärung: Geschichtliche Voraussetzungen und einige zentrale Probleme." In *Judentum im Zeitalter der Aufklärung.* Ed. Günter Schulz. Bremen and Wolfenbüttel: Jacobi, 1977.
Rentschler, Robert. "Lisette, the Laugher." *Lessing Yearbook* 10 (1978), pp. 46–64.
Reuter, Hans-Heinrich, and Werner Rieck. *Geschichte der deutschen Literatur: Vom Ausgang des 17. Jahrhunderts bis 1789.* Berlin: Volk und Wissen Volkseigener Verlag, 1979.
Review of *Lessings Schrifften*, T. 4. *Göttingische Anzeigen von gelehrten Sachen*, no. 70, 13 June 1754.
Review of *Lessings Schrifften*, T. 4. *Jenaische gelehrte Zeitungen*, no. 66, 24 August 1754.
Richel, Veronica C. *Luise Gottsched: A Reconsideration.* Berne: Lang, 1973.
Rieck, Werner. *Johann Christoph Gottsched: Eine kritische Würdigung seines Werkes.* Berlin: Akademie-Verlag, 1972.
———. "Literaturgesellschaftliche Prozesse in der deutschen Frühaufklärung." In *Aufklärung, Absolutismus und Bürgertum in Deutschland.* Ed. Franklin Kopitzsch. Munich: Nymphenburg, 1976.
Riedel, Volker. *Lessing und die römische Literatur.* Weimar: Böhlau, 1976.
Rytz, Hans Rudolf. *Geistliche des alten Bern zwischen Merkantilismus und Physiokratie: Ein Beitrag zur Schweizer Sozialgeschichte des 18. Jahrhunderts.*

Basle and Stuttgart: Helbing und Lichtenhahn, 1971.
Saine, Thomas P. "Scholarship on the German Enlightenment as Cultural History." *Lessing Yearbook* 6 (1974), pp. 139–49.
Sauder, Gerhard. "Sozialgeschichtliche Aspekte der Literatur im 18. Jahrhundert." *Internationales Archiv für Sozialgeschichte der deutschen Literatur* 4 (1979), pp. 197–241.
Schaer, Wolfgang. *Die Gesellschaft im deutschen bürgerlichen Drama des 18. Jahrhunderts: Grundlagen und Bedrohung im Spiegel der dramatischen Literatur.* Bonn: Bouvier, 1963.
Schenda, Rudolf. *Volk ohne Buch: Studien zur Sozialgeschichte der populären Lesestoffe 1770–1910.* Frankfurt/M: Klostermann, 1970.
Schlegel, Johann Elias. *Der Geschäfftige Müßiggänger.* In J. E. Schlegel, *Werke*. Ed. Johann Heinrich Schlegel. Vol. 2. Copenhagen and Leipzig: Proft und Rothen, 1773.
Schlenther, Paul. *Frau Gottsched und die bürgerliche Komödie: Ein Kulturbild aus der Zopfzeit.* Berlin: Hertz, 1886.
Schlingmann, Carsten. *Gellert: Eine literarhistorische Revision.* Bad Homburg: Gehlen, 1967.
Schmidt, Erich. *Lessing: Geschichte seines Lebens und seiner Schriften.* Berlin: Weidmann, 1884.
Schnabel, Johann Gottfried. *Insel Felsenburg.* Ed. Wilhelm Voßkamp. Reinbek: Rowohlt, 1969.
―――. *Insel Felsenburg.* Ed. Volker Meid and Ingeborg Springer-Strand. Stuttgart: Reclam, 1979.
Schneider, Ferdinand Josef. *Die deutsche Dichtung der Aufklärungszeit 1700–1775.* 2d ed. Stuttgart: Metzler, 1948.
Schneider, Heinrich. *Quest for Mysteries: The Masonic Background for Literature in Eighteenth-Century German.* Ithaca, New York: Cornell University Press, 1947.
Schoeps, Julius H. "Aufklärung, Judentum und Emanzipation." In *Judentum im Zeitalter der Aufklärung.* Ed. Günter Schulz. Bremen and Wolfenbüttel: Jacobi, 1977.
Schulte-Sasse, Jochen. "Drama." In *Deutsche Aufklärung bis zur französischen Revolution 1680–1789.* Ed. Rolf Grimminger. Munich: Hanser, 1980.
Seifert, Siegfried. *Lessing-Bibliographie.* Berlin and Weimar: Aufbau-Verlag, 1973.
Seneca, Lucius Annaeus. *Ad Lucilium epistulae morales.* Edited and translated by Richard M. Gummere. Cambridge, Mass.: Harvard University Press, 1970.
Siegrist, Christoph. *Albrecht von Haller.* Stuttgart: Metzler, 1967.
Sombart, Werner. *Die Juden und das Wirtschaftsleben.* Leipzig: Duncker und Humblot, 1911.
Steffen, Hans, ed. *Das deutsche Lustspiel.* Göttingen: Vandenhoeck und Ruprecht, 1968.
Steinhausen, Georg. *Der Kaufmann in der deutschen Vergangenheit.* Leipzig: Diederichs, 1899.

Steinmetz, Horst. *Die Komödie der Aufklärung*. 2d ed. Stuttgart: Metzler, 1971.
Stern, Selma. *The Court Jew: A Contribution to the Period of Absolutism in Central Europe*. Trans. Ralph Weiman. Philadelphia: Jewish Publication Society of America, 1950.
_____. *Der preußische Staat und die Juden: Zweiter Teil: Die Zeit Friedrich Wilhelms I*. Tübingen: Mohr, 1962.
_____. *Der preußische Staat und die Juden: Dritter Teil: Die Zeit Friedrichs des Großen*. Tübingen: Mohr, 1971.
Szondi, Peter. *Die Theorie des bürgerlichen Trauerspiels im 18. Jahrhundert: Der Kaufmann, der Hausvater und der Hofmeister*. Frankfurt/M: Suhrkamp, 1974.
Tawney, R. H. *Religion and the Rise of Capitalism: A Historical Study*. New York: Harcourt and Brace, 1926.
Trautwein, Wolfgang. "Zwischen Typenlustspiel und ernster Komödie: Zur produktiven Verletzung von Gattungsmustern in Lessings 'Die Juden.'" *Jahrbuch der deutschen Schillergesellschaft* 24 (1980), pp. 1–14.
Van Abbé, D. M. "Some Unspoken Assumptions in Gellert's 'Schwedische Gräfin.'" *Orbis Litterarum* 28 (1973), pp. 113–23.
Van Cleve, John Walter. *Harlequin Besieged: The Reception of Comedy in Germany during the Early Enlightenment*. Berne: Lang, 1980.
_____. "Social Climbing during the Age of Absolutism: Personality Distortion and Career Advancement in J. C. Krüger's *Die Candidaten*." *Orbis Litterarum* 35 (1980), pp. 318–26.
Vierhaus, Rudolf. "Deutschland im 18. Jahrhundert: Soziales Gefüge, politische Verfassung, geistige Bewegung." In *Aufklärung, Absolutismus und Bürgertum in Deutschland*. Ed. Franklin Kopitzsch. Munich: Nymphenburg, 1976.
Voßkamp, Wilhelm. "Theorie und Praxis der literarischen Fiktion in Johann Gottfried Schnabels Roman 'Die Insel Felsenburg.'" *Germanisch-Romanische Monatsschrift* 18, no. 2 (1968), pp. 131–52.
Ward, Albert. *Book Production, Fiction and the German Reading Public, 1740–1800*. Oxford: Clarendon, 1974.
Weber, Max. *Die protestantische Ethik und der Geist des Kapitalismus*. Vol. 1 of M. Weber, *Gesammelte Aufsätze zur Religionssoziologie*. Tübingen: Mohr, 1920.
Weber-Kellermann, Ingeborg. *Die deutsche Familie: Versuch einer Sozialgeschichte*. Frankfurt/M: Suhrkamp, 1974.
Wicke, Günter. *Die Struktur des deutschen Lustspiels der Aufklärung: Versuch einer Typologie*. Bonn: Bouvier, 1965.
Wiskemann, Erwin. *Hamburg und die Welthandelspolitik von den Anfängen bis zur Gegenwart*. Hamburg: Friederichsen und de Gruyter, 1929.
Witkowski, Georg. *Geschichte des literarischen Lebens in Leipzig*. Leipzig and Berlin: Teubner, 1909.
Wolf, Peter. *Die Dramen Johann Elias Schlegels: Ein Beitrag zur Geschichte des Dramas im 18. Jahrhundert*. Zurich: Atlantis, 1964.
Wucherpfennig, Wolf. "Nathan, der weise Händler." In *Akten des VI. Interna-*

*tionalen Germanisten-Kongresses Basel 1980.* Ed. Hans-Gert Roloff and Heinz Rupp. Berne: Lang, 1980.

Zorn, Wolfgang. "Schwerpunkte der deutschen Ausfuhrindustrie im 18. Jahrhundert." *Jahrbücher für Nationalökonomie und Statistik* 173, no. 5 (1961), pp. 422–47.

———. "Sozialgeschichte 1648–1800." In *Handbuch der deutschen Wirtschafts- und Sozialgeschichte.* Ed. Hermann Aubin and Wolfgang Zorn. Stuttgart: Union, 1971.

# Index

Abensur family, 34
Addison, Joseph, 40
Adler, H. G., 145 (n. 104), 157
Allerdissen, Rolf, 62, 148 (n. 15), 157
Alps, 45, 47–58, 138
Altona, 22, 34, 73
Americas, 14, 33, 36, 38
Amsterdam, 11, 33, 64, 93, 94, 99, 100, 103
Aquinas, Saint Thomas, 38, 157
  *Summa Theologiae*, 147 (n. 128), 157
Archangel, 100, 101
Arminius, 13
Arnold, A., 152 (n. 3), 162
Arntzen, Helmut, 157
Ashkenazim, 34
Asia Minor, 8
Atlantic Ocean, 65
Aubin, Hermann, 141 (n. 8), 165
Augsburg, 3
Augustus II (the Strong, Elector of Saxony), 15, 16, 35

Baasch, Ernst, 147 (n. 137), 157
Babylon, 129
Balet, Leo, 3, 4, 15, 41, 141 (n. 1), 141 (n. 9), 143 (n. 46), 143 (n. 55), 157
Baltic Sea, 3
Bank of England, 9
Barner, Wilfried, 141 (n. 3), 142 (n. 18), 145 (n. 96), 153 (n. 9), 155 (n. 34), 157
Baron, Salo W., 146 (nn. 113–14), 157
Basle, 45
Baumgart, Peter, 37, 146 (nn. 118–19), 146 (n. 122), 157
Below, Georg von, 147 (n. 137)
"Bergenfahrer-Gesellschaft," 19
Berlin, 6, 15–18, 35–37, 109, 119, 127, 152 (n. 3)
*Berlinische Nachrichten von Staats- und gelehrten Sachen* ("Spenersche Zeitung"), 17
*Berlinische privilegirte Staats- und gelehrte Zeitung* ("Vossische Zeitung"), 17

Berne, xiv, 6, 7, 19–20, 39, 45–58, 144 (n. 65)
Bethmann family, 18
Bible, 6, 22, 24, 29, 38
Biedermann, Karl, 142 (n. 31), 143 (n. 51), 144 (n. 62), 157
Birus, Hendrik, 154 (n. 17), 157
Blackall, Eric H., 157
Blankenburg, Christian Friedrich von, 93
Böckmann, Paul, 148 (nn. 4–6), 157, 161
Boeschenstein, Hermann, 152 (n. 3)
Bonjour, E., 144 (n. 65), 157
Boor, Helmut de, 151 (n. 2), 162
Borchmeyer, Dieter, 137, 155 (n. 2), 157
Borkenstein, Hinrich, 70, 71–76, 81, 90, 109, 149, 157
  *Der Bookesbeutel*, 71–76, 81, 85, 90, 139, 149 (n. 3)
Boxberger, Robert, 152 (n. 4), 158
Braunschweig, 34
Bremen, 19, 21–22, 60
*Bremer wöchentliche Nachrichten*, 19
Breslau, 6
Briegleb, Klaus, 152 (n. 2), 157
Brockes, Barthold Hinrich, 13, 29
Brüggemann, Diethelm, 149 (n. 2), 158
Brüggemann, Fritz, 148 (n. 2), 151 (n. 8), 151–52 (n. 12), 158, 159
Bruford, Walter Horace, 158
Brunner, Horst, 149 (n. 18), 158
Bürger, Heinz Otto, 148 (n. 5), 157
Büsch, Otto, 143 (n. 49), 160
Buxtehude, Dietrich, 13

Calvinism, 146 (n. 125)
Campe, Joachim Heinrich, 158
Castro, Rodrigo de, 33
Catholy, Eckehard, 150 (n. 9), 158
Ceylon, 60
Charlemagne, 13
Charles VI (Holy Roman Emperor), 15
China, 129
Christoph Ludwig (Count of Stolberg), 20, 67–68

## Index

Clemen, Otto, 147 (n. 130), 161
Colbertism, 6, 19, 39, 45–46, 47, 51
"Compagnie prussienne," 17
Crusades, 129
Currie, Pamela, 19, 29, 143 (n. 37), 144 (n. 64), 145 (n. 95), 158

Danzel, Theodor Wilhelm, 110, 152 (n. 4), 158
Davel, Abraham, 20, 46, 48, 50
Defoe, Daniel, 59
  *Robinson Crusoe*, 59
Denmark, 34
Descartes, René, 91
Dessau, 35
"Deutsche Gesellschaft," 14
Dorwart, Reinhold August, 141–42 (n. 14), 143 (n. 51), 158
Dresden, 6, 14, 15
Dunkle, Harvey I., 118, 154 (n. 17), 158

East Asia, 3, 61, 62, 64, 102
Edict of Potsdam, 15
Egypt, 131
Eichner, H., 152 (n. 3), 162
Elbe River, 11, 21, 120
Elias, Norbert, 5, 141 (n. 12), 158
Engel, E. J., 154 (n. 18), 158
Engelsing, Rolf, 6, 21–22, 23, 141 (n. 6), 142 (n. 17), 142 (n. 19), 142 (n. 21), 144 (nn. 71–74), 144 (n. 86), 147 (n. 133), 158
England, xiii, 3, 4, 9, 12, 14, 16, 19, 40, 45, 62–63, 100, 112, 113, 136
"Englische Kompanie," 19
Epictetus, 50, 51
*Epistolae obscurorum virorum*, 89
Eugene, Prince of Savoy, 59

Far East, 17
Farquhar, George, 118
Feilchenfeld, Alfred, 146 (n. 111), 158
Feuchtwanger, Lion, 146 (n. 110)
  *Jud Süß*, 146 (n. 110)
Fleischer and Kober (company), 15
Fontane, Theodor, 27–28
France, xiii, 3, 4, 6, 14, 18, 19, 20, 39, 45
Francke, August Hermann, 91
Frankfurt/Main, 7, 18, 32, 34, 82, 119
Frankfurt/Oder, 64, 65

Freier, Hans, 149 (n. 1), 158
Friederici, Hans, 149 (n. 5), 158
Friedrich II (the Great, King of Prussia), 16–17, 25, 36–37, 39, 146 (n. 118), 146 (n. 121)
Friedrich III (Elector of Brandenburg, King Friedrich I of Prussia), 36
Friedrich Wilhelm (the Great Elector), 15–16, 35–36, 143 (n. 51), 146 (n. 118)
Friedrich Wilhelm I (King of Prussia), 16, 36, 146 (n. 118), 146 (n. 121)

Gebauer, Curt, 26, 144 (n. 85), 144 (n. 91), 158
Geiger, Ludwig, 143 (nn. 51–52), 146 (n. 20), 159
Gellert, Christian Fürchtegott, 19, 70, 91–108, 122, 136, 138, 139, 140, 151, 151 (n. 9), 158, 159
  *Fabeln*, 92
  *Das Leben der schwedischen Gräfin von G\*\*\**, 91–108, 122, 123, 126, 136, 137, 138, 139, 151 (n. 8), 151–52 (n. 12), 159
Glinski, Gerhard von, 144 (n. 82), 159
Glückel of Hameln, 34, 146 (n. 112), 146 (n. 116), 159
  *Memoirs*, 34, 35, 159
Göpfert, Herbert G., 145 (n. 97), 159
Goethe, Johann Wolfgang von, xiii, 32, 159
  *Aus meinem Leben Dichtung und Wahrheit*, 32, 145 (n. 106)
  *Werke: Hamburger Ausgabe in 14 Bänden*, 159
*Göttingische Anzeigen von gelehrten Sachen*, 106, 125, 152 (n. 16), 162
Götze, Alfred, 149 (n. 4), 159
Gompertz family, 36
Gottsched, Johann Christoph, 14, 19, 30, 70–71, 76–77, 83, 86, 89, 150 (n. 15), 150 (n. 17), 159
  *Die Deutsche Schaubühne*, 70, 77, 83, 88, 90, 150 (n. 11), 159
  *Versuch einer critischen Dichtkunst vor die Deutschen*, 70
  *Sterbender Cato*, 77
Gottsched, Luise Adelgunde Viktoria, 70, 76–82, 85–90, 109, 139, 149, 150 (nn. 11–12), 159

Index 169

*Die Hausfranzösinn, oder die Mammsell*, 77–82, 85, 139, 150 (n. 12), 159
*Der Witzling*, 85–90, 99–100, 150 (n. 17), 159
Gotzkowsky, Johann Ernst, 17
Grimm, Gunter, 141 (n. 3), 145 (n. 96), 153 (n. 9), 155 (n. 34), 157
Grimm, Jacob and Wilhelm, 132–33, 146 (n. 115), 147 (n. 130), 149 (n. 4), 155 (nn. 40–42), 159
Grimm, Reinhold, 148 (n. 5), 157
Grimminger, Rolf, 150 (n. 6), 163
Gummere, Richard M., 147 (n. 127), 163
Gumpertz, Aron Emmerich, 118, 125
Guthke, Karl S., 31, 127, 145 (n. 101), 148 (n. 9), 152 (n. 1), 154 (n. 16), 154 (n. 28), 159

Haas, Roland, 149 (n. 16), 159
Haas, Rosemarie, 148 (n. 12), 159
Habsburg, 4
Händel, Georg Friedrich, 13
Hagedorn, Friedrich von, 13, 19
The Hague, 99, 102
Halle/Saale, 59
Haller, Albrecht von, xiii, 19, 40–41, 45–59, 66, 68–69, 81, 121, 137–38, 139, 147, 148 (n. 9), 159
"Die Alpen," xiv, 40–41, 45–59, 62, 69, 71, 74, 75, 90, 121, 124, 147–48 (n. 2), 159
*Gedichte*, 159
Haller, Niklaus Emanuel, 46, 57
Hamburg, 6, 7, 11–13, 18, 19, 21, 23–25, 26–27, 28, 29, 33–34, 35, 40, 60–61, 71, 72, 73, 74, 75, 120, 122, 127, 143 (n. 38)
Hanseatic League, 3, 12
Harz Mountains, 20, 59
Hauser, Arnold, 160
Hecht, Wolfgang, 150 (n. 17)
Heier, E., 152 (n. 3), 162
Heitmüller, Franz Ferdinand, 149 (n. 3), 157
Henderson, W. O., 143 (n. 54), 143 (n. 56), 147 (n. 135), 160
Henzi, Samuel, 20, 46
Hernadi, Paul, 130, 154 (n. 31), 155 (nn. 33–34), 155 (n. 36), 160
Hettner, Hermann, 91, 151 (n. 1), 151 (n. 7), 160
Hillen, Gerd, 154 (n. 21), 160
Hinck, Walter, 149 (n. 2), 150 (n. 9), 150 (n. 12), 158, 160
Hirzel, Ludwig, 147 (n. 1), 159
Hobbes, Thomas, 62
Hoefert, S., 152 (n. 3), 162
Hohenzollern, 4
Hohmann, Peter, 15
Holl, Karl, 149 (n. 2), 160
Holland, 3, 18, 34, 59, 93, 97, 100, 104
Holy Roman Empire of the German Nation, 4, 18
Hudtwalcker, Jacob Hinrich, 12, 22–25, 27, 28–29, 31, 61
Hudtwalcker, Johann Michael, 22–25, 26–27, 28–29, 31, 61, 142 (n. 32), 142 (n. 34), 144 (nn. 75–81), 144 (nn. 87–89), 145 (nn. 92–94), 145 (n. 100), 160
Hudtwalcker, Sara Elisabeth, 26–29, 31
Huguenots, 14, 15–16
Hume, David, 8

India, 3, 17, 112, 129
Italy, 14, 17, 78
Itzig family, 36

Jacobs, Jürgen, 148 (n. 13), 160
*Jenaische gelehrte Zeitungen*, 125, 154 (n. 25), 162
Jersch-Wenzel, Stefi, 15, 37, 143 (nn. 49–50), 146 (n. 126), 160
Jerusalem, 129
Judaism, 31–37, 97

Kahan, Arcadius, 146 (nn. 113–14), 157
Kamenz, xiv, 109, 120
Karl Alexander, Duke of Württemberg, 82
Katz, Jacob, 145 (n. 98), 160
Kellenbenz, Hermann, 146 (n. 111), 160
Kiel, 60
Kies, Paul P., 153–54 (n. 16), 160
Kiesel, Helmuth, 92, 141 (n. 3), 141 (n. 14), 142 (n. 18), 142 (n. 22), 143 (n. 48), 144 (n. 58), 144 (nn. 60–61), 145 (n. 96), 151 (n. 4), 153 (n. 9), 155 (n. 34), 157, 160
Kimpel, Dieter, 93, 151 (n. 5), 152 (n. 17), 160

Kisch, Guido, 106, 145 (n. 103), 152 (n. 15), 160
Klopstock, Friedrich Gottlieb, 19
Knopf, Jan, 149 (n. 17), 160
Kober, Adolf, 146 (n. 111), 160
Koch theater troupe (Heinrich Gottfried Koch), 31
Kockjoy, Wolfgang, 147 (n. 137), 161
König, Dominik von, 154 (n. 31), 161
König, Johann Ulrich von, 13
Königsberg, 6
Kohlschmidt, Werner, 142 (n. 36), 148 (n. 3), 152 (n. 13), 155 (n. 35), 155 (n. 37), 155 (n. 43), 161
Kopitzsch, Franklin, 141 (n. 2), 141 (n. 7), 142 (n. 15), 144 (n. 69), 161, 162, 164
Kramer, Martin, 141 (n. 3), 145 (n. 96), 153 (n. 9), 155 (n. 34), 157
Kregel, Johann Ernst, 15
Kroker, Ernst, 15, 143 (n. 42), 143 (nn. 44–45), 143 (n. 47), 146 (n. 115), 161
Krosigk, Lutz von, 11, 142 (nn. 28–29), 144 (n. 83), 161

Lachmann, Karl, 153 (n. 10), 154 (n. 19), 154 (n. 26), 155 (n. 32), 161
Lange, Victor, 145 (n. 97), 159
Lappert, Hans-Ulrich, 152 (n. 3), 161
Lausanne, 46
Lehmann, Bernd, 35
Leibniz, Gottfried Wilhelm, 8, 14
Leiden, 45
Leipzig, 13–15, 17, 18, 33, 34, 35, 60, 71, 72, 85, 86, 119, 120, 122, 127
Leitzmann, Albert, 147 (n. 130), 161
Lenz, Jakob Michael Reinhold, xiii, 70
Lessing, Gotthold Ephraim, xiii, xiv, 17, 27, 41, 70, 109–36, 137–38, 139, 140, 152 (n. 2), 153 (n. 9), 154 (n. 22), 161
    *Die alte Jungfer*, 154 (n. 22)
    *Die Juden*, 106–7, 116–27, 134–35, 154 (n. 19), 154 (n. 22)
    *Der junge Gelehrte*, 8, 109
    *Minna von Barnhelm oder Das Soldatenglück*, 70
    *Miß Sara Sampson*, 31, 137
    *Nathan der Weise*, 129–36, 155 (n. 32)
    *Sämtliche Schriften*, 161

*Der Schatz*, 109–16, 127, 135, 153 (nn. 9–10)
*Schrifften*, xiv, 152 (n. 16), 154 (n. 25), 162
"Ueber das Lustspiel die Juden, im vierten Theile der Leßingschen Schrifften," 125–27, 154 (n. 26)
Liebmann family, 36
Lillo, George, 40, 137
*The London Merchant, or The History of George Barnwell*, 40, 137
Lisbon, 17
Locke, John, 8, 91
London, 6, 11, 13, 41, 63, 73, 93, 104, 137
Louis XIV (King of France), 9, 14
Lowenthal, Marvin, 146 (n. 112), 159
Ludz, Peter Christian, 145 (n. 98), 160
Lübeck, 60, 64
Lütge, Friedrich, 8, 141 (n. 5), 142 (nn. 23–24), 142 (nn. 26–27), 144 (n. 68), 146 (n. 109), 147 (n. 131), 161
Luther, Martin, 38, 147 (n. 130), 161
    "Von Kaufshandlung und Wucher: 1524," 38, 161

Main River, 18
Maltzahn, Wendelin von, 152 (n. 4), 158
Manitius, Adolph Gebhart, 37
Mann, Otto, 153 (n. 9), 161
Mann, Thomas, 28
Marburg, 24
Martens, Wolfgang, 21, 40, 142 (n. 27), 144 (nn. 69–70), 144 (n. 84), 147 (n. 140), 161
Martini, Fritz, 149 (n. 2), 161
Marx, Assur, 35
Mediterranean Sea, 3, 47
Meid, Volker, 62, 148 (n. 10), 148 (n. 14), 163
Meißen, 109, 120
Mendelssohn, Moses, 125
Menhennet, Alan, 4–5, 141 (n. 10), 142 (n. 20), 161
Metzger, Michael, 116, 119, 153 (n. 9), 153 (nn. 13–14), 154 (n. 20), 161
Metzler family, 18
Meyer, Herman, 148 (n. 4), 148 (n. 7), 161
Meyer, Jonas, 35
Meyer-Krentler, Eckhardt, 151 (n. 6), 161

Michaelis, Johann David, 106–7, 124–25, 126, 127, 136, 139
Middle East, 33, 129, 134
Moscow, 94, 96, 100, 101
Mosse, George, 32, 145 (n. 102), 145 (n. 106), 161
Mottek, Hans, 142 (n. 25), 161
Müller, Andreas, 57, 148 (n. 4), 148 (n. 8), 162
Müller-Seidel, Walter, 148 (n. 4), 161
Müllroser Canal, 11
Münch, Paul, 18, 141 (n. 3), 141 (n. 14), 142 (n. 18), 142 (n. 22), 143 (n. 48), 144 (n. 58), 144 (nn. 60–61), 151 (n. 4), 160
Muncker, Franz, 153 (n. 10), 154 (n. 19), 154 (n. 26), 155 (n. 32), 161

Napoleon, 14
Naumann, Dietrich, 60, 148 (n. 13), 162
*Neue Beiträge zum Vergnügen des Verstandes und Witzes* (*Bremer Beiträge*), 19, 83, 85
de Neufville family, 18
Neuhaus-Koch, Ariane, 113, 153 (n. 11), 154 (n. 22), 155 (n. 33), 162
Newald, Richard, 91, 151 (n. 2), 155 (n. 35), 155 (n. 37), 162
Nixon, Paul, 152 (n. 6), 162
Noltenius, Johann Daniel, 22
North America, 19
Nuremberg, 3, 14

Oder River, 11
Oehlke, Waldemar, 110–11, 123, 126, 153 (n. 8), 154 (n. 24), 154 (n. 27), 162
Offler, H.S., 144 (n. 65), 157

Paris, 6, 41, 73, 77, 78
*Patriot*, 13, 21, 26, 40
Paul the Apostle, 38
Peace of Westphalia, 4
Persia, 129
Persius (Aulus Persius Flaccus), 89
Peru, 49
Peschken, Bernd, 152 (n. 3), 162
Philemon, 110
  *Thesauros*, 110
Pietism, 91, 97, 146 (n. 125), 152 (n. 13)
Pindar, 89
Plautus (Titus Maccius Plautus), 110, 116, 153 (n. 8), 162

*Trinummus*, 110, 152 (n. 6), 153 (n. 9), 162
Poland, 14, 16, 17, 35, 36–37, 91, 92, 106
Pollack, Herman, 145 (n. 103), 162
Portugal, 3, 12, 33
Potter, G. R., 144 (n. 65), 157
Prague, 3, 6
Prussia, 9, 15–18, 25, 36–37, 109, 146 (n. 118), 146 (n. 121)
Pufendorf, Samuel, Freiherr von, 14

Raabe, Paul, 145 (n. 96), 162
Rabener, Gottlieb Wilhelm, 19
Reformation, 8, 46
Rengstorf, Karl Heinrich, 145 (n. 107), 150 (n. 13), 162
Rentschler, Robert, 153 (n. 15), 162
Reuter, Hans-Heinrich, 143 (n. 38), 143 (n. 41), 152 (n. 14), 153 (n. 9), 155 (n. 1), 162
Rhine River, xiii, 18
Rhineland, 14
Richel, Veronica C., 150 (n. 8), 150 (n. 18), 162
Rieck, Werner, 143 (n. 38), 143 (n. 41), 149 (n. 1), 152 (n. 14), 153 (n. 9), 155 (n. 1), 162
Riedel, Volker, 153 (n. 13), 162
Robinson novel, 20, 59, 93, 148 (n. 11)
Rodriguez, Henrico, 33
Roloff, Hans-Gert, 145 (n. 97), 154 (n. 31), 159, 165
Rome, 51
Rousseau, Jean-Jacques, 48
Rupp, Heinz, 154 (n. 31), 165
Russia, 14, 16, 17, 18, 78, 93, 96, 100, 102
"Russische Handelskompanie," 16
Rytz, Hans Rudolf, 19, 20, 39, 142 (n. 16), 144 (nn. 66–67), 147 (n. 134), 162

Sachs, Hans, 9
Saine, Thomas P., 141 (n. 2), 163
Sauder, Gerhard, 141 (n. 2), 141 (n. 7), 163
Saurmann, Nathanael, 19
Saxony, 14, 15, 34–35, 119, 120, 121, 122
Scandinavia, 19
Schaer, Wolfgang, 147 (n. 136), 163
Schenda, Rudolf, 92, 151 (n. 3), 163

Schiller, Friedrich von, 27
Schlegel, Johann Adolf, 19
Schlegel, Johann Elias, 8, 19, 70, 83–85, 109, 139, 149, 150 (nn. 14–15), 163
    *Der Geschäfftige Müßiggänger*, 83–85, 150 (nn. 15–16), 163
    *Werke*, 163
Schlegel, Johann Heinrich, 150 (n. 16), 163
Schlenther, Paul, 150 (n. 8), 163
Schlingmann, Carsten, 151 (n. 7), 163
Schmidt, Erich, 110, 111, 122, 152 (n. 5), 153 (n. 7), 154 (n. 23), 163
Schnabel, Johann Gottfried, 20, 40, 45, 49, 58–69, 70, 81, 139, 163
    *Insel Felsenburg*, 20, 49, 58–69, 70, 71, 74, 75, 124, 147, 148 (n. 10), 148 (n. 14), 163
Schneider, Ferdinand Josef, 151 (n. 11), 163
Schneider, Heinrich, 145 (n. 98), 163
Schönemann theater troupe (Johann Friedrich Schönemann), 13
Schoeps, Julius H., 145 (n. 107), 151 (n. 10), 163
Schramm, Percy Ernst, 142 (n. 32), 160
Schulte-Sasse, Jochen, 150 (n. 6), 163
Schulz, Günter, 145 (n. 107), 154 (n. 28), 159, 162, 163
Seifert, Siegfried, 152 (n. 1), 163
Seneca (Lucius Annaeus Seneca), 38, 50, 51, 147 (n. 127), 163
    *Ad Lucilium epistulae morales*, 38, 163
Sephardim, 33–34, 120, 122
Shaftesbury, Anthony Ashley Cooper, 3rd Earl of, 105, 152 (n. 13)
Siberia, 90, 93, 94, 100
Siebenbürgen, 86, 87
Siegrist, Christoph, 147 (n. 1), 163
Silesia, 12, 14, 17
Sombart, Werner, 37, 146 (n. 125), 163
South America, 3
Spain, 3, 71, 78
*Spectator*, 40
Spener, Philipp Jakob, 91
Spinoza, Benedict de, 91
Splitgerber and Daum (company), 16, 39–40, 143 (n. 54)
Spree River, 11
Springer-Strand, Ingeborg, 62, 148 (n. 10), 148 (n. 14), 163
Steffen, Hans, 149 (n. 2), 163
Steinhausen, Georg, 147 (nn. 132–33), 163
Steinmetz, Horst, 149 (n. 2), 150 (n. 10), 164
Stern, Selma, 36, 37, 146 (n. 117), 146 (n. 121), 146 (nn. 123–24), 164
Stoicism, 51
Stolberg, 19, 20, 67
*Stolbergische Sammlung Neuer und Merckwürdiger Welt-Geschichte*, 59
Storm and Stress, 70
Straube-Mann, Rotraut, 153 (n. 9), 161
Süß-Oppenheimer, Joseph, 82, 146 (n. 110), 150 (n. 13)
Swabia, 14
Sweden, 34, 78, 100, 136
Switzerland, 18, 49, 57
Syria, 129
Szondi, Peter, 40, 147 (nn. 138–39), 164

Tacitus (Publius Cornelius Tacitus), 41, 51
Tawney, R. H., 147 (n. 129), 164
Telemann, Georg Philipp, 13
"Teutschübende Gesellschaft," 13
Texeira family, 34
*Theatralische Bibliothek*, 17, 125
Thirty Years' War, xiii, 3–4, 5, 7, 9, 14
Thomasius, Christian, 14
Tieck, Ludwig, 59
Trautwein, Wolfgang, 154 (n. 29), 164
Trunz, Erich, 145 (n. 106), 159
Tübingen, 45

Uhlich, Adam Gottfried, 70

Van Abbé, D. M., 151 (n. 9), 164
Vanbrugh, John, 118
Van Cleve, John Walter, 142 (n. 35), 143 (n. 57), 150 (n. 18), 154 (n. 30), 164
Vaud, 46
Vergil (Publius Vergilius Maro), 41
Versailles, 45
Vienna, 3, 6, 36
Vierhaus, Rudolf, 142 (n. 15), 164
Voltaire (François-Marie Arouet), 17
Voßkamp, Wilhelm, 148 (nn. 10–11), 163, 164

Wandsbek, 34
War of the Austrian Succession, 17
Ward, Albert, 143 (n. 39), 164
Wars of the Spanish Succession, 59
Weber, Max, 146 (n. 125), 164
Weber-Kellermann, Ingeborg, 144 (nn. 90–91), 164
Weiman, Ralph, 146 (n. 117), 164
Weiße, Christian Felix, 70
Wernicke, Christian, 13
West Indies, 62
Westphalia, 12, 19
Wicke, Günter, 145 (n. 99), 149 (n. 2), 150 (n. 6), 150 (n. 15), 164
Wiedemann, Conrad, 148 (n. 5), 157
Wieland, Christoph Martin, 93
Wilhelmi, Konrad, 21–22
Winthem, Meinert von, 12, 23, 24
Wiskemann, Erwin, 11, 142 (n. 30), 164
Witkowski, Georg, 13, 143 (n. 40), 164
Wolf, Peter, 150 (n. 14), 164
Wolff, Christian, Freiherr von, 8, 14
Wucherpfennig, Wolf, 131, 135, 154 (n. 31), 155 (nn. 38–39), 155 (n. 44), 164
Württemberg, 82

Yiddish, 32

Zevi, Sabbatai, 34
Žmegač, Viktor, 155 (n. 2), 157
Zorn, Wolfgang, 5, 141 (n. 8), 141 (n. 11), 141 (n. 13), 142 (n. 33), 143 (n. 43), 143 (n. 53), 143–44 (n. 58), 144 (n. 59), 144 (n. 63), 145 (n. 103), 145 (n. 105), 145–46 (n. 108), 165
Zurich, xiv, 45